"How we're going about it"

"How we're going about it":
Teachers' Voices on Innovative Approaches
to Teaching and Learning Languages

Edited by

Melinda Dooly and Diana Eastment

Cambridge Scholars Publishing

"How we're going about it": Teachers' Voices on Innovative Approaches to Teaching and Learning Languages, Edited by Melinda Dooly and Diana Eastment

This book first published 2008 by

Cambridge Scholars Publishing

15 Angerton Gardens, Newcastle, NE5 2JA, UK

British Library Cataloguing in Publication Data
A catalogue record for this book is available from the British Library

Copyright © 2008 by Melinda Dooly, Diana Eastment and contributors

All rights for this book reserved. No part of this book may be reproduced, stored in a retrieval system, or transmitted, in any form or by any means, electronic, mechanical, photocopying, recording or otherwise, without the prior permission of the copyright owner.

ISBN (10): 1-84718-431-6, ISBN (13): 9781847184313

TABLE OF CONTENTS

List of Figures ix
Acknowledgements x

Introduction 1
Melinda Dooly

Part I: Tuning into languages: Multiple languages as a resource

Introduction to Part I 12
Melinda Dooly

Chapter One 15
Multiple Language Integration: Introduction
Melinda Dooly

Two-way Immersion in Germany: Notes on Teaching and Learning
Practice 18
Melanie Kunkel, Gabriele Budach

Learning to Communicate Effectively through Intensive Instruction
in French 31
Joan Netten, Claude Germain

Diversity as an Asset: Multiple Language Integration 42
Andrea Young

Recommended Reading: Multiple Language Immersion 54

Chapter Two 56
Task-Based Language Learning: Introduction
Melinda Dooly

Adapting a Task-Based Language Learning Approach to a Spanish
for Specific Purposes Course: "Prácticas comunicativas"
in the University of Antwerp 62
Marta Seseña Gomez

Task-Based Language Teaching in the Netherlands: Dutch L1
and Dutch L2 77
Folkert Kuiken

Task-Based Language Learning in Flanders: Opportunities for Second
Language Acquisition and Beyond 88
Koen Van Gorp

Recommended Reading: Task-Based Language Learning 103

Chapter Three **104**
Content and Language Integrated Learning: Introduction
Melinda Dooly

Conditions for CLIL in Finland: Constructivist Principles, Teacher
Autonomy, and a Supportive National Curriculum 109
David Marsh

All Roads Lead to Rome: A CLIL Social Studies Experience 118
Mercè Barrull Garcia

Talking English to Learn Science: A CLIL Experience in Barcelona 127
Cristina Escobar Urmeneta

Along the Continuum – An Exploration of Integrating Language
and Content Learning in England 139
Do Coyle

Recommended Reading: Content Language and Integrated Learning 152

Part II. New teaching and learning paradigms for the 21st century

Introduction to Part II 156
Melinda Dooly

"How we're going about it": Teachers' Voices on Innovative Approaches   vii
to Teaching and Learning Languages

Chapter Four 159
Technology Integrated into Language Learning: Introduction
Melinda Dooly

Lights! Camera! Action! A Video Project for the Web 2.0 Classroom ... 165
Nicolas Gromik

Engaging Young Learners in Online Intercultural Learning:
The MICaLL Project 177
Melinda Dooly, Carmen Ellermann

Getting the Message: Training Language Teachers in the Theoretical
and Practical Applications of Forums 187
Randall Sadler, Betil Eröz

Recommended Reading: Technology into Language Learning 198

Chapter Five 200
Passport to Pluralism – European Language Portfolio: Introduction
Melinda Dooly

The European Language Portfolio: Developing Presentation Skills
among University Students of German for Business 205
Jennifer Bruen

The Portfolio: Challenges and Experiences in the Portuguese Context ... 216
Cristina Avelino, Francine Arroyo

The European Language Portfolio in Romania and the EuroIntegrELP
Project 225
Liliana Dellevoet, Laura Mureşan

Recommended Reading: European Language Portfolio 241

Chapter Six 243
Exploring New Horizons – Young Learners and Multiple Intelligences:
Introduction
Melinda Dooly

Controversies in Teaching English to Young Learners:
The Polish Solution 251
Hanna Komorowska

Young Croatian Language Learners 261
Jelena Mihaljevic Djigunovic

Using the Multiple Intelligences Theory to Teach Intelligently:
Literature, Poetry and Art in an EFL Classroom 271
Eduarda Melo Cabrita

Recommended Reading: Exploring New Horizons 283

Appendices 284
Contributors 294

LIST OF FIGURES

Fig. 2-1 Evaluation scale 71
Fig. 2-2 Self-evaluation 72
Fig. 2-3 Statistical results of six major criteria for assessment TBLL 73
Fig. 2-4 Course books of Dutch for task-based language teaching 80
Fig. 2-5 Drawing for "Who is the thief?" 89
Fig. 3-1 Learning strategies 122
Fig. 3-2 Tasks for joint construction of knowledge 133
Fig. 3-3 Problem-solving task 135
Fig. 4-1 Part of a student's homepage 180
Fig. 4-2 Students' rap songs 181
Fig. 4-3 Frommer's Travel Board 190
Fig. 4-4 The CMC Forum 191
Fig. 5-1 Extract from the Profile of Language Skills (Passport) 208
Fig. 5-2 Extract from the Self-Assessment Grid (Passport) 209
Fig. 5-3 Can-do Statements for Level C1 209
Fig. 5-4 Example of self-assessment activity 231
Fig. 5-5 "Can-do statements" 233

ACKNOWLEDGEMENTS

This book has been made possible through the generosity and support of many people, not least of whom have been the friends, families and colleagues of all the contributors herein. Special thanks must be given to Marilyn Fillers, Emilee Moore and Gary Motteram for taking time to review this book so thoroughly.

On a more personal note, I would like to express my gratitude to Diana for her unflagging support throughout this project. Despite her own personal struggles in the face of illness, she has always been ready with a joke, smile or hug. Diana, you stand as a model to follow; this book is dedicated to you.

Melinda Dooly
Barcelona, 31 October 2007

INTRODUCTION

MELINDA DOOLY

Why do we need this book?

Diverse demands for language teaching, the incorporation of new technologies into education, an augment of political and social interest in language learning, ever-expanding research and a growing market for theories, methods, materials and research publications have contributed to the general feeling that language teaching is in a state of continuous flux. Inevitably, there are many reasons for the rapid change in policies, training, expectations and information about language teaching, not least of which is the fact that language teaching embraces a wide spectrum of activities, approaches, practices and even beliefs. Moreover, the language learning process must be contextualised in order to truly understand what shapes the way languages are taught. It is quite beyond the scope of this book to cover all these areas and reasons for change, instead it is felt that it is more useful for teachers who are living in this ever-changing context to have access to some descriptive examples of innovative focuses that help face the challenges of all these changes. In particular, we try to look at the way these perspectives are integrated into student-centred learning environments.

Following the year 2001, which was declared the European Year of Languages (CoE, 2001), foreign language teaching has taken on a predominant role in the scholastic curriculum in many countries, especially in Europe. This has put a focus on the need for innovative language teaching approaches. Nonetheless, it has been argued that change and innovation in language teaching really began as early as the 1970s (Richards, 2002) during which period the communicative approach became popular, along with several other novel approaches (e.g. Total Physical Response or the Silent Way). While some approaches, such as the communicative approach or task-based learning are still very much part of language teaching today, many of the other approaches which were considered to be cutting edge in the 70s have almost disappeared. As Richards has put it, we are in the "post methods era" (idem, 4).

Arguably, the "post methods era" is a vibrant, but uncertain time for language teachers. Changes can produce a sense of challenge and opportunity for exploration while provoking ambiguous feelings towards those same changes. The "post methods era" can be confusing —there seem to be no clear-cut methods to follow. Different language teaching and learning approaches often overlap, exacerbated by the fact that there seem to be so many diverse notions and definitions of what it means to "know a language". There are some common strands emerging, however. It is increasingly common to hear voices clamouring for the need to understand the language learning process within its social and psychological context. The fact that most modern language lessons today incorporate, in some way or another, the idea of *communication* (Grenfell, 2000:4) implies that there is now more emphasis on exposure and use of the target language through situational dialogues and practice and a shift away from a focus on discreet grammar. At the same time there is also a growing interest in moving away from *language learning* alone toward *learning to learn languages* just as there is a growing interest in moving beyond "language learning" towards "languaging" (Phipps and Gonzalez, 2004) wherein the purpose of learning and using a language is not an objective in itself – language(s) is/are seen as a material part of the student's life.

This book seeks to address this context of changes constructively and positively by providing an overview of language learning environments which can be considered as having "sprouted" from the "seeds" of the "post method era" and which attempt to put the people involved at the centre of our focus. The book looks at issues and practices related to the classroom —exemplifying situated language learning processes that are largely based on learner-centred, socio-constructivist approaches and which are being implemented in different countries throughout the world. While most of the cases presented are from European countries, there are also examples from Canada, the United States of America and Japan. The contributions included here represent some of the recent (and some not-so recent but influential) perspectives and issues that are currently quite relevant for language teaching. With the backdrop of the aforementioned Year of Languages 2001 behind us, and the declared goals of a plurilinguistic society before us (CoE), we have seized this newfound interest in teaching and learning languages (note the plural suffix, at least two languages apart from the mother tongue are being touted as the ideal goal) as an exemplar moment to highlight some of the practices and experiences of language teaching and learning which are being implemented around the globe.

"How we're going about it": Teachers' Voices on Innovative Approaches to Teaching and Learning Languages

Who should read this book?

This book is principally aimed at language teachers, teacher trainers and trainees interested in finding out about innovative teaching practices, perspectives and approaches which are being implemented in countries around the world. Of course, language teaching approaches must adapt to local environments and will take on characteristics of that environment, however this can sometimes restrict how the approach is actually understood (in a nutshell –one may be unable to see the wood because of the tree). By providing insight into how a variety of approaches are interpreted and put into action in different environments, this book will be of interest to foreign language teachers who are looking for ways to innovate approaches they are already using. It will also have appeal for teachers who are not specialized in foreign language teaching but are interested in cross-disciplinary approaches that encompass language learning. Of course, this book is not limited to teachers and trainers. Anyone who is a stakeholder in educational curricula, such as heads of schools and administrators, even parents, might find this material of interest –especially considering the importance multilingualism has in today's education environment.

While the book is not written as a textbook, it can easily become part of recommended reading for courses specializing in language arts and foreign language teaching. In Europe, it is common practice to have university degrees in this area and teacher trainees are expected to be up-to-date on all current approaches across the European Union. The book can be used as reading for initial teacher training, especially foreign language teacher training, but it reaches beyond that. The growing interest in project-based approaches and content-based language learning, which require cooperation between specialized language teachers and teachers of other disciplines, means that there is a need for accessible reading materials for teachers and teacher trainees across all fields of education.

What is in this book?

This book is divided into two main sections which are, in turn, grouped into sub-sections of descriptive cases. The first section is entitled *Tuning into languages: Multiple languages as a resource.* This section looks at different ways in which multiple language learning is *integrated* into learning activities programmed into the school curriculum. The three subsections are:

- Multiple language integration
- Task-based language learning
- Content and Language Integrated Learning.

The second section, entitled *Emerging Technologies and New Paradigms for the 21st Century,* examines new technologies in language learning, the use of the European Language Portfolio and language teaching to young learners. The axis to these sections is the understanding of emerging technology, research, and education paradigms as resources which can be integrated into the language learning process. Moreover, the notion of the learners as a teaching resource brings us full circle – the learner-centred environment which is absolutely essential for integrative teaching strategies.

The three subsections of section II are:

- Technology Integrated into Language Learning
- European Language Portfolio
- Exploring New Horizons: Young Learners and Multiple Intelligences

A brief introduction of each section provides the reader with some background information about each descriptive case and the common denominators which underlie them. While the book does not intend to delve too deeply into the theoretical issues at play, some key debates inevitably emerge and these are highlighted in the introduction in hopes of sparking interest in further research and exploration in the areas described here. At the end of each section a list of recommended reading is given for readers interested in finding out more about the topics.

What are the key issues addressed?

This book is about approaches in language learning, with a special focus on how resources are employed – especially *human resources.* However, the reader should bear in mind that the notion of "human resource" as it is understood in this book may differ from the more conventional idea of "human resource". The position taken here is that the true stakeholder of any learning process are principally the learners and that this "human factor" must be integrated into any approach taken within education. In an era which is dominated by the "business mentality" and at a time in which education has already assimilated many of the business terms and creeds about how to educate learners (e.g. efficient time management, focus on impact, quality control, accountability, etc.), this human factor often seems to be pushed aside.

Businesses have long recognized the need for setting up "human resources management", "human resources strategies", "human resources development" and most businesses have a human resources department, with its own director and staff. And yet, human resources (or better said, the human factor) is not always taken into consideration in teacher development, curriculum development or lesson planning, despite the fact that the *human resources* (teachers, administrators, parents, community and especially students) are the very backbone of education.

This book will look at the different ways in which available *resources* are being used in language education – thus resource in this book is understood as *anything used positively by the teacher to promote the learning process*. This implies that resource can be understood as computer and Internet connection, policy guidelines, innovative teaching material and of course, the teacher and the student as sources of vital information and interaction which can be channelled into the learning experience. There are many books about how materials are being used, about how to develop classes through different approaches (which may or may not provide materials for the language classes), but there is a need for a book which describes how the *persons* involved in the language classes are *pivotal* to the way in which the language lessons take place, because they are the agents who incorporate the available resources into their students' learning process.

The term resource, defined by Webster's New World Dictionary 2nd College Edition, refers to "available means" and "a source of information or expertise". Starting from there, resources are understood as the means or sources from which learning takes place – a wide definition which allows us to look at the different ways in which language teaching strategies emerge from a learner-centred environment. This theme runs throughout the book. So, when discussing network-based language learning for instance, we are not focusing on the Internet as the main element for learning – the Internet is a *tool* which provides support for *learners* to work together to construct knowledge – thus the emphasis is on the human factor – the participants involved in each particular environment of distanced classes –all working together via the Internet. Likewise, task-based learning emphasizes the learner as the resource for the language use which emerges from the task design. The different types of "immersion" discussed herein, whether through CLIL or plurilingual environments, draw on the students' and teacher's knowledge of the content and languages being studied as the strategy for further language learning. And as the name implies, Young Learners are the human resource for teaching strategies which deal with early language learners.

Of course, another important human resource for education is the teacher. Inevitably, effective language education will depend greatly upon the skills, knowledge and commitment of the teacher. However, for the teacher who would like to stay informed about the different achievements, research, application of new approaches and theories and so forth, he or she may find himself or herself adrift in a vast array of theories, policies and ideas concerning the field of language teaching and learning. Foreign language teaching is a constantly changing field of education; in many places throughout the world language education is perhaps one of the areas of the curriculum which has changed the most in the past two decades. This is largely due to the influences of new research, dissemination of innovative practices, increasing numbers of students and greater interest in educational policy promoting a multilingual society.

The selection of case descriptions to include in this book has not been easy –there are numerous examples of "good practice" being carried out in primary, middle and secondary schools as well as at university faculties and in further education which could deservedly be included. The selection was based on what can be called a "convergence of agenda" for language learning and the way in which knowledge and understanding about this process was transformed into classroom practice. Relevance for the reader was considered – it is the aim of this book that readers will find the information and descriptions transferable to other contexts. So, while it is inevitable that each case described herein is specific to its social, cultural and institutional situation, this fact should not be overly-emphasized either, as it could result in missed opportunities for learning from other practitioners.

Another problem encountered upon starting this book project was how to group the practitioners' experiences into sections in the book. Inevitably, the act of naming is encumbered with many pitfalls, not least of which is the fact that naming (or labelling) immediately evokes particular and often generalized characteristics or features which may or may not be germane to the contextualised circumstances being described. This problem was exacerbated by the fact that we did not want to group the sections according to "approaches" or "methods" and yet we still needed a common axis to distribute the contributions in a framework that made it more accessible for the reader. As we've already mentioned, the idea of the use of resources was important for the outline of the book, so it was decided to focus on the way in which *resources* were put to use in the cases described here. This is the common denominator which delineates each section. Inevitably, this was easier for some sections than others, for instance, an approach which employs new technology has the commonality of using technology as a key tool for language learning. However, the argument remains that there are many different ways to employ technology in teaching and learning so even the supposedly more clear-cut categories were (and still are) open to discussion.

Differences were even more patent when it came to discussing the sections dealing with multiple languages as a resource. For instance, there is a lot of debate about the division between linguistic immersion and Content Language and Integrated Learning (CLIL); we didn't pick the fight – it is already set out for us. On the one hand, CLIL can be considered one particular type of bilingual program, set apart from other bilingual programmes by its institutional and didactical set-up. This argument, in turn, must be contextualised – are we talking about immersion of foreign languages, second languages, or immigrant students learning the vehicular language? Are we discussing educational environments in which bilingualism and plurilingualism are already the norm or is it predominantly a monolingual educational environment? How many hours of exposure to the language can be considered "immersion"? Again, each situation and each experience is a world in itself.

Thus, when trying to pinpoint the most appropriate phenomena to focus upon, it was necessary to ask what is the element that clearly crosscuts the different sets of examples? One such factor is the way in which multilingual resources are employed as a learning resource. As one of the contributors rightly pointed out at the beginning of the writing project, the grouping stems from the outcome rather than the "frame" in which bilingual learning takes place, highlighting the need to group the sections according to both the resources employed and the approach which emerges from that focus. Some may feel that the inclusion or exclusion of a particular practice from a section is an error. However, in the view of the editors, the way in which the cases were grouped prioritized making it reader-friendly rather than focusing on theoretical differences. Arguably, focusing on theoretical variations in the frameworks rather than the outcomes would have made for an entirely different book.

Likewise, some of the cases described in the book could have been defined differently within their socio-cultural contexts. For instance, the question of "Young Learner" was difficult to pinpoint to one age group. Foreign language instruction begins around age six in Austria while in Germany, the average age is eight. In Spain, the compulsory age for beginning foreign language classes has been lowered to six but it is also quite common to find "experimental" schools starting foreign language courses in kindergarten with children as young as two or three. As ambivalent as it may seem, the term "Young Learner" is commonly applied in language learning contexts, as witnessed by associations and conferences which include the title in their names. Therefore our decision was to return to our initial starting point and consider young learners as the (human) resource upon which this approach revolves, rather than limiting the section to a certain age group (although, admittedly, we did keep the age range to below ten) and to include two articles about young learners in the section which describes the expansion of new horizons in learning.

The chapters that follow are made up of contributions from different practitioners with a wide range of experience and expertise in the vast field of language teaching. The transversality of the contributions is not so much the application of specific practices as the *transformation* of knowledge about language learning. This transformation stems from advances in research and through the devising of practices which can be included in a comprehensive teaching programme. This also helps give the book an international scope because the content of the book seeks to provide insight into innovative and inspirational language teaching practices being carried out in different countries. Inevitably, there are many different models, interpretations and definitions of each of the focuses which are the basis of the examples described herein. In many cases the experiences overlap – it is not unusual to hear of a teacher who employs a digitalized language portfolio with students and who includes chats and forums as part of the learning experience –thus combining language portfolios with new technologies. We were interested in providing an overview of language teaching and learning processes which can contribute to further innovation in the field rather than focusing on providing academic debate on where the delineations should be drawn.

It was not an easy task to combine the objective of having as wide a geographic distribution as possible and having relevant representations of experiences in each section. Of course, it is impossible to offer an example from each country or region in the world –impossible for the editors, untenable for the publishers and too daunting for anyone but the most avid reader! We have tried to provide a "sampling" of language teaching which can be considered as efficient, innovative and motivating means to engage students in language learning. It is not our aim to compare or endorse one learning process over another, nor does the exclusion of any area in this book imply that we feel it is not worthwhile. We have chosen these areas for their growing acceptance in language education but which, at the same time, may not enjoy the dissemination as examples of practice which they arguably deserve.

The cases described here are intended only as examples of how teachers and theorists have made use of the resources they had at hand (learners, technological tools, community, school projects, activities and/or new research). Literature written for teachers often provides ample theoretical description of how it "should" be done. While this is doubtlessly important as a basis for sound teaching practice, it needs to be accompanied by sufficient examples of how it has been put into practice inside the classroom. This book is written for all those who are stakeholders in language education and are interested in exploring some of the current practices around the globe. It is our hope that these experiences will serve as inspiration for other teachers and administrators as they see how their colleagues in other parts of the world have adapted these ideas into their teaching.

A final note: in order to avoid sexist language, we have opted for alternating between feminine and masculine referencing instead of using the rather unwieldy s/he, her/his wording. Thus, if 'student' is referred to as 'her' in one chapter, the masculine pronouns will be used in the next.

Works Cited

Council of Europe. 2001. *Common European Framework of Reference for Languages: Learning, teaching, assessment.* Cambridge: Cambridge University Press.

Grenfell, Michael. 2000. "Modern languages – beyond Nuffield into the 21st Century." *Language Learning Journal, 22*, 23-29.

Phipps, Alison and Mike Gonzalez. 2004. *Modern Languages: Learning and Teaching in an Intercultural Field.* London: Sage Publications.

Richards, Jack C. 2002. "30 Years of TEFL/TESL: A personal reflection." *RELC Journal*, 33(2), 1-36.

PART I

TUNING INTO LANGUAGES: MULTIPLE LANGUAGES AS A RESOURCE

Introduction to Part I

Melinda Dooly

Those who know nothing of foreign languages know nothing of their own.
—Johann Wolfgang Von Goethe

This Section has nine contributions, the first three discuss different ways that multiple languages have been integrated into the classroom, followed by three descriptions of task-based language learning (TBLL), and ends with four descriptions of foreign language learning through Content Language and Integrated Learning (CLIL). All of these examples are especially relevant to the current education environment. During the last decade or so, there has been a shift away from decontextualised language teaching towards *integration* of language learning with other learning activities programmed in the school. This may be in the form of content instruction of a subject matter (e.g. Science, Mathematics, History, etc.) or the target language may be used as the vehicular language to carry out a project, or, as is described here, the target language may be used intensively during an established period of time. One of the most frequently cited reasons for this integrated focus is the theory that incorporating meaningful input and communication leads to improved language learning and teaching.

Nonetheless it can be argued that there is not a clear-cut definition of what is meant by the term *integration* of target languages. Indeed, there are several approaches for integrating second language teaching into other areas – such approaches are often broadly referred to as "Immersion". The variety of ways in which the concept of immersion is understood is evidenced by the numerous ways in which it is put into practice across the globe. In some cases the term "linguistic immersion" might be replaced by "intensity of instruction", as both immersion and intensive programs are necessarily intensive, although some may argue that intensive is not necessarily immersion!

For the purpose of this book, we are going to focus on *exposure to and use of the target language as an integrated part of instruction* – although the reader should bear in mind that the area of instruction and the amount of exposure to the target language can have many variants. In short, the focus is on *contextualizing* the language use as a means of *facilitating* its learning. Still, this broad definition becomes problematic when one begins to examine the different ways in which the concept has been and is being applied. Ironically, the definition is rendered almost obtuse *when it is contextualized*! For instance, according to many experts, one of the most widely spread practices in Canada over the past 3 decades is "immersion education" which is principally aimed at the English-speaking majority learning French (see Genesee, 1987; Lapkin, 1998; Lapkin & Turnbull, 1999; Swain & Johnson, 1997). Yet, this "immersion education" must be understood within the context of Canada, which is officially bilingual, with French and English as the two co-official languages. This is a quite different context of language use (e.g. exposure to the language in the school and ample opportunities for its use outside the school) than is the case for the Netherlands, which also has programmes called "bilingual education" which combine the school's vehicular language and English as the second language. In this case, English, albeit frequently used in films and other aspects of everyday life of Dutch youth, is not an official language of the Netherlands.

Likewise, in Germany, some schools employ programmes known as "learning through a foreign language" which often begins in the first year of schooling. In such programmes, half the school day students and teachers use German and the other half a foreign language is used. However, in many cases the so-called foreign language may be the native language of many of the students, since the programmes often focus on languages which are spoken by large populations in Germany (e.g. Italian, Turkish). Inevitably, the different *contexts* in which this *contextualized* focus of language learning is employed will influence the way in which the target language is taught and the results stemming from such experiences.

Still, the theory of linguistic integration as part of the curriculum (with all its variants such as content subject, different target languages, level of intensity of exposure, etc.)—based on the concept of purposeful learning appears to be a wide-spread practice that clearly justifies an examination of such practices. We have chosen the cases here because they exemplify the idea of integrating the language into overall school learning.

The first group of writings is entitled "Multiple language integration". Inevitably, this heading is also applicable for other sections, but in this subsection the focus is not so much on any particular institutional setting, rather the focus is on the *output* of multilingual settings. The next group of writings consists of examples of Task-based Language Learning that illustrate how language learning can be integrated into classroom teaching or across school projects. The last four contributions provide descriptive examples of Content Language and Integrated Learning. In this framework, CLIL is understood as "dual-focused educational context" (Marsh, 2002:1) wherein a language different from the learners' first language is used as a means for teaching and learning in a non-language context. According to Marsh, "CLIL has emerged as a pragmatic European solution to a European need" (2002: 1) and in this book, CLIL is understood as standing apart from other immersion programmes principally based on its institutional setting. This has been the definition used here to separate the different areas of immersion.

Inevitably, as more research goes into understanding the role of bilingualism and multilingualism in life-long language learning, educators will probably be obliged to rephrase and reconfigure many definitions. As Germain and Netten point out in this book, most of the buzzwords seem to refer to the need to integrate the use (and reuse) of the language into all learning processes. This section provides some enlightening examples of researchers and practitioners who are leading the way.

Works Cited

Genesee, Fred. 1987. *Learning through two languages: Studies of immersion and bilingual education.* Cambridge, MA: Newbury House.

Lapkin, Sharon, ed. 1998. *French Second Language Education in Canada: Empirical Studies.* Toronto: University of Toronto Press.

Lapkin, Sharon and Miles Turnbull, eds. 1999. Research in FSL education: The state of the art, *Canadian Modern Language Review (special issue),* 56,1.

Marsh, David. 2002. *CLIL/EMILE—The European Dimension. Action, Trends and Foresight Potential.* Continuing Education Centre: University of Jyväskylä.

Swain, Merrill and Robert Keith Johnson, eds. 1997. *Immersion Education: International Perspectives.* Cambridge: Cambridge University Press.

Chapter One

Multiple Language Integration: Introduction

Melinda Dooly

This section delves into learning that takes place within bilingual and multilingual contexts. Inevitably, this implies an understanding of linguistic competence which goes beyond the traditional sense of monolingual linguistic competence. As we've stated previously, it is our belief that multilingualism should be understood as a resource —the origins and use of that resource may have many variants— but multiple linguistic competences stand as a constant. This moves the focus from language and language learning for their own sake towards the outcomes of different types of programmes cross-cut by the use of intensive exposure and integration of multiple languages.

As societies are constantly transforming and new communities and identities emerge, teachers will be required to adjust their instructional practices to the reality of multilingualism in their classrooms. Teachers must be seen as central stakeholders in the education process and this implies viewing their "practical knowledge and notions" as a broad pool of resources they will employ in the classroom. Therefore it becomes imperative to disseminate examples of situated learning experiences which incorporate multilingual opportunities into the learning process — especially those that embark from the students' own multilingual practices.

Inevitably, there are many different agendas for the promotion of language teaching in society. In many cases there exists an implicit goal of "assimilation" language teaching wherein minority speakers are encouraged to learn the majority language. This is often accompanied by transitional language teaching aimed at enabling minority speakers to be able to "function" in the majority language. Often, these "assimilation" language teaching policies run parallel to education programmes which foster the teaching of a second (foreign) language that is rarely used in the local context —as is often seen in careers or higher education that require a second language (frequently referred to as an "elite" foreign language agenda).

Of course, the above agendas are largely hinged upon a common dichotomy of monolingual versus bi/multilingual teaching, especially when considered within the context of monolingual societies. The notion of monolingual societies is principally based on the ideology that one nation-state is equal to one culture is equal to one language while, in actual fact multilingualism is the norm in most parts of the world. Indeed, just as there are multilingual nations, societies and communities, a large part of the world's population is made up of multilingual individuals. Tapping into that resource is an important challenge for today's educator. Fortunately, many teachers recognise the role of multiple language learning for its cognitive benefits and the contribution language learning can make to advancement in general education.

Multiple language integration is also becoming more predominant in a student-centred approach —students who are multilingual can be the point of departure for other students' language-learning, while validating the multilingual students' language. This perspective challenges the previously mentioned "assimilation" model. In this chapter, the first authors (Melanie Kunkel and Gabriele Budach) present the concept of two-way immersion –including its historical, political and pedagogical implications -within the German context. They focus in particular on the benefits of bilingual literacy; however, they go outside the sphere of foreign language teaching to discuss mother tongue maintenance, and intercultural and social learning. In their article, the authors highlight the nature of multilingualism as a resource, rather than as the sole outcome of institutionally based foreign language learning.

In the second article, Joan Netten and Claude Germaine consider an intensive programme within a literacy-based approach to second language teaching (in this case French in Canada). Seen as an enrichment of an already existent Core Language Programme, it provides intensive exposure to the target language (70% of the school day) for a set period of time (five months) at the end of the students' elementary schooling (between the ages of 11 to 12). The emphasis is on literacy skills (reading, writing and speaking) and is promoted through various activities integrated into the school programme. Different from CLIL, the target language is *not* used as part of the teaching and learning of another subject, the focus in on transferable literacy skills.

Crossing the Atlantic once again, the last section of this chapter discusses a case study in France. Andrea Young is interested in teaching processes that acknowledge and capitalise on the infinitely diverse sets of cultural and linguistic knowledge and skills pupils bring wth them when they come to school. Within this premise, she outlines the "Didenheim project" —a project set up in a French primary school whose aims were "to invent a new teaching and learning model and to make space in the curriculum for dealing with diversity" (Young, this volume). Similar to the Italo-German project described by Kunkel and Budach, this project counted on intensive parental participation, indeed, parents became the "teachers" within the programme. Young outlines the way the project was set up, the importance of teacher-parent cooperation, and the co-construction of knowledge by all the social actors involved.

This section points out how multilingual interaction can lead to exploration of each pupil's knowledge and skills and how this knowledges can, in turn, complement other individuals' knowledge and skills, consequently helping to build trust and mutual respect between parents, teachers and students.

Two-Way Immersion in Germany: Notes on Teaching and Learning Practice

Melanie Kunkel and Gabriele Budach

In the past 14 years, a number of bilingual school sections have been created across Germany, all of them following the model of two-way immersion (Christian, 1996; Cloud, Genesee, & Hamayan, 2000; Torres-Guzmán, 2002). Although the ways in which these programs are set up vary across different contexts, they still share a number of common features. One of these is that the two languages are given equal status as target languages and languages of instruction. This means that pupils from the majority language background are not at an advantage compared to the other language speaking students. (In this particular case, the two languages were German and Italian.) Secondly, half of the class is made up of children with a migrant background with knowledge of the project partner language (again, in this case Italian) and the other half of class is composed of children from a German-speaking background who have no knowledge of the other language prior to schooling. (Some of the children speak other languages apart from these two languages.) A third feature is team-teaching consisting of one German teacher and a teacher with the project partner language and cultural background. Both teachers are in the classroom together most of the time, although at times the children may be separated into different language groups.

This contribution will focus specifically on the model of two-way immersion in a German-Italian bilingual program implemented in three schools in the inner city of Frankfurt. We will be discussing the benefits and challenges of two-way immersion as an innovative model of cross-linguistic and cross-cultural education. In doing so, we will highlight some of the methods and forms of bilingual teaching and learning, such as team teaching and student centred, collaborative project work.

Two-way immersion

Two-way immersion in Germany has a number of goals (Lindholm-Leary, 2001), however, it generally seeks to create benefits for children from a migrant background as well as for children from a monolingual German background. This is extremely important for school success considering that —as happens in other Western societies— children from a German background do comparatively better in schools than children from migrant backgrounds. Two-way immersion is aimed at addressing the needs of both children from migrant and German background.

On the one hand, this approach helps children from migrant background to maintain their linguistic and cultural heritage and to become confident and proficient speakers of German, and on the other this program offers an opportunity for German speaking children to learn a second language and to become bilingual and bi-literate at an early age. At the same time the students can discover and experience another culture. The underlying condition for the project's success is to create a collaborative and cooperative learning culture that values both Italian and German (Gutiérrez, Baquedano-López, Alvarez, & Chiu, 1999; Manyak, 2001). It thereby serves as a basis for developing bilingual identity models as well as meta-linguistic knowledge that will help children learn other languages more easily (Hufeisen & Neuner, 2003).

Some aspects of two-way immersion are shared with another approach known as Content and language integrated learning (CLIL) that is relatively widespread in the German school system (see Chapter Three). Although both models make use of another language apart from German as the language of instruction, there is an important difference between the two language teaching approaches. While CLIL-teaching focuses on a comparison of trans-national contents and culture (e.g. Environmental politics in England given in lessons of Geography and taught through English) two-way immersion is concerned with and primarily addresses linguistic and cultural diversity inside the classroom itself.

Two-way immersion in Germany: a case study in Frankfurt

The Italo-German school project in Frankfurt was started in 1997/98. Being one of the most important migrant communities in the Frankfurt area[1], many of the Italians and their descendents are relatively well integrated, socially and economically. However, the second and third generations of Italian migrants still count among the least academically successful in the province's schools compared to other ethnic groups[2]. Significantly, the project has grown out of an initiative of Italian and German parents – many of them living in mixed marriages – who founded a parents' association in 1995. Its goal was to help the design and implementation of a bilingual German-Italian school project in Frankfurt (Fillia, 2003) thus ensuring an opportunity for migrant children to maintain their linguistic and cultural heritage, and for Italian and German children to develop competent bilingualism and bi-literacy. Initial difficulties had to be overcome at different levels, not least of which finding a primary school in the predominantly German-speaking community that was interested in establishing a bilingual class. Arguments against Italian were largely based on prejudices against Italian children who were considered "too lively and exhausting". Moreover, according to language hierarchies that dominate the German linguistic market, it was argued that English would have been a more valuable and therefore preferred choice for some schools.

However, thanks to the strenuous efforts and support by the parents' association, local migrant institutions and the Italian consulate in Frankfurt, a bilateral treaty between the Republic of Italy and the Land of Hesse was established that created a legal basis for the bilingual program. According to this agreement, Italian teachers are sent to Germany to work with the German teacher as a team partner (paid by the Italian government). In 1997/98 the first bilingual program started at primary school level (Haller & Pagliuca Romano, 2002), which was continued at secondary level in 2003/04 in a gymnasium. (This opportunity is more widely used by children from an Italian background, whose interest in maintaining their Italian heritage is a priority for them, than by children

---

[1] In 2004, Frankfurt had 165 600 inhabitants with a foreign passport (26.5 %), among which 14 494 were inhabitants with an Italian passport. Of course this number does not take into account the inhabitants with Italian background holding a German passport.

[2] The Italian minority is the third largest migrant community in the Frankfurt area, following the Turkish and migrant communities from former Yugoslavia. This is reflected in a school population of migrant origin (2005) consisting of 41,239 students of Turkish origin, 10,475 of Yugoslavian, and 7,528 of Italian origin. The percentage of Italian students sent to special education is higher compared to other migrant groups (in 2005 8.02 % of the Italian group, compared to 7.14 % out of the Turkish school population and 6.25 % of the Ex-Yugoslavian student body). www.statistik-hessen.de/themenauswahl/bildung-kultur-rechtspflege/index.html.

from a German background interested in learning Italian as a second language.) In response to an ever increasing demand, specifically from Italian parents, a second bilingual class at primary school level opened in September 2003.

Organizing the project: Getting the schools, parents and community involved

Organizing a two-way immersion program implies modifying the framework of regular German schooling. Bilingual teaching at secondary level is carried out in focus-areas. Typically, the key areas chosen are mathematics, German and Italian as main subjects that are taught bilingually and (partly) through team-teaching, with biology, history, art and geography being taught in German or Italian alternating the language of instruction each semester or year.

This is best explained through an example. The timetable of grade 6 comprises a total of 29 hours of teaching per week, divided in the following way: Italian and German are taught 2 hours each by the German or Italian mother tongue teacher and 3 hours a week by the bilingual team. Mathematics (4 h/week) is taught one hour by the German teacher and three hours by both in team teaching. Geography (2 h) and biology (2 h) are taught in Italian. Physical education (3 h), religion (2 h) and music (2 h) are taught in German; and art (2 h) is taught by a German teacher who is also fluent in Italian. English is taught 5 h/week by a German teacher.

Another challenge to the bilingual program is how to establish a curriculum that takes into account contents from the German and Italian curricula at the same time. The German curriculum (and more precisely: the version that has been implemented in the context of Hesse[3]) serves as a standard model across Germany, which puts Italian curricular contents in a marginalized position and creates difficulties for integrating both languages and cultures in a balanced manner[4]. Although the bilingual program described here is committed to giving both languages and their respective curricular contents equal status, the implementation of this principle is not always easy. It is achieved through trans-cultural

---

[3] In Germany, educational policy is nearly an exclusive domain of its 16 States (*Länder*). Berlin has been the first *Land* to develop an official curriculum for the middle school of its Italo-German section.

[4] In Germany, educational policy is nearly an exclusive domain of its 16 States (*Länder*). Berlin has been the first *Land* to develop an official curriculum for the middle school of its Italo-German section.

negotiation between the two teachers who are collaborating in the bilingual team.

Another important pillar of two-way immersion is the commitment and participation of parents and communities (Calderón & Minaya-Rowe, 2003). In Frankfurt, the parents' association "biLiS" plays an important role in sustaining the two-way programs. Founded in 1997 by Italian and German parents, the association currently has about 400 members. The association supports the purchase of Italian school material, manuals, dictionaries, audio material, and books for the school library for the three schools involved in the project. Moreover, the association helps provide children's lunch in an Italian-speaking environment and extracurricular activities in Italian (e.g. afternoon art classes with Italian language instruction). Additionally, German parents are offered the possibility to attend Italian language courses. Occasionally, biLiS organises special events, such as an exhibit in the Frankfurt town hall in 2005 presenting the Italian-German project to a larger public; or community events such as a flea market offering literacy resources in Italian, e.g. books, educational games and music.

Collaboration in bilingual teaching and learning

A core feature of the implementation strategy is collaboration, of which two aspects in particular will be discussed here: team-teaching and collaboration in linguistically mixed groups of students. As for team teaching: In secondary school, team-teaching is used for mathematics, German and Italian. During the team-teaching, both teachers are present in the classroom, however, they divide their roles and activities differently. Teachers generally speak exclusively in their native language and avoid doubling content work. Outside of the class, the bilingual teams work together one hour per week to prepare the lessons. During these coordination hours they decide what content to teach, divide it linguistically, choose material and decide how to adapt it to the needs of bilingual teaching. As there is little material of this kind available, the work is very demanding and a real challenge for creative minds.

Teachers in the team do not have fixed roles, but switch according to the teaching situation and the needs of individual children. They intervene in situations when needed, e.g. helping with vocabulary, or creating links with learning situations in prior contexts. When children work individually, they circulate in the classroom and help children by making comments and giving suggestions on the children's work. On other occasions, the class is divided into two groups allowing teachers to differentiate children according to their linguistic repertoire and by creating specific conditions for content and language learning.

In interviews, teachers stated unanimously that team teaching is also an excellent occasion for observing the partner's practice. To see how teachers and children act is understood as a major resource that contributes to reflecting on and developing further their own practice. Moreover, collaboration in general is seen as a source of enrichment. Collaborating in a team, teachers not only get to know different, nationally bound cultures of learning and methods of teaching, they also see and understand the various ways in which intercultural teaching and learning can become a naturalised practice in a (bilingual) school environment.

Admittedly, however, team teaching is a difficult process, since it relies on a highly complex relationship between institutions and individuals (Arkoudis & Creese, 2006). Team teaching must comprise knowledge about contents and norms of institutional culture which teachers then incorporate into cultural capital (valued as part of the curriculum). This capital can be different in nature and status, so its value for teaching must be negotiated continuously. A training program for bilingual team teaching does not exist in the German context, but it would be a substantial help for those interested in teaching in a bilingual program. It would be equally beneficial for teachers wanting to improve their collaboration by helping them to critically reflect on the complex nature of that relationship.

An example of collaborative teaching can be seen in the set up of a maths lesson. If a new topic has been introduced in Italian, pupils are asked to gather their own ideas and comment on the topic in German. With the help of the German and Italian teacher, they search for various possible ways to solve a set problem. They then start dealing with tasks presented in both German and Italian. On both the primary and the secondary level, teachers confirm that mathematics is a suitable subject for bilingual learning and team teaching. Even children with relatively little knowledge of the partner language have equal possibilities of participation as numbers and symbols are universally used. However, verbal expression is equally required and developed in these lessons, for instance, when students are asked to present their results in front of the class and to verbalize their own way of solving a problem.

In lessons of Italian and German, some aspects are evidently different. While some literacy knowledge of text genres (e.g. skills of how to describe a picture, how to do a presentation or to correctly employ conventions for producing specific genres, such as letters) can be taught across languages, specific knowledge of national literature and culturally bound literacy practices has to be addressed specifically. This requires close collaboration between the teachers and an interweaving of content and language learning into a joint and coherent practice that addresses specific contents and particular linguistic grammatical structures in a more pronounced manner than in math teaching.

The principle of contrastive comparison can be used in interesting and fruitful ways. There are various grammatical features that are potentially suitable for this kind of contrastive approach, such as the building of adjectives or the use of the passive voice in German and Italian. The study of specific grammatical features, thereby, can be related to conventions of producing specific genres of texts in literature (e.g. poetry) and literacy practices (addressing genres such as cooking recipes, genres of news-writing) and differences between spoken and written language. Especially in higher grades, the reading and discussion of literature can provide interesting opportunities for contrastive work. For example, in grade 10 a number of poems from World War II and the period shortly after were treated in activities of bilingual learning. Comparing Italian and German texts allowed students to develop a critical understanding of the different points of view about the war on both sides, in Italy and Germany.

As for child-focused cooperative learning as a way to address linguistic and cultural diversity: One goal of two-way immersion is to integrate the children's knowledge about language and culture. A way to address this capital is by organizing group and pair work that encourage learning between peers. To organise cross-linguistic peer work spatially, children from Italian and German background are paired. This strategy is used in primary schools and favours the implementation of bilingual learning routines which systematically integrate the diverse language registers of children with German and Italian background. This practice contributes to the building of a bilingual learning culture in which both languages and cultures have equal status while enhancing mutual collaboration. Thus the knowledge of migrant children is systematically valued, and the process of German children asking for help in Italian whenever it is needed is legitimised (e.g. translation of single words/phrases, explanation of specifically Italian concepts). These activities enhance the contrastive comparison of linguistic structures as well as concepts of culture that children handle competently already in the first years of schooling. Additionally, these practices also reveal that cultural knowledge is not neutral, but rather subscribed to a value hierarchy of linguistic varieties and cultural practices.

This can be illustrated by an example of group work carried out in a geography lesson in grade 6 where the language of instruction is Italian and the topic are the regions of Italy. To explore the knowledge of Italian children in the class, the teachers proposed a project idea to be carried out in linguistically mixed groups. The project output was a presentation of an Italian region, featuring aspects of daily life such as history, culture and geography of that region. As some of the children have a Southern Italian background the teacher suggested Sicily as the topic. The goal of the group work was to create a poster about "Sicilian topics". The children with Sicilian background were named as the "leader" of a group who then chose the other members of their team. After the teams had selected their subjects, the teachers provided some material (such as newspaper clippings, photographs, books, maps, etc.) and the children brought material from home and other (community) resources known to them.

Examples of children's collaborative, multilingual work

The posters proved to be rich and original pieces of work. They included various textual and visual resources (cooking recipes, photos of Mount Etna and other images of the Sicilian countryside, texts about the history and every day life on the island), all creatively assembled and formed into complex multi-modal representations of Sicily. The following examples cast light on aspects of the social interaction taking place between the children while composing and discussing the posters' contents. (Data was collected primarily by retrospective interviews with the children in which they were asked to reflect on their experience of group work.) Focusing on three children from Southern Italian background, the case studies illustrate, on the one hand, the positive impact of group work in valuing children from different backgrounds. On the other hand, they also reveal tensions and the hierarchy of knowledge that contributes to categorisations the children held.

Example 1: Alessandro arrived with his parents from Sicily five years ago. He is highly motivated to participate in the project. He brings a lot of material from contexts outside the school and contributes knowledge and stories that his father told him about fighting against the mafia. He is proud of being seen as a "specialist" of Sicily, and stresses the role his father had by helping him to provide and display his specialist knowledge. This demonstrates the important role of parents in contributing to their children's learning.

Alessandro's contribution is received by the children with mixed enthusiasm: some appreciate it, some do not. Fabian, a German pupil who valued Alessandro's contribution, ascribes him the role of expert that arises from a type of knowledge only someone from an Italian background would have.

> Er hat schon halt viel über so Kultur, eher so in Sizilien so, wie kann man das sagen, von der Bevölkerung her, wir andern können zur Kultur sagen, o. k., *tempi di Agrigento,* aber er kann halt wirklich sagen, wie's innerhalb dieses Staates aussieht [...]. Ich fand interessant, dass er erzählt hatte, dass es in Sizilien ganz schlimm wenige Krankenhäuser gibt, da gibt es wirklich, der wohnt irgendwie in Enna, hier in der Nähe, da irgendwo [zeigt es auf der Karte], genau, und das nächste Krankenhaus ist da [zeigt es auf der Karte], bei Nicósia oder Nicosía [...] und dann wusste er natürlich was übers Essen und so.

> He has talked a lot about culture, well in Sicily, how would you say it, regarding the population, we are only able to talk about culture, like *tempi di Agrigento,* but he is able to tell us how things really are in this state. [...] I found what he told us to be interesting, like that about there being few hospitals in Sicily, it is horrible, there is really, he lives somehow near Enna, near here [he shows the distance marking it on the map], somewhere there, exactly, and the next hospital is there [he shows it on the map again], near Nicósia or Nicosía [...] and then, of course, he knew more things about food and so on. (translation by authors)

In the example Fabian distinguishes between two types of knowledge; a kind of cultural knowledge that every one, especially tourists, can have (e.g. temples in Agrigento, one of the major tourist attractions in Sicily) and a kind of "authentic knowledge" that only someone "from inside" who is sharing the practice of every day life can have. Identifying Alessandro's knowledge as being authentic Fabian assigns him the role of an expert in the group. He thereby appreciates his classmate's knowledge about the scarcity of hospitals in Sicily that reveals a kind of knowledge that is directly linked to his father's and his Italian family's experience.

Example 2: The same task of making a poster on Sicily leads to different points of view from Barbara and Sabine. Barbara's father is Sicilian and her mother is Calabrian; Sabine's parents are both German. Although she has a German background, Sabine feels competent and well informed about Italy, based on previous trips there. Barbara, on the other hand, draws on her Italian background and brings material from home (including books, tourist guides, photographs, etc.) for the poster activity. Being valued by her classmates makes her feels proud.

However, her German classmate Sabine contests Barbara's role as an expert by classifying her knowledge as "tourist" knowledge that is accessible to anyone who travels to the region –regardless of any particular socio-cultural or linguistic background. Coincidentally, Sabine had been to Italy the previous summer —however not to Sicily, but to Naples. Since Naples is not the topic of the task she is not able to contribute her experience in the same way as Barbara does.

> Hätten wir ein anderes Land gemacht, *Napoli*, da war ich auf dem *Vesuvio*, nur haben wir's nicht gemacht.

> If we had been asked to work on a different region, like *Napoli*, I have been there, to *Vesuvio*, but we didn't do that.

As the two examples show, choosing Sicily as the poster topic prioritises the knowledge of children from Italian background and strengthens their social position in the class. This was a specific strategy employed by the teachers to "authenticate their knowledge" —as occurred with Fabian. This did not always work as the students with German background had often travelled to Italy on holidays. Thus, in the second case, Sabine felt she was able to challenge Barbara's expert role.

Example 3: The third example illustrates a situation in which 'insider knowledge' of the type previously described is not accepted by the German members of the group. This was made apparent during a retrospective interview where Marina —whose mother is from Naples and her father from Sicily— remembers the group work as unpleasant and embarrassing, because other members of the group responded negatively about her contribution to the collective work. Marina's knowledge was not only devalued, but also laughed at, as is exemplified in the other students' comments during an interview after the lesson.

> (C=Cristina; V=Vittoria; I=Interviewer)
> C: (über Marinas Beitrag:) Sie hat uns eher was von seinem[5] privaten Leben erzählt.
> [...]
> I: Und das ist nicht interessant?
> V: Nee, das können wir nicht aufs Plakat machen.
> I: Was war denn das zum Beispiel?
> C: Wie viele Bewohner dort wohnen.
> V: Ja, so'n paar und dass da irgendwie nur

---

[5] The use of the possessive pronoun "seine" instead of "ihre" is due to interference: in Italian, there is no distinction between the masculine and the feminine possessive pronoun. Cristina has Italian parents and she attended elementary school in Italy for one year.

C: und dass da seine Oma und seine Großeltern, die hat
V: Cousins und so
I: Aber ist das jetzt, das könnt ihr nicht aufs PLAKAT machen, aber ist das vielleicht trotzdem interessant?
C: Ja, wir haben uns das zwar angehört, aber dann haben wir fast, glaub ich, zwei Stunden so verplempert, um nur seine Geschichte anzuhören, und dann mussten wir uns am Ende beeilen.
I: Aber so ganz persönlich findet ihr das spannend?
V: Ganz langweilig.
C: Langweilig.

C: (about Marina's contribution:) She only told us about her private life. [...]
I: And this is not interesting?
V: No, we couldn't put this on the poster.
I: What did she tell you, for instance?
C: How many inhabitants live there.
V: Yes, very few, and that somehow only
C: and that her grandmother and her grandparents, she has
V: cousins etc.
I: But is this, you can't put it on the POSTER, but is this perhaps nevertheless interesting?
C: Yes, we have listened to it, but then, I think, we have wasted nearly two hours like that, only by listening to her stories, and then, in the end, we were in a hurry.
I But personally, did you find this exciting?
V: Completely boring.
C: Boring.

Marina's stories about private life and family issues were considered boring. Furthermore they were not considered useful for the purpose of the activity, as they could not be used for making the poster. This negative evaluation of Marina's knowledge was partly due to forms of institutional pressure. As the group knew that the poster would be marked in the end, they purposely selected "relevant" and "non-relevant" information, reproducing previously acquired norms of what counts as legitimate, valuable knowledge and what does not. "Story telling" does not count as a valuable genre, although facts and numbers do. But even the information about less dense settlement in Sicily was disregarded, since the input "a few" people as non-countable did not seem to be relevant as a resource to be put on the poster.

The ways in which children remembered their experience of project work demonstrate two types of reaction. While for Alessandro it obviously was a positive experience, Marina had negative feelings about it. Thus, bringing in children's knowledge as a source for positive learning does not work unconditionally. Not all types of "expert knowledge" are valued in the same way because they are submitted to institutional norms of what counts as "legitimate" or "illegitimate" knowledge.

Due to socialized understanding of "knowledge", facts about nature, art, history and political life count more than practices of family and everyday life. Therefore Fabian appreciates Alessandro's stories about fighting the mafia, while Marina's peers devalue her resources and stories that are not used for the collective work. In order to give legitimacy to the kinds of resources that Marina has to contribute, teachers should explicitly invite and encourage discussion about practices that are rooted in the every-day life of families, communities and institutions such as churches. This will legitimise them as a valuable resource to be explored and positively evaluated in discussions and tasks in schools.

Conclusion

Only a few aspects of two-way immersion have been touched on this overview. However, the insights presented here have shown that two-way immersion programs, as they are implemented in German schools, can open new perspectives for including resources coming from children of different linguistic and cultural backgrounds. Arguing from a socio-cultural perspective, this can help children and encourage their learning by creating an environment in which bilingualism and plurilingual identities are legitimate. Furthermore, studies in two-way immersion can contribute to the development of pedagogy in multilingual classrooms, so that such programmes are not confined to the setting of bilingual programs, but rather become part of and enhance learning in mainstream schools as well.

Works Cited

Arkoudis, Sophie and Angela Creese, eds. 2006. "Teacher-Teacher Talk: The Discourse of Collaboration in Linguistically Diverse Classrooms." *Special Issue of the International Journal of Bilingual Education and Bilingualism*, 9 (4): 434-453.

Budach, Gabriele. 2005. "Mehrsprachigkeit in der Grundschule? Betrachtungen zur Praxis von Language Awareness in einem bilingualen Projekt." In *Niemals zu früh und selten zu spät. Fremdsprachenunterricht in Schule und Erwachsenenbildung*, ed. Eva Burwitz-Melzer and Gert Solmecke, 43-52. Berlin: Cornelsen.

Calderón, Margarita E. and Liliana Minaya-Rowe. 2003. *Designing and Implementing Two-Way Bilingual Programs. A Step-by-Step Guide for Administrators, Teachers, and Parents*. Thousand Oaks, London: Sage.

Christian, Donna. 1996. "Two-Way Immersion Education: Students Learning Through Two Languages." *The Modern Language Journal*, 80, 66-76.

Cloud, Nancy, Fred Genesee, and Else Hamayan. 2000. *Dual Language Instruction. A Handbook for Enriched Education*. Boston, MA: Heinle and Heinle.

Fillia, Elena. 2003. "Das bilinguale deutsch-italienische Schulprojekt in Frankfurt am Main." In *Sprache, Mehrsprachigkeit und Migration als Gegenstand und Ressource sozialer Identifikationsprozesse*, ed. Jürgen Erfurt, Gabriele Budach and Sabine Hofmann, 221-226. Frankfurt: Peter Lang.

Gutiérrez, Kris D., Patricia Baquedano-López, Hector H. Alvarez, and Ming Ming Chiu. 1999. "Building a Culture of Collaboration Through Hybrid Language Practice." *Theory into Practice*, 38 (2), 87-93.

Haller, Ingrid and Anna Pagliuca Romano. 2002. *Auf der Reise nach Europa. In viaggio verso l'Europa. Bilinguales Lernen an einer Grundschule*. Witten: pad.

Hufeisen, Britta and Gerhard Neuner, eds. 2003. *Mehrsprachigkeitskonzept- Tertiärsprachenlernen —Deutsch nach Englisch*. Strasbourg: Council of European Publishing.

Lindholm-Leary, Kathryn. 2001. *Dual Language Education*. Clevedon: Multilingual Matters.

Manyak, Patrick. 2001. "Participation, hybridity, and carneval: A situated analysis of a dynamic literacy practice in a primary-grade English immersion classroom." *Journal of Literacy Research,* 33 (3), 423-465.

Torres-Guzmán, Maria E. 2002. "Dual language programs: Key features and results." *Directions in Language and Education*, 14, 1-16.

LEARNING TO COMMUNICATE EFFECTIVELY THROUGH INTENSIVE INSTRUCTION IN FRENCH

JOAN NETTEN AND CLAUDE GERMAIN

In Canada there are basically two types of programs for the learning of French as a second language (FSL): French immersion and Core French. Immersion is a program in which the subjects (such as social studies, science, etc.) are learned through the medium of the second language. There are several variations of this program: early, middle and late, depending on the grade level at which the program starts. Participation in this program is a very effective means of learning to communicate in French. However, for many reasons (political, administrative, social, pedagogical, etc.), only 15% of the English-speaking student population studying French participate in this program; universal participation is not feasible. Thus, 85% of the English student population learns French through what is generally called "Core French". In this program French is normally taught daily for brief periods of time (30 to 40 minutes/day), usually starting in grade 4 (students 9 years of age). Participation in this program tends to be compulsory until the end of grade 9 or 10 (age 14-16), at which time about 90% of the students drop the program. Therefore, despite the fact that Canada is a bilingual country, only a small proportion of its anglophone population speaks French.

Rationale for developing Intensive French

The studies of Core French that have been undertaken in the last 30 years indicate that the results of Core French are not satisfactory (Shapson, Kaufman and Durward, 1978; Stern, 1982; Lapkin, Harley and Taylor, 1995; Calman and Daniel, 1998; Turnbull, 1999). In an attempt to make the program more effective, a National Core French Study was undertaken to bring about a more communicative approach (LeBlanc, 1990). While the suggested changes brought about some improvement, they did not radically change the teaching strategies used in the program. As a result

Core French has not been able to achieve the goal of developing communicative competence for most students.

Since 2002, provincial evaluators have interviewed a large sample of students at the beginning of grade 5 or 6 in four provinces/territories. Results indicate that 98% of the students tested are unable to communicate in French after between 360 to 450 hours of Core French instruction (Netten and Germain, 2005, 2006a). Even at the end of grade 9 or 10, interview results have shown that students are still unable to communicate in French (Atlantic Provinces Education Foundation, 2002; Government of New Brunswick, 2005). Since students do not experience success in the program, motivation to study French declines and attitudes towards learning French become negative.

Intensive French Description of the program

Intensive French was conceptualized by the authors of this article to improve the communication skills and the attitudes of Core French students. It is a five month program that is inserted into Core French in grade 5 or grade 6, when students are 10 to 12 years of age and are still at the beginning of their second language learning experience. The program is open to all students, including those with learning difficulties (Netten and Germain, 2004).

Results are very positive. After five months of Intensive French students are able to communicate spontaneously on topics of interest to them at a level that is congruent with their cognitive development. They also are able to write a narrative composition of one or more paragraphs, without the use of a dictionary, similar to compositions written by native Quebec francophones between grades 2 and 3. These results are based on data collected from over 1500 Intensive French students in five provinces (Netten and Germain, 2006b).

The program began in 1998 as a three year experiment in Newfoundland and Labrador where there was considerable interest in improving Core French due, in particular, to the impossibility of implementing immersion programs in the many very small rural communities. The provincial department of Education decided to adopt the program as an official alternate to Core French in 2002. Once the program was established in this province, it began to expand across the country. Departments of Education or school districts in all the other provinces, except Quebec, and two territories have initiated pilot projects in their jurisdictions. From September 1998 to June 2007, over 10,000 students have participated in Intensive French across Canada, and the number continues to grow.

Differences from the mainstream understanding of a communicative approach to FSL

There are two major changes from the regular Core French program that characterize Intensive French. One is the increase in both time and intensity of exposure to French during five months of the school year. Research has shown that intensity of exposure to second language (SL) instruction increases significantly student achievement (Lightbown and Spada, 1994). Since French is taught for approximately 70% of the school day, instruction in French is increased from the normal 90 hours a year to around 300 hours. In order to achieve this amount of time, no other subjects are taught during the five months of Intensive French except mathematics, and some other specialist subjects, such as religion, art and music, which are taught in English; in the other five months, the students return to the regular timetable where all subjects are taught in English, except French, which returns to only 10% of the curriculum.

The tasks undertaken in the FSL classroom are similar to those undertaken in other subject areas, thus assuring the cognitive development of the students. For example, students do a survey of the musical tastes of their peers, and report the results by using graphs, as they would do in a science class. English language instruction is reduced by 50% as a large proportion of the goals are met through Intensive French, as, for example, communicating ideas effectively or writing paragraphs of various types. All the learning outcomes of the grade 5 or 6 curriculum are achieved because of the transdisciplinary nature of the Intensive French curriculum (Germain and Netten, 2005a and 2007). In this way SL instruction is integrated with instruction in the regular curriculum.

Despite the reduction in time for the other subjects, students show no lags in English language development in the provincial tests at the end of grade 5 or 6. Students also show no lags in the learning outcomes specified for other subject areas, particularly with respect to cognitive processes and skills. Parents and teachers also indicate that the students develop greater learning autonomy in general, and a more positive attitude to the learning of French (Germain and Netten, 2004). The theoretical foundations for this part of the program are found in the work of Vygotsky on the unified nature of cognitive development (1986) and of Cummins on the interdependence of languages (2001).

The second major change is in the teaching strategies used for both oral and written communication. Since the advent of the communicative approach to FSL instruction, the general pattern that has been followed in the development of curriculum resources is based on the need for explicit knowledge of the language patterns to be used. This may be expressed as follows: knowledge of vocabulary, verb forms, and pattern or rule, followed by practice exercises to internalize the pattern, followed by activities to encourage spontaneous communication using the learned structures. An examination of the most widely used curriculum programs in Canada demonstrates this pattern. The underlying assumption is that explicit knowledge becomes a skill which enables students to speak spontaneously. However, this assumption is not supported by recent neurolinguistic research which indicates that knowledge cannot become a skill; the two are located in different areas of the brain, with no direct connection between them (Paradis, 2004). In addition, implicit competence is acquired incidentally and unconsciously (without focusing on it) by using the language. Learning a language for the purposes of oral communication is a constructivist activity on the part of the student; each student must construct his own internal grammar; external grammars are only useful for writing activities. The ability to use a language orally is a skill and is acquired by use in an authentic situation. In Intensive French, oral language learning is contextualized in a real situation.

Current Core French resources also assume that the ability to read and write is simply transferred from the first language. In Intensive French the processes involved in reading and writing are re-taught for use in the second language. For reading, this includes the development of word recognition skills, a new set of sound-symbol relationships and development of strategies necessary for successful comprehension of print material. For writing, the difference between what is heard orally and the written form of the same words or sentences needs to be taught. This is the moment when explicit knowledge can be taught, as in written work students have the time to mentally consult consciously learned information about word forms. The reteaching of reading and writing skills enables students with learning problems to be included. Because of the emphasis on literacy, oral development precedes reading and writing, and the latter two skills are closely related to their oral foundations (Germain and Netten, 2005b). For written communication, which includes both reading and writing, teaching strategies based on a literacy approach to language teaching are used.

Intensive French has many similarities with immersion education. Both programs offer an intensive exposure to the target language in the beginning stages and are based on the acquisition of implicit competence in the language that supports the development of spontaneous communication. Both programs also advocate a literacy approach to the teaching of reading and writing. However, in contrast with immersion instruction, students in Intensive French do not learn subject matter at the same time. In Intensive French, the focus is on the learning of the language first.

Intensive French is very different from mainstream Core French instruction. It begins with an intensive exposure to the target language rather than short periods of instruction. It is based on the premise that oral competence in a language can only be achieved through language use rather than the learning of vocabulary and rules; it is an approach which is centred on the sentence rather than on words. Thirdly, it teaches students how to read and write in the target language; it does not assume that students can transfer these skills from English to the FSL classroom. Consequently, it enables children to develop biliteracy, "the ability to use language and images in varied forms to read, write, listen, speak, view, represent, and think critically about ideas, to share information, to interact with others, to make meaning" (Government of Ontario, 2004) in both French and English. These changes enable FSL instruction to be integrated into the general educational development of the students and the learning of the language itself is contextualized and integrated into the life of the student.

Descriptive example

The four teaching strategies which are crucial to the success of Intensive French are: modeling, use and reuse, and the use of complete sentences in order to make links between the elements of the language, as well as correction. The strategies are not in themselves completely new; many teachers use them from time to time. In Intensive French we require that teachers use them all of the time to the exclusion of use of other strategies.

1. Modelling. Each unit, lesson or pedagogical theme begins with oral modelling. If we suppose the theme is domestic animals with the help of gestures or even pictures, a teacher can say: *J'ai un chien. Il s'appelle....* If the teacher doesn't have a dog, she can talk about a friend's or relative's dog, or about a cat or a bird, as the case may be. Similarly, if the theme is music, the teacher can use the same teaching strategy, and begin by saying, for example, *J'aime la musique pop.* Naturally, still in the interests of authenticity, the teacher would make sure to present right from the beginning some useful negative forms: *J'aime la musique pop mais je n'aime pas la musique country.* This format is important in order to give the model to the student of the sentence that she must use. This personal involvement is necessary in order to motivate the students to want to communicate their real likes and interests. A similar strategy can easily be used to introduce another theme, such as sports, and so on for most themes covered in the classroom in the beginning stages of L2 instruction.

The use of this strategy is in contrast to beginning a lesson or unit with the presentation of new vocabulary words, or examples of structures and rules of grammar out of context. It is more authentic than the latter because it immediately enables the learner to communicate a message; it focuses the attention on the learners and encourages them to become actively involved in the learning process.

2. Use and reuse of the modelled sentence. To encourage use and reuse of the language in the classroom, the teacher creates multiple situations giving the students numerous opportunities to use the previously modelled sentence. It is to be noted that this strategy does not mean that learners repeat without any alteration the sentence modelled by the teacher; each student replies to the question with his own information. Thus, students hear and use the modelled sentence several times, but with slight variations. It is also to be noted that the modelled sentence is not simply "repeated" out of context, as was the case with audiolingual methods. Rather, it is reproduced in a form adapted to the students' personal situation in such a way as to demonstrate effectively that a language is, in fact, a means of communicating through the use of real information. It is this type of use of the language that has been termed the development of "creative automaticity" (Gatbonton and Segalowitz, 2005) as elements of the sentence are changed with its use by different individual learners. In the classroom, this teaching strategy takes four different forms.

a) Asking the question which requires the use of the modelled sentence, slightly adapted according to the personal situation of the student, as the answer. To return to one of the examples given above, suppose the teacher has provided the students with the following linguistic model concerning pets: *J'ai un chien.* The teacher then continues immediately afterwards by asking the question: *Et toi? As-tu un chien? Comment s'appelle-t-il?*

The vocabulary words that students will need to convey their messages are then provided *orally* by the teacher upon request. Vocabulary is much more likely to be retained by learners if it is provided to answer a need, and not in a series of words without a context. It is to be noted that integrating all new vocabulary into a real sentence (*J'ai un chien. Il s'appelle...*) effectively demonstrates that a language is not used primarily to describe, as is implied by the content of most textbooks on the market which begin lessons with *Qu'est-ce que c'est? – C'est...*, but rather, to communicate. It is also important to note that the teacher does not write on the board during the oral part of a lesson, as doing so interferes with the development of the student's auditory memory.

b) Interacting with students. If we return to our example of a discussion on domestic animals, after preparing the students by modelling the sentence, and the interaction pattern, the teacher will then ask students to ask the question to other students in the class, thus ensuring that students can use the question correctly, and at the same time modelling the activity which will follow.

c) Encouraging students to interact with each other. The students engage in short conversations with each other, using the question and answer learned. In pairs, each student in turn asks her partner the questions '*As-tu un chien?*' (*un chat?* etc.) *Comment s'appelle-t-il?* and replies. The students also change patners and ask the same questions a second time.

d) Encouraging listening and participation amongst all students. In order to stimulate interaction in the classroom and as a way of giving students further opportunities to reuse the interaction pattern, the teacher questions the students on what their partners have said as for example: *Quel est l'animal favori de Nicole? Quelle sorte de musique est-ce que Kelly aime?* and so on, referring to the personal answers given previously by the students. After learners have become familiar with the use of this strategy, the teacher can have the students ask the questions.

The development of the ability to communicate includes developing both fluency and accuracy in the L2. In Intensive French specific teaching strategies are required for each of the processes. The next two teaching strategies are related to these two particular characteristics of communication.

3. Using complete sentences to make links. In the beginning stages of learning to communicate, we encourage the use of full sentences in reply to all questions. A student who is asked: *Comment t'appelles-tu?* should answer using the complete sentence *Je m'appelle ...* (rather than by simply stating his or her name). The same applies to answering the question *Quel âge as-tu?– J'ai onze ans* (and not simply: *onze*). While using complete sentences may seem somewhat contrary to our desire to use authentic language in real situations, there are very valid reasons for using this teaching strategy. Through the use of complete sentences in answer to questions, the student becomes adept at making connections between all the linguistic elements (on the phonological, morphological, syntactic, lexical and discursive levels) necessary to speak with fluency in the target language. The use of full sentences also assists the student to develop her internal grammar. How can a student succeed in developing fluency and form hypotheses about the language by using only one word answers, reciting a list of out-of-context vocabulary words by heart or conjugating a verb orally?

4. Correction of language used. Once the teacher has modelled a sentence and has encouraged its use by asking a student the question, the teacher must correct the response of the student, should it be incorrect. The correction is achieved by modelling the correct form, and having the student use the corrected form. Thus, if we return to the example used previously and extend it further:

T. As-tu un chien à la maison, Laura?
S. Oui, j'ai un chien à **le** maison.
T. Tu as un chien à la maison.
S. J'ai un chien à la maison.

It is essential that the teacher immediately give the correct model for the answer given by the student, and that the student repeat this model accurately. All correction must be followed by use by students of the correct form in a complete sentence; it would not be enough to indicate that there is an error because this would produce only declarative knowledge. Furthermore, an explanation of why what was said is incorrect is not necessary. It is also important for the development of the student's internal grammar that the form used be correct.

Once a certain implicit competence of an oral corpus has been developed, attention is then turned to the development of reading and writing skills with this corpus. In the development of these skills the development of both implicit competence and explicit knowledge is addressed. There are three stages in each lesson: pre-reading/writing activities, the teaching of how to read/write, and post-reading/writing activities. The pre- and post- activities are included specifically in order to develop literacy skills, making the links between speaking, reading and writing. All reading and writing activities begin with an oral communication which provides the contextualization of the language skills to be learned. The teacher leads a discussion enabling students to see the relevance of the topic to their lives and also to link what they are able to say (communicate orally) with what they are about to read or write. After the reading/writing lesson has been undertaken, there is further use of the information, integrating what has been read/written with the other skills areas and with previously learned material. This is an essential element of a literacy-based approach to language learning.

In the reading/writing lesson itself, the four strategies of modelling, use and reuse, making links and correction are followed. For reading, the teacher models the text to be read, giving the students a correct model of the words and sentences used, and also ensures its comprehension. Then students read the text aloud for various purposes. During this reutilisation of the text the teacher encourages students to read full sentences with natural intonation, and corrects any errors, such as incorrect interpretation of relationships between sound and graphic symbol, in order to encourage accuracy in reading. Once explicit knowledge of the new system of sound-symbol relationships is developed, students are able to read independently.

For writing, at the beginning stages of the program, the teacher writes a model paragraph from suggestions given by the students for the topic chosen. Once written, students read aloud the paragraph with the teacher, and afterwards the teacher assists the students to see the aspects that could be changed in order for each student to write her own personalized version, using complete sentences. The teacher also assists students to recognize aspects that are specific to written language, such as punctuation, agreements, etc., in order to encourage accuracy in writing that is based on explicit knowledge of language forms. The students then compose their own paragraph. As students advance in the program, they begin to write more and more independently, and use of the writing process (draft, correction, final copy) is encouraged.

These strategies are used to develop both implicit competence in reading and writing in the target language so that students are able to think in French rather than translating what they read and write, and explicit knowledge of how the language functions in order that they are able to read and write with accuracy. In addition, the reading and writing activities follow the speaking activities all in the same day. Once language items have been developed in this way, they are then integrated with previously learned items to pursue a more complex activity, as for example, a project; thus, the language skills developed are integrated to develop literacy in the target language.

Conclusion

Intensive French is a highly effective way for young students to learn to communicate spontaneously in French, as well as to develop literacy skills in the target language. The increase in time and, in particular, intensity enhances the rate of development of these skills. However, its success is due primarily to the teaching strategies used which encourage the development of implicit competence for fluency and accuracy in oral communication and its use of strategies to develop literacy skills. The skills are presented in sequence, but are then integrated in a project or other activity. The whole language learning process is contextualized, from the use of complete sentences in oral discussions to the writing of paragraphs, in authentic communicative situations that have real meaning for the students. This type of approach to the teaching of Core French makes the learning of a second language in a school situation a more valuable educational experience and integrates FSL more effectively in the regular school curriculum.

Works Cited

Atlantic Provinces Education Foundation. 2002. *Core French Survey*.

Calman, Ruth and Ian Daniel. 1998. "A board's-eye view of core French: The North York Board of Education." In *French Second Language Education in Canada: Empirical Studies*, ed. Sharon Lapkin. 282-323. Toronto: University of Toronto Press.

Cummins, Jim. 2001. "The entry and exit fallacy in bilingual education." In *An Introductory Reader to the Writings of Jim Cummins*, ed. Jim Cummins and Nancy Hornberger, 110-138. Clevedon: Multilingual Matters.

Gatbonton, Elizabeth and Norman Segalowitz. 2005. "Rethinking Communicative Language Teaching: A Focus on Access to Fluency," *Canadian Modern Language Review/La Revue canadienne des langues vivantes*, Vol. 61, no 3, 325-353.

Germain, Claude and Joan Netten. 2004. "Étude qualitative du régime pédagogique du français intensif." *Canadian Modern Language Review/La Revue canadienne des langues vivantes*, Vol. 60, No. 3, 393-408.

Germain, Claude and Joan Netten. 2005. "Place et rôle de l'oral dans l'enseignement/apprentissage d'une L2," *Babylonia*, no 2, 11-14.

Germain, Claude and Joan Netten. (2007). "Transdisciplinarité français—langue étrangère et français—langue seconde: les fondements du français intensif," In *Écarts de langue, écarts de culture — À l'école de l'Autre,* ed. Christine Hélot, Elisabeth Hoffmann, Marie Louise Scheidhauer and Andrea Young, 103-112. Frankfurt am Main: Peter Lang.

Government of New Brunswick. 2005. *Report Card 2004-2005*. Department of Education, New Brunswick.

Government of Ontario. 2004. *Literacy for learning – The Report of the Expert Panel on Literacy in Grades 4 to 6 in Ontario*, Ontario Education.

Lapkin, Sharon, Birgit Harley and Shelley Taylor. 1995. "Research directions for Core French in Canada," *Canadian Modern Language Review/La Revue canadienne des langues vivantes*, Vol. 49, no 3, 476-513.

LeBlanc, Raymond. 1990. *National Core French Study – Synthesis. Ottawa: Canadian Association of Second Language Teachers/Association canadienne des professeurs de langues secondes:* Canada: Éditions M.

Lightbown, Patsy and Nina Spada. 1994. "An innovative program for Primary ESL in Quebec." *TESOL Quarterly*, Vol. 28, No. 3, 563-579.

Netten, Joan and Claude Germain. 2006a. "A pedagogical perspective on SLA : Focus on use." Keynote address at the joint Conference of the American Association of Applied Linguistics (AAAL) and Canadian Association of Applied Linguistics (CAAL), Montreal.

Netten, Joan and Claude Germain. 2006b. *Improving the Core French Program.* Report prepared at the request of the Department of Education, Province of New Brunswick.

Netten, Joan and Claude Germain. 2005. "Pedagogy and second language learning: Lessons learned from Intensive French." *Canadian Journal of Applied Linguistics – Revue canadienne de linguistique appliquée*, No 8.2, 183-210.

Netten, Joan and Claude Germain. 2004. "Theoretical and research foundations of Intensive French." *Canadian Modern Language Review/La Revue canadienne des langues vivantes*, Vol. 60, No. 3, 275-294.

Paradis, Michel. 2004. *A Neurolinguistic Theory of Bilingualism.* Amsterdam/Philadelphia: John Benjamins Publishing Company.

Shapson. Stan, David Kaufman and Lynne Durward. 1978. *BC French Study: An Evaluation of Elementary French Programs in British Columbia.* Burnaby, BC: Faculty of Education Simon Fraser University.

Stern, Hans Heinrich. 1982. "Core French programs across Canada : How can we improve them?" *Canadian Modern Language Review/La Revue canadienne des langues vivantes*, Vol. 39, 34-47.

Turnbull, Miles. 1999. "Multidimensional project-based teaching in French second language (FSL): A process-product case study." *Modern Language Journal,* 83 (IV), pp. 548-568.

Vygotsky, Lev. S. 1986. *Thought and Language.* Boston, Mass.: MIT Press.

DIVERSITY AS AN ASSET: MULTIPLE LANGUAGE INTEGRATION

ANDREA YOUNG

Introduction

One of the defining features of our era is the increasing mobility of people on a global scale for professional, personal or economic reasons. Classes containing children of different cultural origins are no longer exceptional but have become the norm for many teaching professionals in schools throughout the world. How are we responding to this relatively recent phenomenon? How can we acknowledge and capitalise on the infinitely diverse sets of cultural and linguistic knowledge and skills which our pupils bring with them to school? How do we welcome these children and their families of diverse cultural heritages into our schools and our communities? How can we help them to feel comfortable, recognising and accepting their individual differences, whilst at the same time inviting them to become a constituent part of the class and the school?

By moving our focus from the individual child to the educational community, a different perspective comes to light and a whole new series of questions arises. How should we be educating all the children in our classes, whatever their cultural and linguistic backgrounds, to respect difference? How can teaching professionals, whether working in large urban schools with a high proportion of children from migrant backgrounds or in small rural schools with less culturally diverse populations, foster curiosity, tolerance and empathy amongst all learners, including those for whom the wider world can seem very distant from their particular local context? In short, what kind of whole school approach (Camilleri, 2007) would allow us to encourage pupils to meet the social challenges facing global citizens of the twenty-first century?

In his recent article Language Education, Identities and Citizenship: Developing Cosmopolitan Perspectives, Starkey defines such processes as education for "cosmopolitan citizenship" (Starkey, 2007: p.59-60) and identifies a need to provide "a space for learners to reflect on and develop new complex identities and articulate these with their understandings of citizenship" in our "multilingual world of increasing hybridity". The issue of space, eking out a place in the already tightly packed school timetable to address issues linked to cosmopolitan citizenship, is also evoked by Garcia et al. who discuss "Weaving spaces and (de)constructing ways for multilingual schools" (Garcia et al. 2006). Garcia too has recognised the growing language and cultural hybridity of the 21st century and the need to invent educational models able to accommodate this hybridity (Garcia, 2004). In order to answer these two fundamental questions concerning how and when to teach about multiple languages and cultures within the school curriculum, a certain degree of creativity is required on the part of teachers.

An account of how one school has chosen to meet these challenges follows below. It is hoped that others may find inspiration from this example and may in turn adapt the approach, which considers diversity as an asset and pupils and their families as a resource for learning about difference, to their own local contexts.

The Didenheim project: Context

The initial problem which propelled the team of teachers at Didenheim primary school to invent a new teaching and learning model and to make space in the curriculum for dealing with diversity was the increasing number of racist incidents within the school between pupils.

At first sight the learning environment could mistakenly be considered to be largely monolingual/cultural (French) with a small minority of bilingual/cultural (Turkish/French) children suffering discrimination at the hands of some of the majority language speakers. As it stands, in France no official statistics pertaining to ethnicity may be systematically collected by schools (see Hélot & Young, 2002 for a discussion of the ideology underpinning this). The only available statistics relate to nationality, not country of origin, and anyone born in France has the right to claim French nationality. Consequently the statistics about nationality do not accurately reflect the cultural heritage of many children currently attending schools in France.

The École la Sirène de l'Ill in Didenheim is a small rural school (just under 100 pupils) situated in the south of the Alsace region of eastern France, near the Swiss and German borders. Its close proximity to national borders has made Alsace a rather distinctive French region, characterised by bilingual, bicultural traditions and population movement. Migrants from Switzerland and Germany have contributed to this regional identity over the centuries and still do so. In 2004 Germans constituted the second largest national group in Alsace (Morel-Chevillet, 2006).

The industrial and economic dynamism of the region has also acted as a magnet, attracting many migrant workers over the centuries. The largest and most recently arrived populations come from Turkey and North Africa, following in the footsteps of European migrants from Portugal, Italy and Poland who came to work in the factories, mines and on the building sites of Alsace. So if we scratch the surface and dig a little deeper than the official nationality statistics for the school population, we very quickly find that there are in fact many more plurilingual and pluricultural family and community members living in and around Didenheim than would appear at first sight.

Identifying resources within the community

The initial difficulty facing the teachers in Didenheim was how to deal with the problem of racism at school swiftly and effectively given their limited available resources. They decided to enlist the support of children, parents and other members of the community and to seek out human resources already present in the local environment. Parents had always responded positively to requests for extra hands to help out during school excursions, fêtes, swimming and art lessons and it was only natural for the school to call upon them to lend their support to the school's new project focusing on learning about languages and cultures. On a practical level, this was also a local, low cost solution to a problem within the local community. A short note was sent home with pupils asking anyone with knowledge about a language and culture other than French and who would like to share this knowledge with the pupils to contact the school. To the immense surprise and great satisfaction of staff, families and friends proposed a wide range of linguistic and cultural skills (a total of 18 languages in all were included in the project, for a full list see Hélot & Young, 2005 or 2006). The problem of resources was solved, but questions regarding space, time and the model to be employed were still outstanding.

Eking out a space in the curriculum

Right from the outset, the teachers went out of their way to welcome parents who had volunteered to participate in the project. It was decided that the sessions should take place at a time which would allow a maximum number of parents to participate in classes during regular school time. Therefore one hour long sessions on Saturday mornings (French children generally attend regular school on Saturday mornings), when most parents were not at work, were dedicated to the project. The first three year groups (a class of 6 year olds, a class of 7 year olds and a mixed class of 8 and 9 year olds) were chosen to participate in the project for two very pragmatic reasons. Firstly school begins at 8am and finishes at 1130am, allowing the volunteer parents or community members to offer three one hour classes and have a break along with the children. Secondly, the children in the remaining upper age group were already learning German or English and it was easier to eke out that illusive space needed for the project in the younger children's timetables. Additionally, it also seemed more logical to precede the study of one foreign language with a more general overview of linguistic and cultural diversity.

A cross-curricula approach

Another factor, which helped considerably in the quest for finding sufficient time in the curriculum to dedicate to the project, was the primary school context in which the class teacher is in the privileged position of teaching the same children for all subjects all day and every day. This afforded a certain flexibility to the project and provided it with an inclusive and cohesive model. Firstly languages and cultures were neither restricted to the "foreign language hour" nor to the "languages and cultures of origin" hour, which usually involves a small number of children leaving the mainstream classroom to attend specific lessons on their heritage language and culture. Instead of dividing up children and compartmentalising school subjects, languages and cultures began to overlap and connect up with geography, history, art, music, cooking, sport and last but by no means least French (the school's language of instruction). This gave the sessions a much wider dimension, made more sense to the learners as more links were made between the different school subjects, allowed all children to pool their resources and experiences and, most importantly, made it possible for the teacher to find time in the curriculum for the project.

The primary class teacher's role in the integration of learning about diversity into the normal curriculum was pivotal. She knew the children (their learning styles, personalities, difficulties, particularities), but also knew what learning had previously taken place in the classroom and therefore how best to link the new knowledge and skills to those already encountered. Therefore she was the one person able to make these interdisciplinary links and to be able to tailor content to individual learner needs, thus helping all children in the class to build on their experience and further their learning. A cross-curricular approach is, however, not only a convenient way of finding space and helping learners to make connections when learning. It is also a fundamental requirement to learning about languages and cultures, as opposed to language learning. In order to appreciate some of the complex issues connected with linguistic and cultural diversity (such as what are the salient features of a language, what constitutes a dialect, a register or an accent, why people leave their countries of origin or why different populations dress, eat or worship differently), other disciplines, such as the national language (in this case French), history, geography and religious education, need to be integrated into the discussion so as to deepen understanding of contextual and environmental factors.

Given that most parents will have little or no experience of such a language and cultural awareness approach and will automatically have a tendency to equate learning about languages with language learning, it is vital to clarify the objectives of this type of education with parents and to clearly differentiate between these two distinct, but complementary, types of learning.

A cooperative home-school model

Good communication between the children's families and the school was the foundation upon which this project was built. In Didenheim, the teachers' first step towards making their school more inclusive, capitalising on pupils' individual assets, giving cultural and linguistic diversity a place and making all children and families feel welcome at school, whatever their backgrounds, was to start with the pupils' families. Parents were invited to school for an initial presentation of the project, its objectives and the basic model which would be adhered to. Obviously this model developed as the teachers acquired more experience of working with parents, but the initial plan (which is still in place today at the school as the project is no longer a project but a constituent part of the school curriculum) involved teachers and parents attending a preliminary planning meeting to discuss content and pedagogical methods. This preceded the actual classroom sessions with the pupils, led by the parent(s) with teacher support as appropriate. Finally there would be a short post class meeting for teachers and parents held directly after the Saturday morning sessions. Parents scheduled to run the sessions planned for the following week would also be invited to this meeting so that participants might reassure each other and benefit from previous experience. These parents would then remain with the teachers to hold their own planning meeting for their forthcoming session.

The teachers in Didenheim took a very democratic and respectful approach towards working with parents, always asking parents what aspects of their language and culture they wanted to share with the children as an initial step, before making suggestions as to how this could be done in a way which would be appropriate to the age and previous experience of the learners. These planning meetings allowed parents and teachers to exchange, to discover how each person's knowledge and skills could complement the others' and to build a relationship of trust and mutual respect. It was clear from their manner, their tone of voice, their observations and their suggestions that the teachers considered the parents as equal educational partners (Cummins, 2001) vital to the effective functioning of the project. This close collaboration enabled parents and teachers to co-construct knowledge in the classroom with the learners. The parents provided endless supplies of cultural knowledge and linguistic skills, the teachers were able to use their pedagogical competences to enable the parents to effectively communicate their knowledge and skills to the pupils.

A further unanticipated, but welcome, consequence of this cooperation was increased understanding between parents and teachers and greater appreciation of each other's skills, professionalism and dedication which led in turn to improved home school relations and a better working environment for all. Parents and teachers saw each other in a new light after working collaboratively. The considerable time and effort which the parents put into preparing their session(s) exceeded all the expectations of staff. Whilst the parents, after teaching solidly for a whole morning, gained inside experience of some of the demands of teaching and were unreservedly appreciative of the teachers' work in the classroom.

This is a very simple, but effective and above all else human project which works through a bottom up rather than a top down approach. The resources are free, provided by the local community of parents and friends who are only too happy to share their knowledge and expertise with the children and their teachers. Who would not be proud to have their personal heritage, their cultural and linguistic capital welcomed into and valued by their local school? The instigators and guardians/guarantors of the success of such an approach are unequivocally the teachers. They are the ones in a position to set the wheels in motion and to guide the learning process.

Teachers empowering parents and pupils

It is the human element which is the key factor in the success of a project such as the Didenheim project. The teacher is the central pivot in the mechanism which facilitates the efficient running of the other components. Rather like a waterwheel, the teacher turns, facilitating the learning process and directing the water. The water wheel, without whom nothing would be set in motion, is rather like the parents. They are the source of the action, they feed the process. If the water dries up (i.e. parental help is not forthcoming), then the wheel has to find an alternative source of power in order create a stimulating learning environment in which pupils may equip themselves with the knowledge and skills they will need for life in the twenty-first century. Efficiency and success are guaranteed by the smooth running of the water in conjunction with the wheel to generate power. If the wheel fails to position itself at the correct angle to harness the full power of the running current, the maximum potential for learning will be lost.

Many parents who participated in the Didenheim project were conscious and appreciative of the teacher's skills in choosing the right moments and ways in which to intervene.

> "C'est bien qu'elle soit là...moi je trouve c'est bien qu'elle soit avec parce que, bon il y en a qui interviennent, il y en a qui n'interviennent pas. Si je me souviens bien la maîtresse du X à l'époque elle n'intervenait pas beaucoup, mais Y et Z elles interviennent, enfin elles n'interviennent pas, mais elles participent...elles sont là un peu comme des élèves...c'est bien ça... parce que je trouve qu'elles ont l'air de s'intéresser plus."

> It's good that they're there...I think it's good that they're with us because, well some of them intervene and some of them don't. If I remember rightly the teacher of class X one year didn't intervene much, but Y and Z intervened, well they didn't intervene, they participated...they were there a bit like pupils...that's good...because I think they seem more interested. (Alsatian mother)

> "J'étais contente... en plus elle fait comme les enfants et puis les enfants, elle elle dit on fait comme ça, on écoute, après on fait, elle fait la même chose, peut être si on fait toutes seules on ne fait pas comme elle fait. Moi d'abord j'explique et après c'est elle qui, avec les enfants, expliquer ou parler, tout ça... on est contentes avec toutes les maîtresses, le maître, il était très sympa et il voulait aider à nous...et puis j'étais trop contente."

> I was happy...what's more she does the same as the children and then the children, she she says do it like this, listen, after they do it, she does the

same thing, perhaps if we do it on our own we won't do it like she does it. I explain at first and then after she does it with the children, explaining, speaking, all that…we are very happy with all the teachers (female), the teacher (male) was very nice and he wanted to help us…and then I was very happy. (Turkish mother).

The notion of power in the waterwheel analogy has been central to this project from the outset. The waterwheel, likened to the teacher who channels the abundance of cultural and linguistic skills and knowledge proffered by the parents, is powered by this "water" and relies on it in order to function. This is indeed a prime example of what Cummins calls an educational partnership (Cummins, 2000). But such a partnership is constructed upon the acceptance of the teacher to concede some of his/her power to the parents. This is not such a straight forward matter as it might at first appear. In many contexts, the class teacher is in control of almost everything that takes place in his class. He decides exactly what will be taught when and how (within the constraints of the national curriculum and directives of course) and class teachers, especially in the primary sector, benefit from a considerable amount of freedom concerning how teaching and learning in the classroom take place.

In France, although some colleagues collaborate and work as a team in some instances, many teachers tend to work in isolation and peer observation is extremely rare. In addition, in spite of the rhetoric published by the Ministry of Education in its official bulletins, parents are not frequently viewed by the teaching profession as partners in their children's education. They will usually be invited to a meeting prior to or at the beginning of the school year and they receive written communication from the class teacher to inform them of school outings, the annual school fête and to ask them for help in preparing and carrying out these events, but they rarely step foot inside the classroom and usually will only be invited to meet the class teacher to discuss their child's learning or behavioural difficulties. In such a culture, the idea of opening the classroom up to virtual strangers, allowing them to experience first hand what goes on there and allowing them to "take the place" of the teacher at the front of the class can give rise to a certain apprehension on the part of some teachers while others may even perceive it as a threat.

In the Didenheim project, the teachers had no such qualms about opening their doors to parents.

"J'ai aussi l'habitude de fonctionner comme ça, c'est vrai que moi j'ai toujours fait appel à des parents…donc j'ai toujours eu des mamans qui venaient me donner un coup de main en arts plastiques…non non dans l'école ce n'est pas nouveau, c'est vrai qu'on fait souvent appel aux parents, c'est vrai qu'on a des relations ouvertes quoi, mais là c'était encore différent parce qu'on leur demandait de prendre la classe en main"

I'm used to working like that, it's true to say that I have always asked parents for help…so I've always had mums in to give me a hand in art classes…no, no this is not new in school, it's true we often ask parents for help, it's true that we have good relations you know, but there it was a different thing again because we were asking them to take the class.
(Teacher of 6 year olds)

They were quite happy to literally take a back seat in their own classrooms, to become one of the learners during the sessions, to symbolically pass their authority, their role, their power as a teacher over to the parents.

"J'étais moi –même en situation d'apprentissage pour certaines langues… Je ne pense pas connaître absolument toutes les cultures et toutes les langues qu'on a pu aborder…après gérer la classe c'est mon travail."

I myself was in the situation of the learner for some languages…I don't think that I know all there is to know about all the cultures and languages which we have looked at…as for classroom management that's my job. (Teacher of 7 year olds)

Some parents initially felt uncomfortable in this role. Prior to the class many were anxious about assuming the role of teacher. Very few had teaching experience and the few who did were secondary school teachers unused to addressing 6 year olds. Once again the support provided by the class teacher was vital in encouraging and reassuring the parents prior to their session.

"Mais en fait on avait surtout, enfin moi surtout j'avais l'impression d'avoir un rôle de les sécuriser, les rassurer, parce que on les sentait très inquiets, bah il faut dire qu'ils commençaient toujours chez moi, donc c'est vrai il y avait beaucoup de parents à rassurer : 'Est ce que c'était bien? Est ce que je dois faire comme ça?' Donc c'est vrai qu'on avait un rôle de conseiller, en tout modestie…Bon après ça c'est le feeling."

In fact we really felt, well especially me, I had the impression that my role was to make them feel comfortable, to reassure them, because you could feel they were very worried, well let's face it they always started off in my class, so it's true to say that there were a lot of parents who needed reassuring: "Was it all right? Should I do it like that?" So it's true to say that our role was to advise, in all modesty…Well after that it's a question of instinct. (Teacher of 6 year olds)

It is important to take these fears into consideration when planning the initial parents teacher meeting to discuss the project. Parents need to be convinced that they are capable, with the support of the teacher, of teaching the children. Concrete examples of the kinds of activities which can be undertaken need to be presented (Young & Hélot, 2003), either by describing them or by showing a short video clip of previous sessions. Once again the teacher is the key initiator in the empowerment process. He nurtures the relationship between educators and learners by establishing a climate of trust and respect and may sometimes even have to challenge patterns of disempowerment (Cummins, 2001) which devalue certain languages, cultures and identities, in order to uphold the basic human rights of his pupils.

Conclusion

It would appear that our post-modern societies have reached an important juncture. As educators, we can choose to respond to the challenges posed by technological developments and increased means of communication and possibilities of mobility; or we can choose to ignore them and in so doing pass over an opportunity to equip a new generation of citizens with appropriate knowledge and skills for a global future.

The teachers in Didenheim have seized this opportunity and although their project has cost very little in financial terms, it has proved itself to be priceless in terms of the knock on effects it has produced: bilingual pupils who blossom as a result of witnessing their home language and culture acknowledged and valued by their school, better home school relations, increased tolerance of difference at school, greater curiosity and motivation to learn languages and about languages and cultures from both staff and pupils (Young & Hélot, 2007).

What the project does cost is time, effort and good will. It requires open minded teachers who are willing to open their classroom doors and give a little of their time to welcome members of the community into school, to take the time to listen to parents, to exchange with them and to support them in their attempts to share their knowledge and skills. The Didenheim project illustrates how teachers who are ready to consider parents as educational partners, to accord them an equal share in a common project, to provide them with a space in the school timetable and a valid role in the classroom, can create new educational models to accommodate the language and cultural hybridity of the 21st century. The skill with which class teachers, such as those working in Didenheim, build bridges between what the children already know and what the parent is presenting; between the language and culture of the family and the language(s) and culture(s) of the country in which the school is situated; between the school and the home environment; is undoubtedly a key factor in the success of such an endeavour. However, without parental participation, none of this would be possible. As the children participating in the Didenheim project remarked:

"La maîtresse elle ne connaît pas toutes les langues... elle ne vient pas de tous les pays...ils viennent du pays dont ils parlent...On comprend mieux quand c'est des personnes de l'extérieur qui viennent présenter les langues...ils parlent bien...ma maman elle sait plus que la maîtresse...c'était bien animé quand des gens sont venus dans la classe."

The teacher doesn't know all the languages...she doesn't come from all the countries...they come from the country they are talking about. We understand better when it's people from outside who come and present their languages...they speak well...my mummy knows more than the teacher...it was nice and lively when the people came into the class.

The joint efforts of parents and teachers, the co-construction of knowledge engendered by the empowerment of parents and children in the classroom, the teachers' willingness to create new spaces and models for an innovative approach to learning about diversity have allowed some of the children in Didenheim to find their voices and to take pride in their multiple identities, whilst all the children participating in the project have been able to lift the lid on the treasure trove of languages and cultures present in their local environment and delve inside.

Works Cited

Camilleri Grima, Antoinette, ed. 2007. *Promoting Linguistic Diversity and Whole-School Development.* European Centre for Modern Languages, Council of Europe, Strasbourg.
Cummins, Jim. 2000. *Language, Power and Pedagogy: Bilingual Children in the Crossfire.* Clevedon: Multilingual Matters.
—. 2001. *Negotiating Identities:Education for Empowerment in a Diverse Society.* California Association for Bilingual Education, Los Angeles.
Garcia, Ofelia. 2004. *Lost in transculturation: The case of bilingual education in New York City.* Linguistic LAUD Agency. Series A, Paper No. 624. Universität Duisburg-Essen.
Garcia, Ofelia, Tove Skutnabb-Kangas and Maria E. Torres-Guzmàn. 2006. "Weaving Spaces and (De)constructing Ways for Multilingual

Schools: The Actual and the Imagined," In *Imagining Multilingual Schools*, ed. Tove Skutnabb Kangas, Ofelia Garcia, and Maria E. Torres-Guzman, 3-47, Multilingual Matters, Clevedon.

Hélot, Christine and Andrea Young. 2002. "Bilingualism and Language Education in French Primary Schools: Why and How Should Migrant Languages Be Valued?" *Bilingual Education and Bilingualism*, (2), Multilingual Matters, Clevedon, 96-112.

Hélot, Christine and Andrea Young. 2005. "The notion of Diversity in Language Education : Policy and Practice at Primary Level in France." *Journal of Language, Culture and Curriculum*. 18 (3), Multilingual Matters, Clevedon, 242-257.

Hélot, Christine and Andrea Young. 2006. "Imagining Multilingual Education in France : A language and cultural awareness project at primary level," In *Imagining Multilingual Schools*, ed. Tove Skutnabb Kangas, Ofelia Garcia, and Maria E. Torres-Guzman, 69-90, Multilingual Matters, Clevedon.

Morel-Chevillet, Robert. 2006. *Les immigrés en Alsace : 10% de la population. Chiffres pour l'Alsace*. N°34, Paris: INSEE (Institut National de la Statistique et des Etudes Economiques).

Starkey, Hugh. 2007. "Language Education, Identities and Citizenship: Developing Cosmopolitan Perspectives." *Language and Intercultural Communication*. 7 (1), 56-71.

Young, Andrea and Christine Hélot. 2003. "Language Awareness and / or Language Learning in French Primary Schools today." *Language Awareness*, 12 : 3&4, 234-246.

Young, Andrea and Christine Hélot. 2007. "Parent Power: Parents as a Linguistic and Cultural Resource at School", In *Promoting Linguistic Diversity and Whole-School Development*, ed. Antoinette Camilleri Grima, 17-23. European Centre for Modern Languages, Council of Europe, Strasbourg.

RECOMMENDED READING: MULTIPLE LANGUAGE IMMERSION

Cloud, Nancy, Fred Genesee and Else Hamayan. 2000. *Dual Language Instruction. A Handbook for Enriched Education.* Boston, MA: Heinle and Heinle.

Creese, Angela and Peter Martin, eds. 2003. *Multilingual Classroom Ecologies: Inter-Relationships, Interactions and Ideologies.* Clevedon: Multilingual Matters.

Cummins, Jim. 2000. *Language, Power and Pedagogy: Bilingual Children in the Crossfire.* Clevedon: Multilingual Matters.

—. 2001. *Negotiating Identities:Education for Empowerment in a Diverse Society.* California Association for Bilingual Education, Los Angeles.

Day, Elaine Mellen and Stan M. Shapson. 1996. *Studies in Immersion Education.* Clevedon: Multilingual Matters.

Freeman, Rebecca Diane. 1998. *Bilingual Education and Social Change.* Clevedon: Multilingual Matters.

Johnson, Robert Keith and Swain, Merrill, eds. 1997. *Immersion Education: International Perspectives.* Cambridge: Cambridge University Press.

Garcia, Ofelia, Tove Skutnabb-Kangas and Maria E. Torres-Guzman. *Imagining Multilingual Schools.* Clevedon: Multilingual Matters.

James, Carl and Peter Garrett, eds. 1991. *Language Awareness in the Classroom.* (Applied Linguistics and Language Study), London: Longman.

Lindholm-Leary, Kathyrn J. 2001. *Dual Language Education.* Clevedon: Multilingual Matters.

Netten, Joan and Germain, Claude. 2005. "Pedagogy and second language learning: Lessons learned from Intensive French." *Canadian Journal of Applied Linguistics/Revue canadienne de linguistique appliquée*, No. 8.2, 183-210.

Paradis, Michel. 2004. *A Neurolinguistic Theory of Bilingualism.* Amsterdam/Philadelphia: John Benjamins Publishing Company.

Torres-Guzmán, Maria. E. 2002. "Dual Language Programs: Key Features and Results," *Directions in Language and Education.* 14/Spring.

Washington, D.C.: National Clearinghouse for Bilingual Education. 1-16.

Valdes, Guadalupe, Joshua Fishman, Rebecca Chavez and William Perez. 2006. *Developing Minority Language Resources*. Clevedon, England: Multilingual Matters.

Chapter Two

Task-Based Language Learning: Introduction

Melinda Dooly

Learner-centred teaching which is organized around tasks designed to engage the learner in communicative activities outside the classroom is becoming increasingly popular. Commonly known as task-based learning (TBL), it is sometimes considered to be congruent with Project-based learning (PBL) —albeit there are some theorists who feel they should be kept separate. Due to need for brevity, that debate will not be presented here and we shall refer to all the contributions in this section as task-based language learning.

Advocates of task-based language learning (TBLL) highlight the fact that a key element to its success is its responsiveness to learners' specific communicative needs. TBLL also has the potential of developing functional language proficiency without forsaking grammatical accuracy. TBLL teachers try to present a coherent, theoretically motivated approach to a language teaching program which includes student needs' analysis, programme and materials design, and final evaluation. In other words, it is an approach that integrates the task(s) into the overall learning process. This stands in contrast to many supposedly task-based proposals which merely present recommendations for materials and application of materials for a miscellany of single tasks-tasks which are often out of touch with actual learner needs and end up being little more than "mini-tasks" that replace drills but do not have an overall cohesion to the entire programme. Ellis (2003:28) draws attention to these differences by distinguishing between "task-supported" language learning and task-based language learning. TBLL, with its focus on communicative language teaching, creates a base for tasks to be both the what and how of language teaching.

Nunan considers a pedagogical task to be work that engages the learners so that they are purposefully interacting in the target language. This implies that while they are focusing on conveying meaning, they are deploying their grammatical knowledge (1998: 25). In this context, a task-based approach is understood as a meaningful unit around which teachers can plan, deliver, and review lessons (see Shavelson and Stern, 1981; Swaffer et al., 1982). The lessons are focused on an overall task completion, instead of decontextualised activities carried out in the language classroom. Different from decontextualised activities that are individually focused on textual, lexical or grammatical features, the language lessons are related to other activities required of the students.

This does not mean that individual, stand-alone texts are not part of the lessons, however they are incorporated into the task distribution —text production could be keeping record of task accomplishment (as a spoken or written by-product of other tasks) or an integral part of the task –for example, writing a letter to the local politician asking for a bigger school playground. This is one of the main differences between text-based and task-based lessons. Language learners do not study the target language as a decontextualised object; instead the target language is used and experienced as an integral part of the process needed for completion of the task. The premise is that new knowledge is better integrated into long-term memory and more easily retrieved if the learner is able to connect it to real events and activities.

Based upon cognitive and interactionist Second Language Acquisition (SLA) theory and research findings, TBLL proposes the use of tasks rather than texts as the focus unit for learning; tasks are used to promote "learning by doing"; input, which should be richly varied. The tasks help pupils learn how to negotiate meaning, for example getting the learners to interact with the input by modifying and elaborating on it. Students will "want to know" and will be engaged in resolving the tasks because the activities are contextualized in such a way that they are personally relevant. TBLL is often set up through problem-solving and frequently involves collaborative work which is elaborated around an activity that is relevant to all the learners involved. Moreover, TBLL tries to take into consideration individual learning differences and learning strategies which can be pinpointed and the tasks adapted during the process; consequently adaptation and autonomy are long-term objectives. (For further information, see, Doughty, 2001a; Doughty and Long, 2003; Long and Robinson, 1998; Robinson, 2001; Skehan, 1998).

Another important feature of TBLL is that it draws the learner's attention to form so feedback should involve error-analysis and student "recasts". This approach also takes into account the learner's interlanguage, by inducing "noticing" (Schmidt, 2001). Therefore the timing of feedback on errors is critical, so that learners are able to make some sort of comparison between the information provided in the feedback and their own preceding utterance (Doughty, 2001b).

Inevitably, texts have a relevant role in TBLL, however, the texts used are usually neither so-called "authentic" texts, which may be too complex for most learners, nor are they simplified texts, which are unnatural and tend to be self-contained and have little in common with real discourse. Texts used in TBLL are "elaborated" input. This term is used to refer to the different ways in which native speakers modify their discourse during interaction with non-native speakers (different stages of scaffolding). This same term is applied to the elaborated input in TBLL. These texts incorporate the different strategies for comprehension used by non-native speakers. This means that the modifications are student-directed and are principally modifications which occur during negotiation of meaning. (See Gass, 2003). This is evident in the texts created by the students themselves as part of the task (making lists, recording events, explaining results and so on).

Simplifying significantly the overall complexities of any type of learning process, we might say that a task based learning syllabus can be defined as a complex classroom activity, structured in a series of phases that prepare the learners to do the target task. These phases are made up of both pedagogical and communicative sub-tasks. The principle aim of the pedagogical tasks is to provide the grammar, lexical and socio-cultural knowledge (usually by deductive or inductive processes) students need to carry out the final task successfully. The principle aim of the communicative sub-tasks is to involve the student in an activity which is focused on a particular linguistic feature. The communicative sub-task also provides genuine exchange of meaning in a real context—although it must be related with the target task.

Teachers should select the TBLL input according to the communicative necessities required by the target task (although this is not necessarily established *a priori*). During all the TBLL process the four skills must be practiced. This means that target task selection can only be carried out after the learners' needs have been analysed. This is then used to establish the topics and the situations in which the students will communicate in the real world outside the classroom.

The steps in designing task-based program are:
- Subjects and situations selection (according to students' interests and needs)
- Target-task selection.
- Objectives and components definition (communicative, grammar, lexical, socio-cultural...)

"How we're going about it": Teachers' Voices on Innovative Approaches to Teaching and Learning Languages

- Pedagogical and communicative subtasks creation.
- Evaluation- Self-evaluation.

(For a theoretical approach see Estaire y Zanón, 1994 & Zanón, 1999, for a more practical outline, see Fernández, 2001).

Inevitably, there are issues which come up with task-based learning, not least of which is the difficulty of setting up pedagogical situations wherein the teaching is actually task-based rather than isolated "chunks" of work which are not integrated into a complete learning process. There are also inherent socio-cultural difficulties in the adaptation of task-based learning to learning environments which are not traditionally learner-based. This can produce student anxiety as they may feel confused or that they are not improving their language skills. Also, because the language lesson is not explicitly focused on language practice, student use of mother tongue may be more prevalent; however use of the target language can be negotiated between the teacher and students during the pre-task phase.

As foreign language education becomes a major educational goal for many countries, this approach to language teaching is seen by some as a logical link to content-based instruction. As an example of this type of relationship, we have three descriptive cases in this section. Firstly, Marta Seseña Gomez explains how a task-based language learning approach was adapted to a Spanish course at the University of Antwerp. The course was held in the faculty of Business and Economy where Spanish is taught as a foreign language during a mandatory period of two years to Engineering and Economy students. TBLL was implemented as a means to close the gap between the students' grammar and lexical knowledge (which was quite good) and their evident lack of ability to interact in a fluent and effective manner in an authentic communicative context. Seseña Gomez describes two target tasks that were created within this framework in order to increase students' accuracy and "automaticity".

In the next contribution in this chapter, Folkert Kuiken outlines the different ways in which task-based language learning has gradually been integrated into different teaching contexts in the Netherlands. The author describes and then compares four TBLL course-books, noting the difference in content and approach. The books have been written for different contexts: in primary and secondary education for a multilingual classroom, a Dutch course-book for newcomers to secondary education and a Dutch course-book for adult immigrants. Next, Kuiken discusses how task-based language learning has contributed to significant changes in language teaching in the Netherlands; changes in the teacher and students' roles, changes in the physical make-up of the classroom; new space in language teaching for media and technology, extracurricular activities, (self)evaluations and, finally, how TBLL has brought strategic language learning to centre stage.

Finally, Koen Van Gorp discusses the ways in which task-based language learning is used in multilingual classrooms in Flanders (Belgium) to promote language and content based education. He exemplifies how the carefully designed materials and tasks encourage children's collaborative problem-solving. Students are enthusiastic about the learning task because they are playing detective. Solving crimes, mysteries and puzzles motivates them to perform the task. Next, Van Gorp outlines how TBLL can be used to create a positive environment in which pupils and teachers learn to "deal with multilingualism as a resource or richness —rather than a problem" (Van Gorp, this volume). In a captivating example of a multilingual primary classroom in a rather poor district of Antwerp, the author describes a project called Radio Tika in which the students worked cooperatively while exploiting their own multilingual resources.

Works Cited

Doughty, Catherine. 2001a. "Principles for CALL pedagogy." Paper presented as the plenary address at the Hawaii Association of Language Teachers, March 2001a, in Honolulu, Hawaii.
—. 2001b. "Cognitive underpinnings of focus on form." In *Cognition and Second Language Instruction*, ed. Peter Robinson, 206-57, Cambridge: Cambridge University Press.
Doughty, Catherine and Michael H. Long, eds. 2003. *Handbook of second language acquisition*. New York: Basil Blackwell.
Ellis, Rod. 2003. *Task-based language learning and teaching*. Oxford: Oxford University Press.
Estaire, Sheila and Javier Zanón. 1994. *Planning classwork: A task based approach*. Oxford, Heinemann.
Fernández, Sonsoles, ed. 2001. *Tareas y proyectos en clase*. Madrid, Edinumen.
Gass, Susan M. 2003. "Input and interaction." In *Handbook of second language acquisition*, ed. Catherine Doughty and Michael H. Long, 224-255, New York: Basil Blackwell.
Long, Michael H., and Peter Robinson. 1998. "Focus on form: Theory, research and practice." In *Focus on form in second language acquisition*, ed. Catherine Doughty and Jessica Williams, 15-41, Cambridge, UK: Cambridge University Press.

Nunan, David. 1998. *Designing Tasks for the Communicative Classroom.* Cambridge, UK: Cambridge University Press.

Robinson, Peter. 2001. "Task complexity, cognitive resources, and syllabus design." In *Cognition and second language instruction*, ed. Peter Robinson, 287-318, Cambridge: Cambridge University Press.

Shavelson, Richard J. and Paula Stern. 1981. "Research on teachers' pedagogical thoughts, judgments and behavior." *Review of Educational Research*, 51, 455-498.

Skehan, Peter. 1998. *A cognitive approach to language learning.* Oxford, England: Oxford University Press.

Swaffer, Janet. K., Katherine Arens, and Martha Morgan. 1982. "Teacher classroom practices: redefining method as task hierarchy." *Modern Language Journal*, 66(1), 24-33.

Zanón, Javier, ed. 1999. *La enseñanza del español mediante tareas.* Madrid, Edinumen.

Adapting a Task-Based Language Learning Approach to a Spanish for Specific Purposes Course: "Prácticas Comunicativas" in the University of Antwerp

Marta Seseña Gómez

Following theories concerning communicative competence and the idea that a "language" is above all, a way to communicate, it is clear that the one of the most important elements in the language learning process is to develop communicative skills as opposed to more grammatical ones. Despite the apparent simplicity of this concept, second language teachers are daily faced with the challenge of finding the best way to implement this concept in classroom practice. This leads to the issue of which is the best method to achieve this. Which is the best approach that will motivate the students? How can a method be utilized in order to increase accuracy, automaticity[1] and fluency in learners? And perhaps more importantly, how can an approach, valued for its language learning potential, be integrated into a pre-established syllabus?

With these initial questions in mind, this article discusses the difficulties encountered during the implementation of a task-based language learning (TBLL) approach in a Spanish for specific purposes course at the University of Antwerp, Belgium. The objectives were to increase the accuracy, "automaticity" and fluency of the learners. The article will describe how the adaptation of TBLL to the already existent framework of the course (within the University syllabus) was managed in such a way to achieve remarkably good results.

---

[1] Automaticity could be defined as the subconscious condition wherein "we perform a complex series of tasks very quickly and efficiently, without having to think about the various components and subcomponents of action involved" (DeKeyser 2001 : 125)

The starting point will be the description of the context in which the TBLL adaptation was made (type of course, the method used in the classes, the pre-established syllabus, number of hours per week and year, learners' level and ages, etc.), followed by a discussion of the reasons for choosing the TBLL method to increase the communicative competence of the students in the course. An outline of the factors which led to the decision to adapt the approach and how this was carried out is provided. Finally, a critical evaluation of the proposal is given.

The context

The Spanish for Specific Purposes course discussed in this article was developed at the University of Antwerp, more specifically at the Faculty of Business and Applied Economics. It is a two-year compulsory course, with the option of taking the course for a third year. Business students (in their second year) must make the choice between German and Spanish as a second language (the first foreign language is always French). Once they have chosen one of these two languages they are committed to completing the whole two year period. Learners are divided in groups of 20 or 30 people who attend classes of two hours weekly during two terms of twelve weeks each. There is a gap of seven weeks between the two terms (exams period). The main goal of the course is to give the students the communicative tools they will need in a future conversation in Spanish in the frame of their work (Business and Economics).

The method originally used for this course had a strong focus on form[2] component and was divided into three stages. The first phase consisted of the implicit input of the course content, framed within a communicative context. The second phase consisted of explicit mastering of content through drill practice, and the third phase returned to the implicit use of content within a communicative context. Despite the focus on Communicative Teaching during two of the three phases, it was noted that students managed to achieve a good command of grammar but were not competent in oral communication skills. They had no fluency, they had deficient vocabulary and they were overly preoccupied with prescriptive elements of language related to grammar rather than focusing on communicative skills. Students were able to complete the drill exercises correctly, they successfully acquired grammar rules that had been "discovered" together in the classes, and they had developed strategies to do communicative exercises. Nonetheless, the students could not discuss

---

[2] Focus on form provides some type of implicit focus on grammar during communicative language teaching. (Fotos, 1998: 301)

any topic which had not been prepared previously, even if the functional structures, vocabulary or grammar were already known. These communicative deficiencies were even more apparent in the second year than in the first one, probably due to the fact that the students' knowledge of Spanish was greater (in theory, at least), thus creating higher expectations from the teachers.

Why task-based language learning?

The real goal of a second language course (according to Krashen, 1981:61) is not to make the students learn but to acquire and develop an "intermediate competence" that serves as the starting point for the student to begin to understand what is being said outside the classroom, in the real world (authentic contexts where the target language is being used). From this knowledge base, students can then improve their skills on their own. Nation (2005: 385) provided further argument for selecting task-based language learning as the ideal solution for the situation described above. According to Nation, the chances of achieving the intended transfer— that is the ability to use adequately and fluently previously acquired knowledge in a new context— can be improved substantially by adding to the traditional communicative structure a creative phase. This phase is based on inventive and original use of the course content in a new communicative situation.

This meant that an extra phase needed to be added to the original three-phase communicative course. The additional phase had to provide a motivating communicative content in which students could put the input from the previous stages into practise. By the end of this last phase, the output should demonstrate accurate, correct, fluent and acquired knowledge of the input. However, questions still remained on how to best carry out these propositions and which would be the best method for this fourth new phase. After careful consideration, it seemed clear that the features of task-based language learning could provide the needed support for the main intentions of the new fourth stage.

Nunan defines a "task" as:

> A piece of classroom work that involves learners in comprehending, manipulating, predicting or interacting in the target language while their attention is focused on mobilizing their grammatical knowledge in order to express meaning and in which the intention is to convey meaning rather than to manipulate form. The task should also have a sense of completeness, being able to stand alone as a communicative act in its own right with a beginning a middle and an end. (Nunan: 1998: 25)

With this in mind, it was decided that the course should be developed in such a way that the students' tasks represented a part of the real context in which they would use the Spanish language in the real world. It was important that the tasks were not isolated exercises, but a complex activity divided into achievable parts—directed towards the holistic acquisition of the target language.

Firstly, it is necessary to summarize the principle components of TBLL in order to understand the adaptations needed to ensure the integration of the approach into the pre-established syllabus. Following Zanón and Estaire, a task is composed of: a) sub-communication tasks[3], similar to Nunan's "general tasks"; b) enabling tasks which provide support for communication tasks, that is, the linguistics tools needed to carry out a communication task as well as the final task. (These tasks must be as meaningful as possible but their focus is on linguistic aspects rather than meaning; c) evaluation-self evaluation tasks—an integral part of the learning process and which is not uni- directional because the student evaluates his own work and the whole task, while the teacher evaluates the students' work and the task design.

Sheila Estaire and Javier Zanón (1994:49) present this scheme in order to clarify the necessary steps to design a task:

- Determine the interest area.
- Plan the final task.
- Determine unit objectives.
- Specify necessary contents to carry out the final task, related with each of the objectives.
- Determine the communication and enabling tasks.
- Plan the procedure for the evaluation of the process and the product.

"Las Prácticas comunicativas": An example of adaptation of TBLL

In order to link TBLL with the pre-established syllabus already existent at the University, language workshops—known as "Talleres de prácticas comunicativas"— were created to give the students the opportunity of putting in practise the linguistic elements they had learned (not acquired) during lessons in a semi-real context related with their

---

[3] Sheila Estaire and Javier Zanón prefer this second name (Estaire and Zanón, 1994: 13-19,34-35).

interests (Business and Economics). These are the general characteristics of these special classes:
- Student numbers: 100-120 (in four rotating groups)
- Student language levels: II year Spanish course (A2-B1 level)
- Number of sessions: 5 per semester (10 in total).
- Length of sessions: 50 minutes.
- Characteristics of the "Talleres de prácticas comunicativas": Optional (students had the choice between participating in the workshops or sitting an oral exam).

Following the schema proposed by Estaire and Zanón, it was clear that certain phases and elements of TBLL had to be adapted to fit the circumstances of the Spanish for Specific Purposes course. For instance, it is generally suggested that the topics of the tasks be decided by students themselves—guided by their teacher—because they can be a good source of motivating ideas that are relevant to their own world, interests and preferences. However, in this particular case, the large number of students required a pre-selection of the topics, because it would have been impossible to get all the students to agree on one topic. Besides, with the division of the general group in four sub-groups, it was predictable that, in each of these sub-groups, the interest area chosen would have been different from the others and, consequently, also the final task, resulting in a wide disparity of objectives in each case.

It was impossible to relate the content of the different tasks to the final task—as is stipulated by TBLL—because the classes included an optional characteristic and not all the students participated in the same phases of the course. Thus, from the beginning, the "prácticas comunicativas" (language workshops) were conceived as a support to the regular classes and as a way to help the students assimilate the knowledge learnt in the classes. Moreover, the activities from each of the "Prácticas Comunicativas" (communicative practice sessions) were designed as "communication sub-tasks" and not "enabling tasks". The "enabling sub-tasks" were developed into the regular classes which the students attended in the two terms of the year.

The question of including evaluation in the learning process required certain flexibility as well. Because participation in the "Prácticas Comunicativas" meant exemption from the oral exam, evaluation had to be based on daily work and effort involved in the process leading up to the final task. The evaluation-self evaluation phase was adapted slightly so that in each of "Prácticas Comunicativas" workshop sessions there was a conventional evaluation (necessary since they were exempted from the oral exam and final evaluation is required by administration), with self evaluation at the end of the entire learning process.

An example of TBLL in a Spanish workshop

A practical example of the language workshop is given below (first term of Year One task). First, the general outline of the task descriptions is given. This is followed by an example from the evaluation-self evaluation phase of the course.

Determine the interest area:
- Business and Economics.

Plan final task:
- To acquire a good knowledge about Business and Economics and to develop the strategies necessary to act in different situations related with work. (Students will reach this task through the accomplishment of the five communication subtasks that are proposed in each session).

Determine unit objectives (principal objective of each "taller" or workshop session)
- To describe ideal work conditions for a firm.
- To write a curriculum vitae in order to apply for a job and to hold an interview.
- To understand and know how to create a firm.
- To write a decalogue for business success.
- To create a new firm based in the possibilities of real franchise.

Specify content which is necessary to carry out the final task, related with each of the unit objectives (listed above):

1. Describing ideal work conditions for a firm

Communicative objectives:
- Describe ideal work conditions for a firm: space, relationships with colleagues, etc.

Functional objectives:
- Introduce oneself.
- Recognise the different components of a formal letter.
- Express one's likes and dislikes.
- Describe things related to the job.

- Express an opinion.

Grammatical objectives:
- Gustar, encantar, preferir, etc. [to like, to enjoy, to prefer, etc.]
- Ser, estar, haber, etc. [to be, to have done, etc.]
- Creer, pensar que, etc. [to believe, to think that, etc.]
- Porque, es que... [because, it is such that...]
- Para mí, según [in my opinion, according to...]

2. Writing a curriculum vitae in order to apply for a job and hold an interview.

Communicative objectives:
- To write a curriculum vitae.
- To participate in an interview.

Functional objectives:
- To talk about oneself.
- To talk about the past.

Grammatical objectives:
- Imperfecto/ Indefinido. [imperfect, indefinite]
- Los interrogativos. [interrogatives]
- Ser y estar. [to be]

3. Understanding and knowing how to create a firm.

Communicative objectives:
- To understand and to know the creation process of a firm.

Functional objectives:
- To understand conversation and talk about the past.

Grammatical objectives:
- Imperfecto/indefinido/pretérito [imperfect, indefinite, preterite]
- perfecto/ pluscuamperfecto. [perfect, pluperfect tenses]
- Conectores temporales. [time adjuncts]
- Reciclaje de elementos vistos con anterioridad. [review of previous items]

4. Writing the advice Decalogue for business success.

Communicative objectives: To write the advice Decalogue for business success.
- To solve problems.

Functional objectives:
- To give advice.

Grammatical objectives:

"How we're going about it": Teachers' Voices on Innovative Approaches to Teaching and Learning Languages

- Imperativo afirmativo y negativo. [affirmative and negative imperatives]
- ¿Por qué no...?, ¿y si...?, ¿qué tal si...?, etc. [why not? What if...? How about...]
- Los pronombres de complemento. [relative clauses]
- Las oraciones con si. [conditional phrases]

5. Creating a new firm based on the possibilities of real franchise
Communicative objectives:
- To create a new firm based on the possibilities of real franchise.

Functional objectives:
- To express the impersonal.
- To express obligation.
- To give an opinion.
- To make a proposal.
- To reject proposals politely.

Grammatical objectives:
- El se impersonal. [impersonal reflexive]
- Tener que, deber, etc. [have to/must]
- Creer, pensar que, etc. [to believe, to think that, etc.]
- Porque, es que, etc. [Because, thus, etc.]

Workshop contents

In order to determine the communication and enabling tasks, careful planning of the learning process was imperative. To do so, the designed activities (outlined above) were integrated into both the language workshops and the regular classes. (For the sake of brevity the workshop activities are not fully described here[4].)

In Taller 1 (Workshop 1) we proposed to the students that they compose a formal letter business letter, followed by a group of questions related to the type of letter and the content itself. In this way we could practice not only the way of writing formal letters in Spanish but also the reading comprehension. The second and last part, related with the content of the letter, dealt with the ideal work conditions in a firm (physical space and the worker's character).

---

[4] Readers interested in exploring these activities further should have a look at http://www.sgci.mec.es/be/publicaciones/mosaico.htm (numbers 12, 13 and 15, section "Fichas"), where three of the five activities are explained in detail.

In Taller 2 (Workshop 2) the students' work was related to a job offer. The students had to write their CV and an application letter (we supplied them with an example of each of this type of documents). The final goal of this workshop was to "attend a job interview" for the position they had written their application letter for (role-play).

In Taller 3 (Workshop 3) we presented the students with two versions of the same text about the creation process of one of the most important and successful Spanish firms, Zara. The phrases on the text were not in the correct position and there were information gaps that could be completed with the information of the other version. Students were asked to put the phrases in the correct order and complete the gaps. They did this through pair-work—each partner had the other, correspoding text version. Finally, students had to add some more details into appropriate parts of the text and then write a similar text about the creation process of a real or imaginary firm.

In Taller 4 (Workshop 4) we explained to the students that they would be participating in the setting-up of a new firm. The students were divided into groups and each of them represented a different department in the firm. Their task, in this case, was to create an advice Decalogue for business success for their departments.

Finally, in Taller 5 (Workshop 5) the students were required to create a new firm, based on the possibilities from a real franchise. This sub-task was done in an Internet classroom. The students were provided with a list of web links to real franchise firms that had been previously researched in Internet. Students had to search the web site of the firm they had chosen, select needed information and write an introductory text of their chosen franchise.

Evaluation and Self-evaluation

The evaluation questionnaire was created to get the students to reflect on different points related with the method and the activities they had done in the five sessions. The assessment questionnaire was divided into three different sections:

The first one is made up of some statements related to the method itself. Students only had to place an X next to the phrases which they agreed with. An example of some of the statements included in this part were:

- This type of learning is amusing.
- I don't like learning Spanish this way.
- I think that this type of learning is very useful.

"How we're going about it": Teachers' Voices on Innovative Approaches   71
to Teaching and Learning Languages

- This type of learning and practising Spanish helps me to communicate better in real contexts.

In this part of the evaluation we could not only find out the degree of satisfaction that students felt when doing this task, but also their difficulties related with this method, along with their ideas about their own learning process.

The second part of the evaluation/self evaluation sheet allowed us and the students to know how they are able to perform in the different functional components that are supposed to be acquired at this point of the learning process. In order to do this, we have created a second group of statements but in this case, they were all related with the ability of the students to "perform" with Spanish language components. In this case, students have to reflect about their abilities in the different functional objectives that were defined by each part of the task and to place them in a scale from "very good" to "bad".

Some examples are given below.

Fig. 2-1 Evaluation scale

I'm able to:

VERY GOOD   GOOD   AVERAGE   BAD
- To describe ideal work conditions for a firm
  [ ]   [ ]   [ ]   [ ]

- To introduce myself
  [ ]   [ ]   [ ]   [ ]
-To recognise the components of a formal letter
  [ ]   [ ]   [ ]   [ ]

The third and last part is related with an evaluation of the whole task, and gets the students to reflect on improvements that could still be made. Students should think about their own participation in the different parts of the task. In this case we present to the students some open-ended statements that they have to complete individually. In this way we could know their implication in the process of the task, their opinion about the results and their interest areas for further activities.

Some examples of this part of the evaluation are given in figure 2-2.

Fig. 2-2 Self-evaluation

- I would like the next task to be about
_____

- In this task it's still possible to improve
_____

- My participation in this task has been_____

Critical evaluation and discussion

In order to check the effectiveness of the TBLL experience, a study was carried out after one year. The two groups were separated to make up an experimental group and a control group. Results concerning "automaticity" were compared between the two groups. Both groups were taking the same theoretical classes, the only difference in the two groups' training lies in their attendance to the Prácticas Comunicativas (language workshops) or not (attendance was optional). Thus, the control group was made up of students who had decided not to participate in the "Prácticas Comunicativas" workshop and opted for sitting the exam. This group was composed of 35 subjects. The data compiled for the study came from their individual dossiers, which contained material they had developed after reading 12 different texts found in specialized Spanish business newspapers and magazines. The students' performances in an oral test—which consisted of giving a brief presentation on each of these companies—were also included in the data. The experimental group was made up of 33 students and the study data came from the practical activities they had done during the workshops.

Next, criteria for evaluating students' output was established which would help determine whether the adaptation of a TBLL approach had helped improve the students' "automaticity". It was decided to base the criteria on the Common European Framework of Reference for Languages: Learning, Teaching, Assessment, adjusting the framework criteria to the specific course. The main criteria were: pronunciation, fluency, intonation, sociolinguistic competence, lexical competence and grammatical competence. Each of these criteria were divided and specified in a detailed list of subcriteria which cannot be reproduced here due to need for brevity. However, interested readers can consult the article entitled "Task-based language learning put to the test: The case of the prácticas comunicativas in Spanish as a foreign language for Business and Economics"in the Proceedings of the 5th International AELFE Conference (2006) and De Ridder, Isabelle; Vangehuchten, Lieve and Seseña Gómez, Marta 2007. "Enhancing automacity through Task-based Language Learning" in *Applied Linguistics* 28/2: 309-315, Oxford, Oxford University Press. Briefly, the table below gives statistical results on the six major criteria (in percentages):

Fig. 2-3 Statistical results of six major criteria for assessment TBLL

Criterium	Condition	Mean	SD	Min.	Max.	N
Pronunciation	Control	74.76	22.28	25.00	100.00	35
	Experimental	58.58	14.36	33.33	83.33	33
Intonation	Control	70.71	23.02	25.00	100.00	35
	Experimental	54.92	24.59	25.00	100.00	33
Grammar	Control	63.27	18.18	28.94	89.47	35
	Experimental	88.89	16.59	43.75	100.00	33
Vocabulary	Control	65.89	23.64	25.00	100.00	35
	Experimental	91.18	11.90	44.44	100.00	33
Social Adequacy	Control	68.57	29.61	25.00	100.00	35
	Experimental	85.92	22.48	25.00	100.00	33
Fluency	Control	67.50	24.47	25.00	100.00	35
	Experimental	74.00	25.74	25.00	100.00	33

As can be inferred from these results, the TBLL group proved superior in the areas of grammar, vocabulary, social adequacy and fluency. However, regarding pronunciation and intonation, the control group outperformed the experimental group. This fact can be explained by the different situation in which students of both groups were using the target language. In the experimental group, students were interacting in groups, whereas the students in the control group participated in a one-to-one interaction with the evaluator (a native or near-native speaker).

It is likely that one of the most important deciding factors of why the experimental group outperformed the control group in aspects such as grammar, vocabulary, social adequacy and fluency is motivation. Indeed, the experimental group had decided to choose an extra class in which they could practise grammar contents in a semi-real context, with the aim of improving their performance in Spanish. This implies that they were more motivated to learn, to acquire the language and more open-minded to using the structures with which they had been in contact and less inclined to worry about making mistakes. This is especially true in the case of the workshops, which was not a "normal" class for them. While these factors must be considered, it does not detract from the fact that TBLL in general, including the adaptation we did to our course, provides a learning environment in which students are relaxed and more self-confident. This helps ensure a better learning process and students improve their use of the language more quickly.

On the whole, the students' reactions in the "evaluation- self evaluation" phase of the experience were very positive. Following the success of the initial proposal —proven not only by the results of the study, but also by the enthusiastic reaction of the students' themselves— this experience has been repeated three more times, always with similar outcomes. In the light of statistical results and students' opinions, it is easy to argue that TBLL is an excellent way to increase the accuracy, automaticity and fluency of the learners, and that it is indeed possible to adapt this approach to the specific conditions and general framework of different teaching environments.

Works Cited

DeKeyser, Robert M. 2001. "Automaticity and automatization" in *Cognition and Second Language Instruction*, ed. Peter Robinson, 125-151, Cambridge: Cambridge University Press.

De Ridder, Isabelle, Lieve Vangehuchten and Marta Seseña Gómez, Marta. 2007. "Enhancing automacity through Task-based Language Learning," *Applied Linguistics* 28/2: 309-315, Oxford: Oxford University Press.

Eguiluz, Angel. 1998. *De los procesos a las tareas: el concepto de tarea. Trabajo de investigación de M.E.L.E.* Salamanca: Universidad de Salamanca.

Estaire, Sheila. 1990. "La programación de unidades didácticas a través de tareas," *Cable*, 5: 36. Madrid: Difusión.

—. 1999. "Tareas para el desarrollo de un aprendizaje autónomo y participativo," in *La enseñanza del español mediante tareas*, ed. Javier Zanon, 53-72, Madrid: Edinumen.

Estaire, Sheila and Javier Zanón. 1994. *Planning classroom: A task based approach*. Oxford: Heinemann.

Fernández, Sonsoles, ed. 2001. *Tareas y proyectos en clase*. Madrid: Edinumen.

Fotos, Sandra. 1998. "Shifting the focus from forms to form in the EFL classroom", *ELT Journal*, 52/4: 301-307. Oxford: Oxford University Press.

Fried-Booth, Diana L. 1986. *Project work*. Oxford: Oxford University Press.

Gatbonton, Elizabeth and Norman Segalowitz.. 1988. "Creative automatization: principles for promoting fluency within a communicative framework." *TESOL Quarterly*, 22, 473-492.

Krashen, Stephen D. 1981. *Second language acquisition and second language learning*. New York, NY: Pergamon Press.

Nation, Paul. 2001. *Learning vocabulary in another language*, Cambridge: Cambridge University Press.

Nunan, David. 1989. *Designing tasks for the communicative classroom*, Cambridge University Press: Cambridge.

Ribé, Ramon and Núria Vidal. 1993. *Project work step by step*. Oxford: Heinemann.

Seedhouse, Paul. 1999. "Task-based interaction," *ELT-Journal*, 53/3: 149-156. Oxford: Oxford University Press.

Segalowitz, Norman. 2003. "Automaticity and second languages," In *The handbook of second language acquisition*, ed. Catherine Doughty and Michael H. Long, 382-408. Malden/Oxford/Carlto: Blackwell.

Vangehuchten, Lieve and Marta Seseña Gómez. 2006. "TBLL put to the test", in Proceedings of the 5th International 5th international conference of the European Association of Languages for Specific Purposes Conference, 14-16 September, in Zaragoza, Spain.

Zanón Javier. 1990. "Los enfoques por tareas para la enseñanza de las lenguas extranjeras," *Cable* 5, 19-27.

Zanón Javier, ed. 1999. *La enseñanza del español mediante tareas*. Madrid: Edinumen.

Web page

Common European Framework of Reference for Languages: Learning, Teaching, Assessment, Strasbourg: Council of Europe, 2001 (Spanish version at http://cvc.cervantes.es/obref/marco/)

TASK-BASED LANGUAGE TEACHING IN THE NETHERLANDS: DUTCH L1 AND DUTCH L2

FOLKERT KUIKEN

Introduction

Task-based language teaching started in the Netherlands in the 1990's, resulting at the end of that decade in two course books for students in secondary education. For mother tongue education Schoolslag was published, while Zebra was designed for students who learned Dutch as their second language. In 2002 a course book for pupils in primary education appeared, entitled Taalverhaal, whereas one year later Code was launched for adult learners of Dutch as a second language. This means that there are now task-based language syllabuses available both for younger and older learners, and for mother tongue education as well as for Dutch as a second language[1].

Although the target groups of these syllabuses differ, there are many similarities between them, as they all take the principles of task-based language teaching as their starting point. Further on, we will illustrate the way in which the syllabuses resemble each other. There are, however, also differences between the course books and in section 3 we will explain what these differences are. Next we will demonstrate in section 4 how the task-based language approach has changed the practice of language learning. These changes have to do with the respective roles assigned to the teacher and the students in the task-based language approach, the arrangement of the classroom and the use of various media, extracurricular activities, the importance attached to (self-) evaluation and the emphasis on strategic language learning. In the fifth and last section we will discuss

---

[1] Task-based language teaching has also been implemented in the teaching of foreign languages to Dutch students. One of the projects for foreign task-based language teaching was TABASCO, which stands for task-based school organisation for the acquisition of languages in Europe. However, in this chapter we will restrict ourselves to the teaching of Dutch as a mother tongue (L1) and Dutch as a second language (L2).

some current developments related to task-based language teaching. These issues concern other language teaching approaches, ICT and language policy.

Similarities between courses of task-based language teaching

We will start with some examples of tasks that are presented to the students in the Dutch classrooms: first primary education, then secondary education and finally adult education.

Primary education, Dutch L1: Taalverhaal (Van den Berg et al. 2002) is a course book for teaching Dutch at primary school to pupils from 7 to 11 years (2nd to 6th grade). The course is meant to be used in a multilingual classroom, given the fact that many pupils speak languages other than Dutch at home. Therefore a lot of attention is paid to vocabulary acquisition in the course. Every course book for a particular grade is divided into several units which are centered on a specific theme. For instance: the second theme of grade book 4 is "Arts". Some of the tasks that are presented to the pupils in this theme are: choosing a theatre performance (from a set of several options), finding out how to go there by public transport, and expressing opinions on a painting by Van Gogh. All tasks are divided into a preparatory phase (Du. bedenken = to devise), a performative phase (Du. doen = to do) and a reflective phase (Du. terugkijken = to look back).

Secondary education, Dutch L1: A couple of years before Taalverhaal was issued a course book of Dutch for students in secondary education was published, entitled Schoolslag (Asscheman et al. 1998). Like its antecedent in primary education, Schoolslag is intended for the multilingual classroom and therefore the authors have integrated sections on academic language proficiency, strategic language learning and systematic vocabulary training into the course. The course consists of eight volumes, divided into volumes for the lower forms of secondary education and the higher ones, covering four school years in total (7th to 10th grade). Like in Taalverhaal the tasks presented to the students have been grouped into themes. Some examples in year 1 are: "Nature and environment", "From the past till now", "Media" and "Discovering and investigating".

In the latter theme all tasks refer to interviewing a scholar or researcher. Similar to Taalverhaal the tasks in Schoolslag consist of three parts: Du. voorbereiden (= to prepare), Du. uitvoeren (= to perform) and Du. terugkijken (= to look back). In the preparatory phase the students learn to formulate their main question, how to start an interview, what questions they should ask in order to get an answer to their main question, and how to close an interview. During the performative phase they do the interview and submit the interviewee to the questions they have prepared in advance, while in the reflective phase they consider if they have indeed received answers to all their questions.

Secondary education, Dutch L2: Zebra, which appeared one year after Schoolslag, has also been written for secondary school students, i.e. for newcomers and other students who do not yet master the Dutch language enough to be able to participate in regular class (Alons et al. 1999). Zebra and Schoolslag have been developed around the same time in close cooperation with each other. In this way 12 to 16 year old newcomers who learn Dutch by means of Zebra can smoothly continue with Schoolslag in regular class. Zebra consists of four parts, which can be worked through in one to one and a half years, depending on factors like language aptitude, intelligence level and motivation of the students. One of the tasks presented in part 1, theme 8 ("Who are you?") is "to read and understand personal ads". In the preparation for the task (Du. hoe moet het? = how to do it?) the students are confronted with 12 personal ads which they are supposed to read. In the performance of the task they have to find out what the ads have in common (Du. doen! = do it!). After finishing the task they are asked to consider if they could understand the information contained in the ads and if they were able to make matches between the ads (Du. hoe gaat het? = how is it going?).

Adult education, Dutch L2: Code is, like Zebra, intended for speakers of Dutch as a second language. But whereas Zebra has been designed for 12 to 16 year olds, Code has adult learners of Dutch L2 as its target group. The course consists of three volumes for a period of one to one and a half years, after which the students are supposed to have reached a proficiency level in Dutch that enables them to participate in Dutch higher vocational education or university[2]. Again the tasks have been grouped into themes (food, transport, music, health, sports, humor, etc.) with 15 themes in each volume. The theme of chapter 23, entitled "Young and old", in volume 2 is "generations", and the second task in this chapter is called "to gather information about the composition of the population in your country". In the first part of this task (Du. voorbereiden = to prepare) the learners are confronted with a table and a text on the composition of the population in the Netherlands. In the second part (Du. uitvoeren = to perform) they have

---

[2] The first two volumes of *Code* have been based on principles of task-based language teaching, but remarkably enough the authors have abandoned this approach in volume 3.

to collect information about the population in their home country using the Internet, and then write a text of about 200 words on the composition of the population in their country. In the third and last part of the task (Du. afronden = to round off) they are asked to discuss with their fellow students the similarities and differences between the composition of the population in the Netherlands and their home country.

The four course books for Dutch that have been designed on principles of task-based language teaching cover the period from primary education to adult education. In order to present the subject materials in convenient pieces they have all been distributed across several volumes. The tasks that are presented to the students have been grouped into larger thematic units. In all courses the tasks have been subdivided into three stages: the preparation of the task, the performance of the task itself, and a stage in which the students look back on how they have performed the task (see Fig. 2-4).

Fig. 2-4 Course books of Dutch for task-based language teaching

	Taalverhaal	*Schoolslag*	*Zebra*	*Code*
Author & year	Van den Berg et al. (2002)	Asscheman et al. (1998)	Alons et al. (2002)	Boers et al. (2003)
Dutch L1/L2	Dutch L1 (multilingual classes)	Dutch L1 (multilingual classes)	Dutch L2 (newcomers, adolescents)	Dutch L2 (newcomers, adults)
Type of education	Primary education (7-11 years)	Secondary education (12-16 years)	Secondary education (12-16 years)	Adult education (> 18 years)
Term	5 years (2nd-6th grade)	4 years (7th-10th grade)	1-1.5 year	1-1.5 year
Volumes	5	8	4	3
Task division	1. *bedenken* (to devise) 2. *doen* (to do) 3. *terugkijken* (to look back)	1. *voorbereiden* (to prepare) 2. *uitvoeren* (to perform) 3. *terugkijken* (to look back)	1. *hoe moet het?* (how to do it?) 2. *doen!* (do it!) 3. *hoe gaat het?* (how is it going?)	1. *voorbereiden* (to prepare) 2. *uitvoeren* (to perform) 3. *afronden* (to round off)

So far it seems that the courses, despite the different target groups they have been written for, resemble each other to a large degree with respect to their design. This is indeed the case, which is not surprising as they are all based on more or less the same principles. However, there are also some substantial differences among the four courses, as we will see in the next section.

Differences among courses of task-based language teaching

We will now discuss the differences between the four courses with respect to the characteristics of task-based language teaching. These characteristics are: tasks as a starting point for language teaching; integration of skills; an analytic approach of language teaching; and a focus on the process of language acquisition.

Tasks as a starting point for language teaching: The examples of tasks given in the preceding section all demonstrate that the authors have organized the subject matters into real-life tasks: choosing a theatre performance, interviewing a researcher, reading and understanding personal ads, writing a text on the composition of the population in a particular country, etc. In the instances where this is not the case they present pedagogically relevant tasks to the learners. In so far there is not much difference between the courses.

Integration of skills: The same is true with respect to the second characteristic: integration of skills. Task-based language teaching means that different skills (listening, speaking, reading, writing) are integrated into one single task, as is the case in normal, real-life tasks. Choosing a theatre performance with a bunch of people includes reading, listening and speaking; interviewing a researcher means listening and speaking; reading and matching personal ads with fellow students involves reading and speaking; gathering and presenting information on a particular topic implies (at least) reading and writing. This means that the four courses confront the learners with tasks in which several skills are integrated and they do not differ very much from each other on this point.

An analytic approach to language teaching: There are, however, differences between the courses with respect to the other two characteristics of task-based language teaching. The first difference concerns the fact that language teaching is analytical, in the sense that learners are confronted with a task as a whole: in performing the task they become aware of all that is needed for the task (words, putting these words in the right order, making a coherent argument, etc.) and they learn how to analyze and break up the task into smaller elements. This is in contrast with a synthetic approach where, the other way round, earlier acquired pieces of language are put together to form larger units. What can be noticed is that one course is more analytical than the other. Some task-based language teaching courses do no more and no less than presenting tasks to the learners e.g. the Belgian syllabuses Klaar? Af! (Werkgroep Anderstalige Nieuwkomers 1998) and Taalkit (Werkgroep Anderstalige Nieuwkomers 1999), whereas in other courses tasks are alternated with sections in which some particular elements of language are highlighted. This is for instance the case in Atlas (Nunan 1995) where a clear distinction is made between "task chains" and sections which are labeled "language focus".

Atlas has served as a model for Zebra in which a similar distinction has been made between what in Zebra is called "tasks" and "building blocks". In these building blocks attention is paid to sounds, intonation, words, sentence structure and language functions. In some cases the building blocks introduce elements that can be used in the task that follows, whereas in others their function is to consolidate elements that had to be used in the preceding task. In Atlas and Zebra the division between "task chains" or "tasks" and "language focus" or "building blocks" is more or less balanced, but in Schoolslag the task sections are much shorter than the building blocks. In Code, on the other hand, there are not many language focus sections, but here the preparatory phase of a task is often much longer than the performance of the task itself, whereas in the third phase, which is meant to be reflective, learners are often requested to perform a second task. In those cases the term "eclectic" would be a better characterization for the course than "task based", and this is indeed a term which is used by the authors in some of the manuals.

Focus on the process of language acquisition: The last characteristic of task-based language teaching regards the emphasis on the process of language learning. It was shown in section 2 that in some way all courses have included a phase during which the learners are forced to reflect on the task they have just performed. Zebra seems to be the most demanding with respect to this point, as the students are not only requested to reflect on each task after having performed it, but also to evaluate themselves after every theme and subtheme. The result of this is that in the end students often become bored with these continuous reflections on their language acquisition process. The authors of Code, which appeared some years later than Zebra, have learnt from this experience and have therefore given another interpretation to the reflective phase. In some cases this has led to the performance of a second task instead of an evaluation of how the task has been performed. To characterize this phase they use the term "to round off" (Du. afronden) instead of "to look back", "to reflect" or "to evaluate". It should be remarked, however, that this "rounding off" cannot be considered as a reflection on the acquisition process, as is meant originally by the task-based language teaching approach.

All in all, what these examples illustrate is that there is considerable variation in what are labeled task-based language courses. However, if we think of the various ways in which communicative language courses have been designed, this is certainly not a new phenomenon.

Changes in the practice of language teaching

Despite the differences that can be discerned between several course books, in general the task-based language teaching approach has led to substantial changes in the daily practice of language teaching. The changes we want to discuss here, are: the role designed for the teacher and the students, the arrangement of the classroom and the use of various media, extracurricular activities, the use of (self)evaluations and the emphasis on strategic language learning.

The role of teachers and students in task-based language teaching: In comparison with earlier methods of language teaching, for instance the communicative approach, the roles attributed by task-based language teaching to teachers and learners have changed. Instead of omniscient teachers who pass on their knowledge to the students in a teacher-fronted setting, their role during task-based language teaching is expected to be more that of a counselor or a coach who guides the students through the language acquisition process. They attribute tasks to the students, walk around while the students prepare or perform the tasks and may be consulted by the students for help or advice. Teachers are, in short, the ones who supervise and manage the language acquisition process of their students.

Likewise the role of the students has changed. They are no longer passive consumers of language lessons, but are stimulated to take their language acquisition into their own hands. This is a very important point in the light of new regulations with respect to citizenship in many (European) countries. In the Netherlands for instance newcomers have to pass an exam in Dutch before they are granted Dutch citizenship and they are supposed to obtain the required level all by themselves. Task-based language teaching fits into these new developments, given the fact that the role of learners is assumed to be self-organizing, self-discovering and creative.

The arrangement of the classroom and the use of various media: The changing role of teachers and students in language learning has its repercussions for the arrangement of the language classroom. In a classroom where teacher-fronted teaching is out of the question, students are not supposed to sit in a square or one behind the other, but in small groups in which they try to solve the tasks with their fellow students. This setting was already common in primary education in the Netherlands, but in secondary and adult education both teachers and students had to get used to this new arrangement.

Whereas in more traditional approaches speaking activities were alternated with listening, reading and writing, in task-based language teaching these skills are integrated with each other. This implies that all media need to be available at any moment. A well-equipped classroom should therefore include shelves with reference books (grammar books, dictionaries), computers to use internet and equipment to watch video and listen to CDs. Implementation of task-based language teaching does not only require a change of mindset in the students and teachers, but leads also to a change in the physical arrangement of the classroom. Paradoxically, however, authorities sometimes seem to have fewer problems in financing at once a whole new concept including all the necessary facilities than when they are asked continuously to pay for smaller purchases. This is at least the experience we had in the Netherlands when Zebra was introduced.

Extracurricular activities: With the use of (real-life) tasks as proposed by task-based language teaching the gap between language learning inside and outside the classroom has become smaller. Of course, some (real-life) tasks can only be performed outside the classroom. All courses mentioned above include extracurricular activities where students are asked to complete assignments outside the classroom. These assignments vary from watching the daily news (Code), gathering information about Dutch magazines (Zebra) to setting up a research project (Schoolslag). Since the introduction of the new law on civic integration in the Netherlands as of January 2007 such tasks have become extremely important, as newcomers in the Netherlands are obliged to compile a portfolio with samples of real-life tasks in order to pass their civic integration exam.

The use of (self) evaluations: In a society where competence-oriented learning has become more and more influential, it is important for citizens to know what their qualities are and what they can and cannot do (yet). Therefore they should be able to evaluate themselves. Both teachers and students are often afraid of self-evaluations: what if they overestimate or underestimate themselves? In the beginning this may indeed be the case, but it turns out that after some exercise learners are very well able to evaluate their language skills quite adequately. The next problem then is how often one should ask learners to evaluate themselves (not too often as we learnt from Zebra) and what kind of feedback teachers should give their students if these have not yet acquired a particular skill or level of proficiency.

The emphasis on strategic language learning: If learners come across an unknown word in a text they have many ways to find out what it means: they may recognize a part of the word, they can guess the meaning of the word, they may infer the meaning of the word with the help of the surrounding context, they can reach for a dictionary, etc. Not all learners are so creative that they will think of all these possibilities. However, in order to solve a language task the self-discovering capacity of the learners is important, as we saw above. In task-based language teaching learners are stimulated to develop this self-discovering capacity in at least two ways. After having performed a task they are asked to reflect on the way they have performed the task and to compare with their fellow students if there are other ways to solve the task that lead perhaps to a better or quicker solution. Besides that, some course books have included general suggestions and more specific tips for language learning. Examples are: "Be clear. Ask if everybody has understood you" (Taalverhaal); "Make an outline. It can be useful to put the information of a text into an outline" (Zebra); "Choose the right way to listen. Before you are going to listen to a text, think of what you want to know. Sometimes you have to remember everything. But often you only need to listen to a part of the text to get the information you need" (Schoolslag). By means of these kind of clues learners are stimulated to find out which strategies work best for them in order to become competent language users.

Task-based language teaching and current developments

The success of task-based language teaching does not stand on its own. It is attached to historical developments in language teaching, political circumstances and technological inventions. In this final section we want to discuss some of the developments that are connected to task-based language teaching. These issues concern the relationship between task-based language teaching and other alternative approaches, such as ICT.

Task-based language teaching and other approaches: The task-based language teaching approach has some features that it shares with other approaches. The focus on functional, communicative activities for instance is a characteristic shared by the communicative approach. In content-based language teaching tasks also play an important role, albeit that an essential aspect of these tasks concerns the integration of language and subject matter. In this sense task-based language teaching demonstrates the continuity in the range of language teaching approaches rather than discontinuity. The link with content-based language teaching is particularly strong (see the chapter on Content and Language Integrated Learning in Section I). This can be illustrated by the fourth volume of Zebra, where language goals have been attached to subject matters like history, social studies, geography, art history, biology, chemistry, physics, etc. This was done in order to bridge the gap for newcomers between their acquisition of Dutch and participation in regular classes. Another illustration of this close link can be found in adult education in the Netherlands, where task-based and content-based language teaching come together in so called "dual" or "integrated routes" for newcomers: in these programmes the content of the language tasks the participants have to perform is dictated by the vocational training they receive in a specific field.

Task-based language teaching and ICT: The rise of task-based language teaching coincides more or less with the development of the information and communication technology. This means that in task based language teaching one can take advantage extensively of digitalized audio and video files, the use of Internet, dictionaries and other reference books that are available on CD-ROM or on the web, etc. The use of these resources fits the role attributed to the student as a self-discovering, self-organizing learner. The courses presented here are all multi-media courses, where text books are complemented with audio- and videotapes, CDs and CD-ROMs, and where the learners are regularly referred to the Internet. The use of Internet has, however, also its disadvantages: Internet addresses change quickly and are rapidly outdated, and if learners do not get clear indications on where to look for specific information they can easily get lost on the web.

Task-based language teaching and language policy: In many European countries the Common European Framework of Reference (CEFR; Council of Europe 2001) has become a yardstick for assessing and classifying the performance of language learners. Although the CEFR does not favour a particular language teaching approach in order to obtain a specific level, it goes without saying that the way the levels in the CEFR are conceived of fit the task-based language teaching approach perfectly. In the Netherlands many teaching institutes have already organized their courses in terms of CEFR levels. According to the law on civic integration newcomers are compelled to pass an exam of Dutch at A2 level. One can easily infer from these facts that task-based language teaching profits from these developments. However, the more the CEFR gets known, the more it becomes subject of criticism. These criticisms concern both the lack of a theoretical base of the CEFR as well as the question of which tasks should be part of a particular level and how they should be assessed and evaluated (Hulstijn 2007). Lately, research has started in order to gain more insight into these issues. Meanwhile, the practice of task-based language teaching seems more inclined to expand than to diminish.

Works Cited

Alons, Lies, Nanette Bienfait, Astrid Kraal, Folkert Kuiken, Marianne Molendijk and Willemijn Vernout. 1999. *Zebra. Nederlands als tweede taal voor anderstaligen in het voortgezet onderwijs.* Amsterdam: Meulenhoff Educatief.

Asscheman, Marijke, Carien Bakker, and Nanette Bienfait. 1998. *Schoolslag.* Amsterdam: Meulenhoff Educatief.

Berg, Hetty. 2002. *Taalverhaal.* Utrecht/Zutphen: ThiemeMeulenhoff.

Boers, Titia, Nicky Heijne, Marten Hidma, Vita Olijhoek, and Carola van der Voort. 2003. *Code. Basisleergang Nederlands voor anderstaligen.* Utrecht/Zutphen: ThiemeMeulenhoff.

Council of Europe. 2001. *Common European Framework of Reference for Languages: Learning, teaching, assessment.* Cambridge: Cambridge University Press.

Hulstijn, Jan H. 2007. "The shaky ground beneath the CEFR: Quantitative and qualitative dimensions of language proficiency," *Modern Language Journal*, 91, 662-666.

Nunan, David. 1995. *Atlas. Learning-centred communication.* Boston: Heinle & Heinle Publishers.

Werkgroep Anderstalige Nieuwkomers. 1998. *Klaar? Af! Eerste start voor de onthaalklas secundair onderwijs.* Leuven: Steunpunt NT2.

—. 1999. *Taalkit. Verdere opvang in de onthaalklas secundair onderwijs.* Leuven: Steunpunt NT2.

TASK-BASED LANGUAGE LEARNING IN FLANDERS: OPPORTUNITIES FOR SECOND LANGUAGE ACQUISITION AND BEYOND

KOEN VAN GORP

Introduction

The implementation of task-based education has been a nation-wide project for the past seventeen years in primary and secondary education in Flanders (Belgium). Task-based education was promoted as one way to enhance the quality of Dutch language education in primary and secondary schools, as well as in courses of Dutch as a second language for newcomers under the Educational Priority Policy (EPP) issued by the Flemish government from 1990 onwards (Van den Branden, 2006).

For primary schools, task-based syllabuses both for language as well as content based education, specific task-based language teaching materials for writing and reading, and task-based language tests were designed, enabling primary EPP schools to devise and implement task-based education according to their own specific needs (Colpin & Van Gorp, 2007). In this section I will begin by briefly illustrating the tenets of task-based second language teaching in Flanders using a problem solving task. Secondly, I will illustrate how tasks not only have potential to enhance acquisition of the target language, but can also be used to promote multilingualism in primary schools. I will do so by describing the process the learners take to tackle such tasks.

Tenets of task-based language teaching in Flanders

Since task-based language learning is basically learning by doing, the best way to start is by reading and performing the following short language task:

Who is the thief?

Grandmother Mouse came home through the back door. Her arrival frightened a thief. On entering she heard him running away through the front door; she also heard a metallic tool hitting the ground. But she was too late to see the thief.

Her friend the fox detective Sherlock Holmes arrived promptly. He entered through the back door accompanied by the two major suspects: the bear and the stork. They were the only people working nearby, so one of them had to be the thief.

Sherlock looked about the living room. After inspecting the front door and noticing the wrench he immediately knew who the thief was.

Who is the culprit: the bear or the stork?

Fig. 2-5 Drawing for "Who is the thief?"

The "Who is the thief?" task is part of De Toren van Babbel (a pun on the tower of Babel; "Babbel" being colloquial Dutch for "talking"), a language syllabus for primary school children. 11 to 12-year-olds perform this task as part of a larger theme about crime and detectives. In this theme they explore the world of police detectives, crimes and clues by performing relevant and challenging tasks.

A task is defined as "an activity in which a person engages in order to attain an objective, and which necessitates the use of language" (Van den Branden, 2006: 4). By using language for meaningful purposes, for communicating about oneself and the world, and by creating joint acts (Clark, 1996) the pupils learn language. In order to guarantee the language learning potential of a task Van Gorp and Bogaert (2006) describe the main features of tasks in a language teaching syllabus as follows:

a Tasks involve relevant and natural language as a means of reaching a motivating goal.
b Tasks contain a gap that challenges the learners and provides opportunities for learning language at the learners' own level.
c Tasks inherently elicit interaction and feedback (combining focus on meaning and focus on form).

In the case of Who is the thief? most pupils, except those that have an aversion against solving crimes, mysteries and puzzles, will be motivated to perform the task. Both the content (a crime scene) and the goal (solving the crime) appeal to most young people (as well as adults). Task-based language education underscores the importance of motivation (Van Gorp & Bogaert, 2006) since motivation is of crucial importance for language learning (Dörnyei, 2001) and motivation is often lacking in traditional language activities (Appel & Vermeer, 1996). Although Who is the thief? is a pedagogical task (Long & Crookes, 1993), and not a real target task, relevant and natural (language) skills (reading comprehension, selecting and combining relevant information, discussing clues) that are important for functioning at school, are central to task performance.

The task addresses the pupils' "zone of proximal development" (Vygotsky, 1978) or "zone of next potential" (Williams & Burden, 1997). Reaching the goal is not self-evident, but provides a real challenge. The pupils will have to put their minds to work and process the linguistic and visual information the task provides to find the solution to the problem. Some Agatha Christie or Enid Blyton-fans will probably solve the puzzle at one glance, but most learners will not find the solution immediately and will have to look for the answer in the text. They start re-reading the text; they will stumble across words that they do not know, like "wrench" or "culprit" or information that is not clear at once: "Why did Sherlock enter through the back door? Is the metallic tool the wrench?"

Learning skills and expanding one's linguistic repertoire require the learners to do things with language that they have not done before or have not as yet fully mastered. But the linguistic repertoires of all language learners differ from each other. Task-based language learning does not expect language learners to learn the same things at the same time in the same way, but exploits the heterogeneity of the language learners' linguistic repertoires and as such provides opportunities for all learners to advance their linguistic skills according to their own needs (Van den Branden, 1997). One pupil will encounter the word "wrench" for the first time, another one will consolidate his knowledge of the concept "culprit", a third one will practice his speaking skills explaining why the fact that Sherlock entered through the back door is important in a crime investigation. And a fourth one will learn how clues in the text focus the attention of the reader to crucial information, e.g. "After inspecting the front door and noticing the wrench he immediately knew who the thief was." So the language learning potential of the task is eventually reached in the social interaction it elicits (Coughlan & Duff, 1994).

Not finding the solution to the problem, a language learner will naturally turn to his neighbour and ask: "Do you have any idea? Could it be the stork? Why?" Shoulders are shrugged, or someone answers "No, the stork can't hold the wrench" or "Of course it's the stork." In task-based education meaningful interaction is enhanced in as many ways as possible for many purposes (Van Gorp & Bogaert, 2006): enhancing motivation and persistence to tackle the task, creating a sounding board for ideas and opinions, providing feedback both at the linguistic and cognitive level, engaging in collaborative dialogue, etc. Peer interaction does not only enhance the motivation of the learners, but also augments the language learning potential of the task, especially if pupils work in heterogeneous groups (Lantolf, 2000; Van den Branden, 2000). Well-designed tasks promote peer interaction (Pica, Kanagy & Falodun, 1993). However, when tasks do not result in the meaningful interaction that they are supposed to elicit, the teacher has to intervene and try to set things right (Van den Branden & Van Gorp, 2000).

The role of the teacher as coach and provider of feedback and motivational and supportive interaction (Van Avermaet, Colpin, Van Gorp, Bogaert & Van den Branden, 2006) can not be underestimated. Concerning Who is the thief? all the information (linguistic and non-linguistic) is present in the task to solve the problem. But the relevant information has to be deduced and connected. In order to do so, the pupils have to comprehend what they read, make explicit the implicit information in the text (e.g. the fact that the metallic tool falling is probably the wrench in the picture); they have a notion of what a culprit is, and tap their knowledge of the world of crime investigations (e.g. understand the importance of a crime scene in which everything is left untouched). If the pupils do not succeed or have doubts about the value of specific information, the teacher can mediate the thinking process of the pupils and help them to focus on relevant pieces of information: "Why is the front door still open? Have a closer look at the wrench. Why is it lying there? What happens if you open the door further? Do you think that the bear could have fled out of the door as it is?" (Indeed, the stork is the culprit. The position of the wrench makes it clear that the thief had to be thin to escape through the open door. Since a crime scene is not tampered with, the wrench lies at the exact place the thief had dropped it when grandmother Mouse entered through the back door.)

Having read and discussed the information in the text and the picture, and having combined this information with their own knowledge of the world, the pupils have performed a task that necessitates the use of a lot of natural and relevant academic language. If such a task is performed and the above mentioned task features are carried out, the language class becomes a powerful environment for language learning. This powerful language learning environment can be depicted in the form of three circles as seen in the diagram in Appendix A. These three circles can be read from the perspective of the different participants in the classroom, capturing the tenets and strengths of a task-based language learning approach. How these circles should be read from the language learner's perspective and from the teacher's perspective can be seen in Appendix B.

These two perspectives underscore the fact that language learning is a joint activity that takes place in a social setting (Clark, 1996; Lantolf, 2000). In Flanders task-based education is predominantly used to provide opportunities for second language acquisition irrespective of the multilingual nature of the social setting or classroom. As a result the multilingual repertoires that second language learners bring to the classroom are often disregarded. But tasks do not only provide the means of developing a specific linguistic repertoire in a particular target language, like the Dutch academic language of pupils. They also provide great opportunities to promote multilingualism or, at the least, create a positive environment in which pupils and teachers learn to deal with multilingualism as a resource or richness rather than a problem (Ruiz, 1984). How this potential can be reached I will illustrate in the next paragraph.

The role of tasks in promoting multilingualism: Radio Tika

In Flanders Dutch is the (sole) medium of instruction in official education. Bilingual or multilingual education is, except for a small bicultural project in six schools in Brussels (Leman, 1991), almost non-existent. For historical and ideological reasons (Jaspers, 2005) allowing other languages as a medium of instruction is a very sensitive political issue in Flanders. Recently, the Flemish Minister of Education expressed his concern that multilingual education might lead to "zero-lingualism". The idea that multilingualism has a negative effect on the acquisition of Dutch is widespread amongst teachers (see also Roslon, 2006). In primary school classrooms teachers rely mostly on monolingual instruction strategies (Ramaut, 2000). Most teachers in schools that are densely populated with L2-learners are reluctant to allow the home language of the children in the classroom and even on the playground (Van Gorp & Van den Branden, 2003), although some teachers realise that allowing space for the home languages of the children might have a positive effect on the well-being and involvement of the children (Berben, Van den Branden, Van Gorp, 2007). Task-based education could be an ideal approach to cautiously promote multilingualism in a classroom with only one medium of instruction. In order to do so, at least some of the tasks in a task-based syllabus need to actively employ the multilingual resources the pupils bring to the classroom. I will illustrate this point by discussing the performance of the task, Radio Tika, in a classroom combining the fifth and sixth grade (10-12-year-olds) of a multilingual primary EPP school in a rather poor district of Antwerp (the largest city in Flanders) (see also Berben, Van den Branden, Van Gorp, 2007).

The task

The task Radio Tika (see Appendix C) invites the pupils to create a radio news bulletin for the radio station "Tika" from the fictitious multilingual country "Tikaland". The pupils work in small groups and practice both their cooperative and language skills producing a radio news bulletin of their own and listening to other groups' news bulletins. Each group also provides the audience of their news bulletin with a listening task; they formulate three questions in Dutch about the news item they present. The audience has to listen attentively and try to answer these questions.

Radio Tika is a task that meets the criteria of task-based education mentioned above (see Appendix A and Appendix B). Constructing a news bulletin involves a lot of relevant (academic) language about the world of radio broadcasts (domestic news, foreign news, sports, a weather forecast) that are relatively abstract and unknown to the children. Creating a news bulletin is a motivating activity; one that challenges the pupils but also allows them to construct messages at their own level of proficiency. The peer interaction and interaction with the teacher that the task elicits, and especially the limited time allotted to the news bulletin (e.g. three minutes), will "push" the output of the children to a higher level of proficiency (see below).

The syllabus developers had one additional goal in mind when developing this task, i.e. promoting multilingualism. The task instructions invite the teacher to mention explicitly that the pupils should be asked to produce a news bulletin in which different topics are covered in different languages. In order to do so, the teacher is invited to compose multilingual groups. At the end of the activity, after all the news bulletins have been presented, the teacher is invited to discuss the use of the different languages with his/her pupils. As such, the issue of multilingualism becomes a central topic in a classroom where all pupils are multilingual while the official medium of instruction is only Dutch.

The role of the pupils and the teacher: co-operation and support

Let us now look at how the performance of this task turns out in real classroom conditions, i.e. at how a group of 10- to 12-year-old children combine forces and resources to construct the domestic news of their radio broadcast in English.

Of the group of four children, Jamila, Sihame and Aicha were born in Belgium and speak Berber at home. Michael, the fourth pupil, is originally from Ghana and has only been in Belgium for a couple of years. All the children speak Dutch and learn French (e.g. from grade 5 onwards) at school. It is important to keep in mind that these children have never formally been taught English. The "little" English they know, they know from television, songs and in the case of Michael because it is one of his home languages.

Group work: In short, the group work goes as follows. The four pupils first decide on which news items they are going to broadcast and which languages they are going to use. Next, they devise the contents and construct the news items in Dutch. The home news about the king of Tikaland tells about the king's birthday, and the fact that he is giving a party. Then they decide who is going to tell the item: Sihame will present the domestic news in English; Jamila will talk about foreign news in Dutch; Michael will bring sports in French, and Aicha will bring the weather forecast in Berber. When the teacher intervenes and urges them to work in pairs because they can work faster that way, they more or less do so. With respect to the home news item Sihame collaborates with Aicha and Michael to get the message right and written down in the target language. When the children practise the news report they find out it only lasts thirty seconds instead of three minutes. The teacher encourages the pupils to expand the news items, for instance by telling something about the food the king likes; a suggestion Sihame will follow. Since the time left to finish their news bulletin is very short everybody is concerned with his or her own news item. The final "assembling" of the news items happens when the children present their news report to the classroom.

Getting the message right: With respect to the translation of the message the pupils help each other. In translating the message all their linguistic knowledge is called into play.

Excerpt 1
<pre>
    Sihame: Hoe zegde "koning" int Engels? The queen?
                 (How do you say "king" in English? The Queen?)
    Michael: The king.
    Aicha: The king ja.
                 (The king yes.)
    (Translated by author)
</pre>

Aicha even uses her knowledge of French, whereas Sihame sighs that she can not speak English – although she finds the right words herself.

Excerpt 2
<pre>
    Sihame: Hoe zeggen ze "hij is jarig" in het Engels?
                 (How do they say "It's his birthday" in English?)
    Aicha: Bon anniversaire!
                 (Happy birthday!)
    Michael: {laughter}
    Sihame: The queen is today…
                 Verjaard. Ja die is, kan geen Engels!
                 (birthday. Yes she is, I don't know English!)
    Sihame: The queen is vandaag happy birthday.
                 (The queen is today happy birthday.)
    Aicha: Today is the birthday of the king.
    Michael: Ja.
                 (Yes.)
    (Translated by author)
</pre>

Michael and Aicha support Sihame's meaning construction in English by acknowledging her input and even expanding on it or correcting it when needed. It becomes clear that Michael is the more proficient English user when he suggests changes to Sihame's English in order to enhance accuracy in the intended message. Corrections are on a morphological level ("years"), a syntactical level ("is" instead of "become") and lexical level ("fifty years old"). Michael's focus on form pays off in Sihame's presentation.

Excerpt 3

Sihame:	He is fifty year. {*laughter*}
Michael:	Ja das waar. Das toch fifty years.
	(*Yes that's true. It is fifty years.*)
Sihame:	Kijk, luister hé.
	(*Look, listen.*)
	The queen is today euhm, today is the birthday of the queen.
Michael:	King
Aicha:	King
Sihame:	He's become fifty years.
Aicha:	Ja. Juist.
	(*Yes. Correct.*)
Michael:	He is fifty years old.
Teacher:	En?
	(*And?*)
Aicha:	Ja. He is fifty fifty fifty years old.
	(*Yes.* He is fifty fifty fifty years old.)

(Translated by author)

As Excerpt 3 already shows, Shihame wrestles with the translation of "koning" (king in Dutch). She believes it to be "queen" (see excerpt 1) and has much difficulty in switching and sticking to the accurate word "king". Michael and especially Aicha, emphasize to Sihame that she has to say "king" instead of "queen". Also the teacher plays her part in explaining the accurate word to Sihame.

Excerpt 4

Sihame:	Juffra juffra today is the birthday of the queen. He's 50 years…
	(*Miss miss today is the birthday of the queen. He's 50 years…*)
Aicha:	The king!
Sihame:	Today is the birthday of the queen.
Aicha:	The king!
Sihame:	He's 50 years old. He's gonna ha… he's gonna hold a party, he is … he is gonna invite all the people to his party.
Teacher:	Perfect.
	(*Perfect.*)
Aicha:	Juffra maar da is geen queen, das king!
	(*Miss but it's not queen, it's king!*)
Sihame:	Ewel!
	(*So!*)
Teacher:	En wa, king, van wie?
	(*And what, king, whose?*)

Sihame:	Das toch ne man. King?
	(*It's a man.* King?)
Aicha:	Jama gij zegt queen.
	(*But, you are saying* queen.)
Teacher:	Ja want een queen das een vrouw hé?
	(*Yes, because a* queen, *is a woman, isn't she?*)
Sihame:	Ewel, today is the birthday of the king.
	(*So,* today is the birthday of the king.)
Aicha:	Ja ma gij zegt altijd queen!
	(*Yes, but you are always saying* queen!)

(Translated by author)

Sihame keeps practising what she has to say, often mistaking "queen" for "king", and being most of the time corrected by Aicha, and occasionally by the teacher.

The teacher regularly checks the progress of the pupils and encourages them a lot with phrases like "well done" and "perfect". Occasionally, the pupils ask the teacher to help them with their translation. But the teacher does not really offer help in translating the Dutch sentences in English – although she helps Michael in translating his French message, probably due to the fact that French is a school subject and Michael a relative "newcomer". Instead, the teacher encourages the pupils to help each other: "Help each other, Aicha, perhaps you have an idea. Michael help each other, help them along." Michael has a look at Sihame's written English which enables Shihame to produce a news item in almost fluent English without much hesitation.

After the domestic news item turns out to be too short, Sihame elaborates her news item on her own, following the teacher's suggestion concerning content. Sihame's final presentation goes as follows:

Excerpt 5

Sihame:	Ik ga in het Engels beginnen. Today is the birthday of the ... king. He's 50 years old. He's gonna hold a party, he's gonna invite all the people of his country. The king is gonna serve all kinds food. But the favourite food of the king is chips.
	(*I am going to start in English.* Today is the birthday of the ... king. He's 50 years old. He's gonna hold a party, he's gonna invite all the people of his country. The king is gonna serve all kinds food. But the favourite food of the king is chips.)

(Translated by author)

The fact that Aicha and Michael were not involved as much with the last part of the message as with the first part is shown in the one lexical error "kindes" Sihame makes. On the whole, Sihame's contribution in translating the message is quite impressive, e.g. the decision to use "gonna hold a party" instead of "gonna have a party" (see excerpt 4).

With the help of her fellow pupils, Sihame has constructed a rather complex, and almost accurate message in a foreign language, English, that she has not been formally taught yet. The pupils discussed, translated, corrected and negotiated language. Supporting each other, they were able to combine and balance a focus on meaning with a focus on form in constructing their message.

The teacher also played an important but essentially supportive role. She intervened when necessary, she encouraged pupils but never really told them what they had to say. She also differentiated in her support (e.g. helping Michael with his French translation, and not helping Sihame with the English one). In general, Radio Tika is, like the previous example of Who is the thief?, a clear example of the way tasks create cooperative language learning opportunities, not only for the second language, but for all the languages the pupils bring to the task.

Conclusion

As exemplified in the first part of this article, task-based language learning and teaching is a way to provide high-quality language education which is appealing to the students. In Flanders, task-based language syllabuses are used by hundreds of EPP schools to teach all pupils —but especially minority children and children at risk— the language of the school (academic Dutch). Tasks like Who is the thief? show how opportunities for second language learning are commonly created in Flemish classrooms. Still, the use of such tasks seems to underline the monolingual character of the classroom, and threatens to ignore the multilingual repertoires the pupils bring to that same classroom. It is argued here that a task-based language approach has more to offer than only teaching the language that is the medium of instruction.

The potential to use tasks for appealing to the pupils' multilingual resources is still largely untapped. Tasks, like Radio Tika, exploiting the multilingual resources of the children show that if pupils are offered the chance to show their expert skills in their home or other languages, they take that chance. In a cooperative classroom environment the children help each other understand and produce messages in all kinds of languages. Allowing multilingualism in the classroom does not equal opening

Pandora's box, as many Flemish teachers think. They are afraid to lose control because they do not understand what children are saying, and are afraid that allowing languages other than Dutch in the classroom or even the school is detrimental to the learning of Dutch.

Bringing multilingualism out into the open in a classroom where other languages apart from Dutch (except French as a foreign language) have no particular place may be an efficient way to underscore the value of the children's home languages, to foster respect for multilingualism and boost the children's pride in being able to speak more than Dutch. Experimenting with tasks that allow for the use of different languages, exploiting the multilingual repertoires of children in a positive and safe environment may give L2-learners a sense of pride and belonging, especially in contexts like Flanders where bilingual education is almost non-existent and monolingualism is felt to be the educational norm. It may enable pupils to find and develop their own voice to the fullest; a voice which is multilingual in nature. Researching and exploring how tasks can help promote second language acquisition and allow for multilingualism at the same time—and even enhance one another in the same classroom—may be a real challenge for teachers. But it will be a challenge which might have a very positive influence on the equal opportunities of many L2-learners and which may be faced with well-designed tasks.

Works Cited

Appel, René and Anne Vermeer. 1996. "Van oude methodes en verschillen die nog niet voorbij zijn: over NT1 en NT2 in het basisonderwijs," In *Het verschil voorbij. Onderwijs Nederlands als eerste en tweede taal in Nederland en Vlaanderen*, ed. Sjaak Kroon and Ton Vallen, 75-92, Voorzetten 51. Gravenhage: SDU.

Berben, Martien, Kris Van den Branden, and Koen Van Gorp. 2007. "We'll see what happens: Tasks on paper and tasks in a multilingual classroom," In *Tasks in action. Classroom-based research on task-based language education*, ed. Kris Van den Branden, Koen Van Gorp and Machteld Verhelst, 32-67, Cambridge: Cambridge Scholars Publishing.

Colpin, Marleen and Koen Van Gorp. 2007. "Task-based writing in primary education. The development and evaluation of writing skills through writing tasks, learner and teacher support." In *Tasks in action. Classroom-based research on task-based language education*, ed. Kris Van den Branden, Koen Van Gorp and Machteld Verhelst, 194-234, Cambridge: Cambridge Scholars Publishing.

Clark, Herbert H. 1996. *Using Language*. Cambridge: Cambridge University Press.
Coughlan, Peter and Patricia Duff. 1994. "Same task, different activities: Analysis of a second language acquisition task from an activity theory perspective." In *Vygotskian Approaches to Second Language Research*, ed. James P. Lantolf and Gabriela Appel, 173-194. Norwood, NJ: Ablex Press.
Dörnyei, Zoltán. 2001. *Teaching and Researching Motivation*. Essex: Pearson Education Ltd.
Gysen, Sara, Kathleen Rossenbacker and Machteld Verhelst. 1999. *Kleuterobservatie-instrument Taalvaardigheid (KOBI-TV)*. Leuven: Steunpunt NT2.
Jaspaert, Koen, ed. 1996. *De Toren Van Babbel. Nederlands voor de lagere school. Tweede leerjaar. Deel 0. Deurne: Plantyn.*
Jaspers, Jürgen. 2005. *Tegenwerken, belachelijk doen. Talige sabotage van Marokkaanse jongens op een Antwerpse middelbare school. Een sociolinguïstische etnografie*. Brussel: VUB Press.
Lantolf, James. 2000. *Sociocultural Theory and Second Language Learning*. Oxford: Oxford University Press.
Leman, Johan. 1991. *Between Bi- and Intercultural Education: Projects in Dutch-Language Kindergartens and Primary Schools in Brussels*. In *Ethnic Minority Languages and Education*, ed. Koen Jaspaert and Sjaak Kroon, 123-134. Amsterdam: Swets & Zeitlinger.
Long, Michael and Graham Crookes. 1993. "Units of analysis in syllabus design: The case for task." In *Task and Language Learning: Integrating Theory and Practice*, ed. Graham Crookes and Susan Gass, 9-54. Clevedon: Multilingual Matters.
Pica, Teresa, Ruth Kanagy, and John Falodun. 1993. "Choosing and using communication tasks for second language instruction." In *Tasks and language learning. Integrating theory and practice*, ed. Graham Crookes and Susan Gass. 9-34. Clevedon: Multilingual Matters.
Ramaut, Griet. 2000. "Language Norms in a Multilingual Flemish Nursery School." In *Man schreibt, wie man spricht*. Ergebnisse einer international vergleichenden Fallstudie über Unterricht in vielsprachigen Klassen, Interkulturelle Bildungsforschung. Bd. 7, ed. Ingrid Gogolin and Sjaak Kroon, 41-61. Münster: Waxmann Verlag.
Roslon, Anna. 2006. *Meertaligheid, wel of geen onderwerp? Onderzoek naar communicatieve behoeften van de ouders van meertalige kinderen. Wetenschapswinkel Taal, Cultuur en Communicatie*, Rijksuniversiteit Groningen: Hogeschool van Amsterdam.

Ruiz, Richard. 1984. "Orientations in Language Planning." *NABE Journal*, 8(2), 15-34.
Van Avermaert, Piet, Marleen Colpin, Koen Van Gorp, Nora Bogaert, and Kris Van den Branden. 2006. "The role of the teacher in task-based language teaching." In *Task-based Language Education: from Theory to Practice*, ed. Kris Van den Branden. 175-196, Cambridge: Cambridge University Press.
Van den Branden, Kris. 1997. "Effects of negotiation on language learners' output" *Language Learning,* 47, 589-636.
—. 2000. "Does negotiation of meaning promote reading comprehension? A study of multilingual primary school classes," *Reading Research Quarterly*, 35, 426-443.
—. 2006. *Task-based language education: from theory to practice.* Cambridge: Cambridge University Press.
Van den Branden, Kris and Koen Van Gorp. 2000. "How to evaluate CLIM in terms of intercultural education?" *Intercultural education* 11 S42-S51, Supplement 2000.
Van Gorp, Koen and Kris Van den Branden. 2003. "Hoe vernieuwend denken studenten in de lerarenopleiding over taalonderwijs? Een onderzoek naar de percepties van eerstejaars— en derdejaarsstudenten kleuteronderwijs en lager onderwijs op het vlak van taalvaardigheidsonderwijs", in *Naar meer gelijke kansen in en door onderwijs*. Studiedag georganiseerd door het Vlaams Forum voor Onderwijsonderzoek (VFO), Gent, 24 oktober 2003, http://www.cteno.be/downloads/publicaties/van_gorp_van_den_branden_2003_studenten_in_lerarenopleiding.pdf.
Van Gorp, Koen. 2004. "Taakgericht onderwijs: uitdagend taalvaardigheidsonderwijs voor zowel NT1 en NT2-leerlingen." In *Jong geleerd is oud gedaan. Talen leren in het basisonderwijs*, ed. Rian Aarts, Peter Broeder and Anne Maljers, 63-78, Den Haag: Europees Platform voor het Nederlandse Onderwijs.
Van Gorp, Koen and Nora Bogaert. 2006. "Developing language tasks for primary and secondary education," In *Task-Based Language Education. From theory to practice*, ed. Kris Van den Branden, 76-105, Cambridge: Cambridge University Press.
Verhelst, Machteld. 2006. "A box full of feelings: Promoting infants' second language acquisition all day long." In *Task-based language education: from theory to practice*, ed. Kris Van den Branden, 197-216, Cambridge Applied Linguistics Series, Cambridge: Cambridge University Press.

Vygotsky, Lev. 1978. *Mind in Society. The Development of Higher Psychological Processes.* Cambridge: Harvard University Press.

Williams, Marion and Robert Burden. 1997. *Psychology for the language teacher. A social constructivist approach.* Cambridge: Cambridge University Press.

RECOMMENDED READING:
TASK-BASED LANGUAGE LEARNING

Bygate, Martin, Peter Skehan, and Merrill Swain, eds., 2001. *Researching Pedagogic Tasks: Second Language Learning, Teaching and Testing.* London: Longman.

Ellis, Rod. 2003. *Task-based Language Learning and Teaching.* Oxford: Oxford University Press.

Leaver, Betty Lou and Jane R. Willis, eds., 2004. *Task-Based Instruction In Foreign Language Education: Practices and Programs,* Washington, D.C.:Georgetown University Press.

Littlewood, William. 2002. "Cooperative and collaborative learning tasks as pathways towards autonomous interdependence." In *Learner Autonomy 7: Challenges to Research and Practice,* ed. Phil Benson and Sarah Toogood, 29-39, Dublin: Authentik.

Nunan, David. 2005. *Task-Based Language Teaching.* Cambridge: Cambridge University Press.

Van den Branden, Kris, ed. 2006. *Task-Based Language Education: From Theory to Practice.* Cambridge Applied Linguistics series. Cambridge: Cambridge University Press.

Willis, Dave and Jane Willis. 2001. "Task-based language learning. In *The Cambridge Guide to Teaching English to Speakers of Other Languages,* ed. Ronald Carter and David Nunan, 173-179, Cambridge: Cambridge University Press.

Willis, Jane. 1996. *A Framework for Task-Based Learning.* Harlow: Longman.

Chapter Three

Content and Language Integrated Learning: Introduction

Melinda Dooly

As it has already been pointed out, there are many variants of linguistic immersion as a teaching and learning strategy. Because of its growing role in foreign language teaching, this section has four contributors. They have been grouped together because they fit the European term for "content language and integrated learning", with an emphasis on the teaching of other subjects through the medium of a foreign language. In the cases described here, the target language is a foreign language within the home society; it is not used by minority speakers of large immigrant populations as might be the case for other immersion programmes and it is used specifically as the language of academic instruction in a clearly defined subject area (e.g. History, Geography, Civics, Art).

While the CLIL context for language instruction has not become a part of "mainstream" curriculum practices, there is a growing interest in the movement in several countries across Europe and many researchers are interested in finding ways to make CLIL more accessible to a wider range of public schools. At the foundation of this movement lies the perspective that language is used for the purpose of communicating and that it must be purposeful communication. Therefore, in the school, the foreign language should be used as part of the holistic learning process, wherein the communication holds purpose and meaning for the student. It has also been argued that CLIL can be influential in increasing the language learner's motivation and confidence as well as produce more positive attitudes towards the language and the language learning process (Ullmann, 1999; Coyle 2002).

Due to its very nature of integration into other subjects, CLIL can be influential in the empowerment of the student since language learning and multilingualism will no longer be only for advanced linguists (Coyle, Op. Cit.). It might be added that it also moves language learning away from academic "elitism", especially if the content area is an obligatory, core subject for all students. *Integration* of the learning process of the target language and the subject learning is a key component to CLIL. Both the academic content of the subject being studied and the language used for acquiring that content are relevant to the student's overall learning, no matter which subject. Moreover, because the opportunities of learning the language are expanded to contexts beyond the walls of the language classroom, all student are better prepared for language use in diverse social situations or in other academic domains.

Of course, as with any learning paradigm, complex problems emerge from the very tenets of the paradigm itself. While it may seem intuitively obvious that language is embedded in any process of learning –of any subject across the curriculum— the learning of a subject must be described as learning the particular discourse of that subject. This implies that the students must become socialised in the discourse community inherent to each subject and that teachers must be aware of both the discourse acquisition processes of learners as well as the subject matter discourse. This inevitably foregrounds the question of which discourse community should be emulated —native or non-native speakers? In other words, in exploring how people are socialised into different contextualised discourse communities, it is imperative that the discourses themselves are studied as they emerge (in workplaces, in academic settings, between native or non-native speakers and so on).

Arguably, one way of dealing with this complexity is through the integration of theories of language acquisition and content acquisition (see Valdes, 1992). By highlighting this need for integration of learning processes of different discourse communities, the role of socio-constructivist learning can be brought into play. Van Lier (1996) highlighted the role of social interaction in the classroom wherein learning is an interdependent, jointly negotiated activity. This emphasizes the negotiated meaning stemming from the learning process. It also emphasizes the learning process as much as the learning outcomes and implies that both the teacher and learners involved in the process will be, in part at least, responsible for the emerging discourse. Through negotiation, the stakeholders (in this case, the teacher and the learner) are in better positions to decide jointly what discourse community to belong to, how it can be accessed most efficiently as well as deciding exactly why that discourse is needed and how the discourse will be deployed.

Throughout the years of discussion of language learning methodologies, one of the clearest dichotomies which emerged is the debate between what could be called "traditional" language teaching, with a focus on products and knowledge; and the "communicative approach" with the focus on functions and process. However, with the communicative approach, too often the focus on process (doing "things" to promote language use) is often at the cost of content – indeed it neglects the fact that communication is all about content, or what might be called "shared knowledge" (Soetaert & Bonamie, 1999).

For CLIL to be effective, it must necessarily be accompanied by serious reflection on what conception the stakeholders have about what "language" means and what conception they have about "content". A conception of language which is fundamentally structural will have different results in a CLIL context compared to a conception of language as multiple competences in a state of constant flux. Likewise, the understanding of knowledge of the disciplines themselves will influence the way in which language and content can be integrated. Canonical, hierarchical understanding of knowledge in disciplines has been problematized by the advent of the "post-modern, digital" era (discussions about the Western literary canon; blurring of borders between literature and media texts and between "real" and "virtual") but there are many movements to put "traditional" content back on the scholastic agenda (Wolff, 1999).

Needless to say, the conceptualization of what counts as real content and what does not and whether content knowledge is hierarchical or not will deeply influence the way in which CLIL will be implemented. Similarly social, political, economic, cultural and technological trends will have an impact on the way in which CLIL will be implemented, although these trends may have less impact than the actual conceptualization of the learning process held by the stakeholders involved.

There are other, perhaps more technical issues, which often come up when discussing CLIL. Because CLIL is not explicitly focused on language learning, students may feel that they are not improving in the target language, or they may feel confused or uncertain about the overall linguistic objectives. Learners may be used to clearly defined "mini-objectives" or learning cues from previous language lessons and feel disoriented by this type of immersion. The teacher may need to include some form of explicit language features —as warm-up or follow-up exercises.

As the classes are not overtly "marked" as language lessons, students may prefer to use their native language –using their L1 in class may seem much easier and quicker for them. Herein lies the negotiation between the stakeholders about the discourse community rules which was referred to earlier. If the students do not see the benefits of using the target language, they are more likely to use their mother tongue. Also, finding the adequate materials can be a problem; as can be the use of the target language to share information about the content being studied. This can be broached several ways –by combining texts in the students' mother tongue with tasks and student output in the target language; by designing tasks that allow the students to evaluate, draw conclusions or give opinions about the material at their language level and then slowly raising the level of challenge or other types of adaptation to the context. These are just some of the challenges faced by CLIL practitioners.

Notwithstanding these challenges, proponents of CLIL outline the empowerment of learners as one of the underlying principles of the approach. Through negotiation of the learning process, focused on the students' inclusion in different (otherwise frequently inaccessible) discourse communities, learners will become engaged with and challenged by their own learning process of both the language and the content. This can be seen in the descriptions given here. In the first article, David Marsh provides the reader with an overview of how CLIL is conceptualised in Finland and how it has been implemented on a nation-wide basis at many different education levels. Next, Mercè Barrull i Garcia describes an optional course for Middle School that uses English as the target language for a Social Studies project about Roman history in Catalonia (Spain), followed by an article by Cristina Escobar Urmeneta describing the development of CLIL materials for teachers (also in Catalonia). In the last article, Do Coyle provides a general overview of the recent expansion of CLIL in England. As one of the European countries that it is taking a firm step towards official endorsement of CLIL as a part of the national curriculum, Coyle's article provides the reader with relevant information about research into CLIL, as seen from the basis of England's national policy.

Works Cited

Coyle, Do. 2002. "Toward a reconceptualisation of the MFL curriculum." In *Teaching Modern Languages in Secondary Schools: A Reader*, ed. Ann Swarbrick, 56-172. London & New York: Routledge.

Soetaert, Roland and Bart Bonamie. 1999. "Reconstructing the Teaching of Language: A View Informed by the Problems of Traditional Literacy in a Digital Age," *Journal of Information Technology for Teacher Education*, 8(2), 123-149.

Ullmann, Michael. 1999. "History and Geography through French: CLIL Curriculum in a UK Secondary School." In *Learning Through a Foreign Language*, ed. John Masih, 96-105. London: CILT (Centre for Information on Language Teaching and Research).

Valdes, Guadalupe. 1992. "Bilingual minorities and language issues in writing." *Written Communication*, 9, 85-136.

Van Lier, Leo. 1996. *Interaction in the Language Curriculum: Awareness, Autonomy & Authenticity.* NY: Longman Group Ltd.

Wolff, Janet. 1999. "Cultural studies and the sociology of culture." In *In[ ]visible culture. An electronic journal for visual studies*, 1, Winter 1998.
(http://www.rochester.edu/in_visible_culture/issue1/wolff/wolff.html)

CONDITIONS FOR CLIL IN FINLAND: CONSTRUCTIVIST PRINCIPLES, TEACHER AUTONOMY, AND A SUPPORTIVE NATIONAL CURRICULUM

DAVID MARSH

Introduction to Finland

Finland is close to the size of Germany, but sparsely populated (5.2 million). Language learning has been an important factor in education over the last 50 years for two reasons. First, to support language policy whereby Finnish and Swedish act as official languages, with Sami (Lapland), Sign Language and Romany considered minority/regional languages. Second, to ensure that the population has sufficient language skills for an internationalized working life.

About 75% of the population completes secondary education, and 33% have higher education or other tertiary qualifications. Some 67% of all households have internet access, of which about 57% is broadband. Children (7-14 years) spend relatively fewer hours in schools than in most OECD[1] countries, and public spending on education is the second-highest in Europe as a proportion of Gross Domestic Product (2005 National Data).

In 2000 and 2003, Finland was placed in overall first position in PISA (Programme for International Student Assessment/OECD) which gave special attention to skills in reading literacy, mathematics, and problem-solving. This test is a three yearly appraisal of about 250 000 15 year olds (2003) in some 41 countries, of which 30 are in the OECD. The average Finnish scores were some 50 points higher than the OECD average of 500.

---

[1] The OECD (Organization for Economic Cooperation and Development) is an international body composed of 24 member nations. Its objective is to coordinate economic and development policies of the member nations.

This has indirect bearing on language learning because of methodologies used in schools across the curriculum.

Since the 1950s Finland has swiftly transformed from being a largely agricultural economy into one focused on high technology. A key milestone was the reform of comprehensive education in the 1960-1970s. One aspect of this was to enable the whole school population to have access to foreign language learning. In the 1970s this provision was extended to vocational education, which by European standards, was a landmark decision. Since then Finland has devoted considerable attention to the teaching and learning of foreign languages and often been quick to introduce innovations in schools. Focus on widespread foreign language learning for all in the 1970s, was followed by attention being given to practical means by which to internationalize education from the 1980s onwards.

Language Learning as a Finnish Educational Priority

The original usage of the term "information society" in 1975 (OECD) had direct bearing on why the teaching and learning of foreign languages was considered then, as now, to be of the utmost importance in Finland. The major language of the country, Finnish (96% of population), is not an Indo-European language, and the learning of a global lingua franca was considered pragmatic and essential.

In the 1970-1980s Finland had already developed forms of communicative language learning to a high extent. However, alternative ways of further improving language learning, especially when dealing with the broad school population, were also examined. It was evident that even if language teaching was of high quality, time was rarely sufficient within the curriculum to achieve optimal goals. The search for radically new means for achieving these goals took place in the early 1990s.

Within language education, academics and teachers analysed the outcomes of research resulting from experience of immersion and languages across the curriculum in Canada and Southeast Asia. This was done alongside examination of methodological trends such as task-based and cooperative learning. The positive outcomes reported prompted interest in developing an adapted approach which could be applicable in different educational contexts and countries. This became a European initiative, led principally through Finnish-Dutch cooperation, and led to the development of Content and Language Integrated Learning (CLIL). This educational approach was dual-focused: an additional language is used for the learning and teaching of both content and language.

Finland already had a very small number of schools offering education partially, or fully, in a foreign language (English, French, German, & Russian). The reputation of these schools, and a wish to further promote egalitarianism of educational opportunity, involved examining how any advantages might be transferred across to mainstream education.

The 1991-1996 National Development Plan for Education in Finland states that "language teaching, cross-cultural understanding, foreign language content instruction, and other forms of instruction which are important from the point of view of increased international contacts and internationalization of the working life, are systematically supported and developed at all levels of the Finnish educational system". In addition, the report stated that by the year 2000, all upper secondary level students should be able to pursue studies or work experience abroad. This had direct consequences for further improving English language teaching, and CLIL was one means to achieve this.

The emergence of CLIL in Finland can be summarized according to:
- Philosophy: The wish to adapt and introduce approaches found in certain countries, areas (often border regions), and schools, into mainstream education to boost egalitarianism and prepare the future workforce for predicted post-millennial communication expectations and demands.
- Educational Perspective: The view that language learning needs to suit the diverse language learning styles of young people; and that this could be achieved by embedding language learning further into the curriculum. In professional circles, CLIL was viewed as a 1990s development and extension of the functional-notional approach introduced into foreign language learning in the mid 1970s.
- Impetus for Action: Action resulting from a combination of pressure which has been top-down (parliamentary approval, ministry directives and change of education laws) and grassroots (parental and student demand).

CLIL is found in primary, secondary, and vocational education through English, Finnish, French German, Russian, Sami and Swedish. In higher education, Finland, alongside the Netherlands, has been identified as offering the highest number of programmes taught in English as a second/foreign language in Europe (2002, ACA).

Language and Communication, the Individual Learner, and the National Curriculum

The Finnish National Core Curriculum for Basic Education (2004) is a key resource in enabling innovation in how languages are learned and taught. It supports three fundamentals of good practice concerning teacher autonomy, constructivist educational principles, and is based on transversal principles. It contains a number of cross-curricular themes which are generally integrated into the learning of subjects, including languages.

These themes concern:
- Personal growth
- Cultural Identity and Internationalism
- Media skills and communication
- Participatory citizenship and entrepreneurship
- Responsibility for the environment, well-being, and a sustainable future
- Technology and the individual

The curriculum acts as a basic framework, the contents of which are to be observed by schools which build "local curricula". Each local curriculum, usually school-based, needs to develop these "core contents", and embed them into the learning of subjects. Thus, Finland has a curriculum which allows a high degree of school and teacher autonomy. This is one very important factor in understanding how innovations such as CLIL can be implemented in this environment. The curriculum describes the types of methods which should be used to achieve these cross-curricular goals. These are particularly significant in relation to constructivist learning pedagogies which often focus on "learning by doing" and giving learners the opportunities to "co-construct knowledge". They are of considerable significance in local implementation of CLIL because they involve "important methodological principles established by research on foreign language learning, such as the need for learners to be exposed to a situation calling for genuine communication" (Eurydice 2006:9).

CLIL and Language Awareness

The constructivist learning approach which is so prominent in the Finnish national curriculum lays a strong foundation by which to integrate learning across subjects. CLIL is one example where language learning is combined with some form of non-language content in order to achieve overall educational objectives. What is crucial is how the curriculum places the child, and children, at the centre of the learning process.

The language learning focus often found in Finnish CLIL invariably rests on developing aspects of language awareness. Van Lier (1995: xi) describes this as "an understanding of the human faculty of language and its role in thinking, learning and social life. It includes an awareness of power and control through language, and of the intricate relationships between language and culture". Finnish CLIL practice invariably attempts to draw on and develop higher learning capacities which are a major focus in language awareness. This is one feature which differentiates CLIL from types of language learning approaches which are also content-oriented.

As in other countries, language teachers face major challenges in developing language learning and language awareness for reasons often linked to context, methodologies and time. To begin with, the context of the language learning classroom is usually artificial because language learning is perceived by pupils as the main aim. This means that these learners then view it, and the activities within it, as lacking relevance and authenticity. Finnish CLIL teachers often view CLIL as complementing language learning classes, and giving more "time" for language development in the curriculum. Therefore, CLIL is often an extra platform for developing language learning, and not an alternative to what happens in the language learning classrooms. As found across Europe, in Finland it "enables languages to be taught on a relatively intensive basis without claiming an excessive share of the school timetable" (Eurydice, 2006:9).

Working in rich communicative environments, typical of good CLIL practice, means that the learners engage in performative action which both engages the individual, and helps develop holistic language awareness. This is difficult to achieve in a language lesson where the main focus is on "doing things with words", rather than "using words to achieve actions". In Finnish CLIL, the target language goes beyond being a "vehicular language" towards being a "mediation language" – one in which focus is not on form and function, but rather on content transmitted through the language, and language transmitted through the content.

Researchers in Language Awareness have described the need for conceptual shift, whereby the individual develops in a performative, or otherwise procedural way, from less aware to more aware about "explicit knowledge about language and conscious perception and sensitivity... in language use" (Garret & James 2000). Drawing on the cognitive, cultural, communicative, and content input of methodologies, CLIL provides a procedural platform by which the student can undergo such a conceptual shift, both experientially and intellectually.

These features of an extra platform for developing language learning is what enables it to become meaningful for the student both in terms of its structure, and how it is used in real-life contexts. Thurlow (2001:214) introduces the notion of "communication awareness" to describe how communication becomes "meaningful, to young people themselves; ...how they articulate their own understanding and experience of communication". CLIL methodologies often serve to enact this experience both in terms of the second language, and the first language to some extent. And this closely suits the objectives found within the national curriculum.

It is no surprise that CLIL emerged in the 1990s, because this was a period of substantial change in both Finnish society and the wider world. The advent of the knowledge revolution in education resulted mainly from increasingly widespread access to the Internet and the new technologies. Finnish CLIL can be seen as a practical application of the "Knowledge Triangle" which integrates education, innovation and research. "Some would argue that one effect of this on young people concerns the purposefulness of education and an increasing reluctance to postpone gratification. Teachers and others argue that some students are no longer willing to learn now for use later, which is a form of deferred purpose, but prefer to learn as you use and use as you learn which suits the immediacy of purpose common to the times" (Marsh, 2002: 66).

Finnish CLIL Practice: An Eclectic Approach

In the mid 1990s, during the early days of Finnish CLIL expansion, the key aims reported involved:

- increasing interest in learning foreign languages
- developing students' language proficiency
- promoting internationalization
- improving the school's image (Nikula & Marsh, 1997: 18 – 23)

Later, in 2000, a European survey was carried out on the major reasons for implementing CLIL. Finnish respondents reported the following main aims, which differed in emphasis according to education levels:

- Capacity-building for internationalization

- Developing intercultural communication skills
- Preparing for future studies / working life (Marsh et al., 2001)

The Finnish CLIL continuum ranges from very short project-based experiences, through to large-scale and long-term implementation. The range is very wide. This may involve whole subjects, of themes within and across subjects. International connection through projects, visits, forms of exchange, are common.

The teachers are mostly content teachers, or class teachers at primary level. Language teachers are by definition, a minority within any school, and thus this is not surprising. Teamwork between language and content teachers is a common, and successful operating formula. Thus the Finnish approach to CLIL can be considered "eclectic". A wide variety of approaches are used, at different educational levels, for differing reasons. A specific approach adopted will depend on the aims identified.

Inclusion of learners with special needs into mainstream classes has been an important national development from the 1990s onwards. Some 20% of Finnish students are considered to have special learning needs at some point in their schooling, and the levels of inclusion into mainstream classes is very high. Schools use different means for selecting pupils into CLIL classes, but there is a high ethos of egalitarianism and equal opportunity within education. Thus, whereas various forms of testing may be done in cases of large-scale learning in the second language, generally such selection processes are not used.

The most common subjects taught in English in comprehensive school (grades 1-9) and upper secondary schools are as follows

Grades 1-5
- Environmental Science
- Music
- Mathematics
- Visual Arts
- Physical Education

Grades 7-9
- Home economics
- Biology
- Geography
- History & Social Studies
- Mathematics

Grades 9-11 (Upper Secondary)
- History & Social Studies
- Geography
- Biology
- Chemistry
- Psychology (Eurydice 2006: Finland National Report)

Conclusion

The Finnish CLIL "generic umbrella" includes many variants. Some of these may be considered as primarily language teaching. Some can be seen as mainly content teaching. The essence of CLIL leads to it having status as an innovative educational approach which transcends traditional approaches to both subject and language teaching. It is the existence of a highly supportive national curriculum alongside a high degree of school autonomy which enables different types of models to be implemented. School-by-school, class-by-class, these emerge, flourish, and decline, according to the situation in a school at any given time.

CLIL serves as one form of educational integration which leads to methodological adaptation and change. In 2007, a national advisory group reported on the future of language education in the country. CLIL features in the recommendations, particularly with respect to learning languages other than English. It also focuses on the positive results which can be obtained from small-scale implementation, and suggests that these be increased in schools across the country (KIEPO 2007).

The issue of how young people learn English language is a very significant one in this environment. The arguments put forward by Graddol (2006) on how the status of English is changing in certain societies means that English has shifted from being a foreign language, to that of a de facto second language in this country. The learning of this language is not just coming from intentional learning contexts such as classrooms, but also through incidental learning from exposure and use of the language in the wider environment. This change happened within a short period of time and is directly linked to use of the new technologies. English is increasingly being viewed as a basic core competence which all school leavers have to a greater or lesser extent. As it becomes a widespread competence, the added value to the individual diminishes.

The future of CLIL in Finland is not easy to outline, but there are already indicators suggesting that it should be more widely spread on a low exposure level. Thus, more young people would learn in this way, and this learning would often be geared up to achieving individual affective outcomes. This, in turn, impacts on how other languages are taught. If youngsters react positively to, for example, CLIL in English, it is possible that they will react adversely to alternative forms of language learning which are not as stimulating. Thus, it is possible that there will be a knock-on effect from English language CLIL implementation which will lead to this approach being more widely used to teach and learn other languages.

Works Cited

Eurydice. 2006. *Content and Language Integrated Learning (CLIL) in Europe.* Brussels: Eurydice.
Garret, Peter and Carl James. 2000. "Language Awareness." In *Encyclopedia of Language Teaching and Learning,* Michael Byram (ed.). London: Routledge.
Graddol, David. 2006. *English Next.* London: British Council.
KIEPO. 2007. *Towards Tomorrow's Language Education. Report on Finnish Language Education Policies project.* Jyväskylä : University of Jyväskylä.
Marsh, David, ed. 2002. *CLIL/EMILE – The European Dimension: Actions, Trends and Foresight Potential.* Brussels, DG EAC, European Commission.
National Core Curriculum for Basic Education. 2004. Helsinki: National Board of Education
Nikula, Tarja and David Marsh. 1997. *Vieraskielinen Opetuksen Tavoitteet ja Toteuttamin.* Helsinki: National Board of Education.
PISA. 2003. *Programme for International Student Assessment.* Paris: OECD.
Thurlow, Crispin. 2001. "Communication Awareness in Mid-Adolescence," *Language Awareness*, 10 (2/3): 213-231.
van Lier, Leo. 1995. *Introducing Language Awareness.* London: Penguin.

ALL ROADS LEAD TO ROME: A CLIL SOCIAL STUDIES EXPERIENCE

MERCÈ BARRULL I GARCIA

Introduction

The Department of Education of Catalonia (Spain) wants to promote knowledge of foreign languages through the teaching and learning of non linguistic content areas in the target foreign (CLIL). One initiative to promote CLIL is through the financing of "experimental frames of action" available to teachers for a period of between 6 months to one year (basically this is within a framework of funded classroom research). Within this context, I applied for and was awarded funding by the Catalan government to design and implement a research project that intended "to explore the incidence that CLIL can have on both the linguistic and non linguistic learning of my pupils and to offer the teaching staff at my school and beyond specific methodological options based on piloting of a CLIL project that is "adapted to the reality of the Catalan classrooms". Apart from my work as an English teacher, I also hold a degree in Geography and History, thus facilitating my opportunities for implementing cross-curricular content teaching.

The language goal of the project was two-fold: to enable my students in Year 2, Middle School to acquire the necessary communicative skills (through explicit in-class tasks focused on communicative strategies in the target language) and to help them develop autonomy and awareness of different possible tools and strategies according to their individual needs.

Part One: Description of the project

A quick but honest look at the real situation in an every day English class in Spain underlines the difficulty of getting pupils to use English as the vehicular language unless they are working on a specific task under the watchful eye of the teacher. This is not to say that the students are not interested or that they do not make an effort, but too often they lack the assuredness of their own language abilities, combined with insufficient communicative strategies. At the same time, students are usually unable to self-assess in order to know what or how to study in their own time in order to complement the few hours of formal foreign language instruction they have in the school.

These difficulties are further exacerbated by the fact that most textbook activities designed for speaking practice are usually grammatically or lexically focused but few are accompanied by explicit strategies to improve oral interaction during pair or group work. Strategies such as opening or closing rituals, turn-taking, interactive repair-work, etc. are needed for carrying out pair work or group work and for the eventual completion of tasks. If the students do not have these strategies in the target language, they will inevitably lapse into their own language once they become involved with negotiating the running of the task at hand.

Based on the situation described above, this project had two different parts:

1) The first step was to encourage spontaneous oral interaction between pupils by helping them to learn and use communicative strategies to "get them through" difficulties encountered during the interaction. In order to do so, I first tried to pinpoint the most important needs that students had during their interaction, when carrying out different classroom activities. After that, I spent some sessions introducing and allowing time and practice of some of the communicative strategies that the students and the teacher had agreed were needed. At the same time, students were introduced to self-assessment questionnaires.

2) During the second part the students carried out the specially designed CLIL activities entitled "All roads lead to Rome." These activities integrated history and social science content topics (Ancient Rome), academic language development (giving presentations), and direct instruction and practice in using learning strategies to acquire both procedural and declarative knowledge (O'Malley and Chamot 1990). In this second phase the students, working in groups, had to complete different tasks in order to learn some facts about ancient Rome. At the end of the activities they were expected to be able to give an academic presentation to their classmates.

Both parts have common objectives:
- Develop the necessary competences needed to interact orally in English by providing them with tools and opportunities to practice in "natural" contexts.

- Increase learners' autonomy by involving them in their own learning process and developing their capacity to evaluate the extent and success of their learning (metacognitives strategies).
- Promote cooperative work with other students through the development and sharing of both factual and process knowledge (social/affective strategies).
- Help the learner, especially the less successful students, to become aware of a wide variety of learning strategies so they can choose the ones that work best for them, based on their individual capacities and competences, learning style or developmental stage.

The project was implemented at IES Vil•la Romana, a public secondary school situated in a town called La Garriga, near Barcelona. The students at this school were predominantly middle class; 12% of whom were non-natives, mostly from South America and Morocco. The learners involved were aged between 12 and 13 years old and had studied English for five years prior to participating in the project. In general the students claimed that they liked studying English (67.8% of the 56 students said that they quite liked it or liked it a lot) but surprisingly they did not like *speaking* English very much (73.2 answered they did not like speaking English at all or not very much). Not surprisingly, trying to find strategies to overcome the students' reticence to speak in English is designed into further development of the project.

Description of the learning strategies and process

First, the 56 students involved completed a questionnaire about their likes and dislikes and what strategies they thought they used to keep the conversation going when they were interacting in English. The four strategies they mentioned were cooperative strategies: asking for repetition (85%), repeating if the others did not understand (85%), asking for clarification (83%) and asking for help (83%). These same questions were repeated at the end of the first part of the project with the aim of comparing the results with the results of two control groups at the end of the learning strategies process (discussed further on).

In the beginning, 20 students of mixed ability were chosen as the reference group. They worked in pairs or groups of four during seven one-hour sessions from February to March. The students used a voice recorder during the oral activities to be able to listen to themselves and analyze the strategies and language used.

The process of teaching the learning strategies used followed four of the six steps described by Grenfell & Harris (1999) and Harris et al. (2001) and was very similar to the process explained by O'Malley & Chamot (1990).

Step 1: Consciousness/ Awareness raising: the purpose was to encourage learners to reflect on their learning process and to develop their awareness of different possible learning strategies.

To start with, the students carried out a task designed for oral interaction (not related to the CLIL activities), which they recorded. Then they listened to their recording and completed a questionnaire, thus analysing the strategies they had used during the task. (Later the author interviewed two groups to compare their answers with the tape script.) Following this session, the students were asked to think during the week about the strategies they usually used when they spoke in their L1.

In the next session students brainstormed their lists of strategies and filled in a questionnaire, reflecting on the problems they had with English fluency and the strategies they needed to improve their interactive competences. Each group explained their conclusions and the group wrote a definitive list of strategies to learn. The majority of the students said that remembering words and "proper grammar" were the biggest problems when talking, which prompted them to use their L1. So they started working on strategies which could compensate this: mime or non-verbal strategies, circumlocution (describing or paraphrasing the word), synonyms, coining words (saying the word in their L1 but with an English accent or inventing a word translating from L1; Macaro 2003:p.111) and using words or patterns to give them time to think.

Step 2 & 3: Modelling and Practice: The aim was to develop student knowledge about strategies by presenting, describing, naming and modelling the new strategies. A poster was hung on the wall and each student got a paper copy.

Students watched some scenes from the film Ladies in Lavender where two English women tried to communicate with a Polish boy who couldn't speak or understand English. The objective was to analyze the different strategies they used: mime, facial expression, asking for clarification etc., completing a chart as they watched. This was followed by a general practice of the selected strategies in different oral activities set up by the teacher **(step 3)**.

Step 4: Action planning; goal setting and monitoring: Learners identified their own targets, the particular strategies that would help to achieve them and the means by which they could measure success (Grenfell and Harris, 1999). In this phase, students listened to their recordings daily and filled in an evaluation chart analysing the things they did better, things they still needed to improve and the things they were going to do in order to continue improving their speaking.

Results

On the whole, the students felt that working on strategies had been useful for them and after having worked on them they tried to use more English in class (50%). They also collaborated more with the classmates when speaking (44.4%), and they tried to make an effort to do the oral activities better (38.9%) and they thought more how they learned (33.3%).

In the second questionnaire, the reference group (the ones who worked on strategies) said that they had increased the number of strategies they used while the other two control groups had actually decreased in their use of strategies.

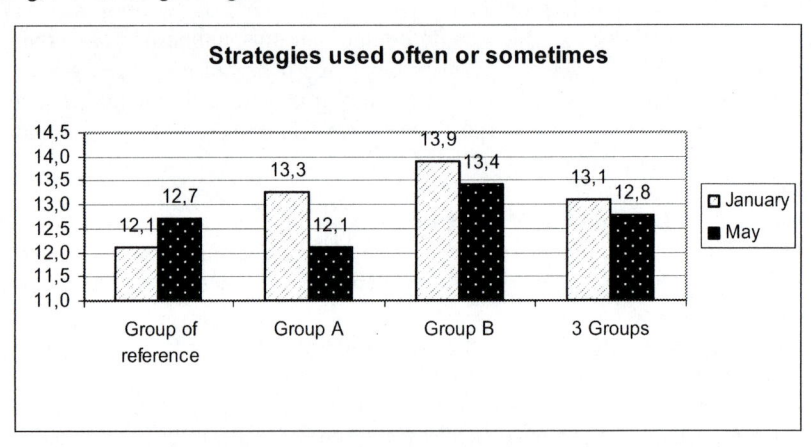

Fig. 3-1 Learning strategies

Strategies used often or sometimes

Group	January	May
Group of reference	12,1	12,7
Group A	13,3	12,1
Group B	13,9	13,4
3 Groups	13,1	12,8

Part two: The CLIL activities: All roads lead to Rome

This topic was chosen because there are ruins of a Roman bath near the school and students were familiar with the Roman culture. The activities are designed for 11 to 13 year old students. They are working on content (learning about their Roman heritage), acquiring language knowledge (principally focused on speaking skills), learning strategies (metacognitive and speaking strategies) and acquiring general knowledge and skills (ICT, e.g. using Power Point for giving presentations).

During the CLIL activities, two teachers (the author and a teaching colleague) worked with 11 students from the three different classes. The students either worked in pairs or groups of three. They were expected to work mainly on their own but counted on teacher support during the third term of the school year (the project was part of a free elective course). Each group had a digitalised dossier (a personal electronic file) and a voice recorder (one group was also video recorded). Six speaking sessions were recorded and then evaluation charts filled in. (Extracts from the CLIL activities are included in Appendix D).

The process of the activities was the following:

First, students began with a questionnaire about Ancient Rome in order to reactivate previous knowledge they had about the topic. They were then introduced to some websites they could use to help complete it. Next, students began to look for more information based on activities designed to learn about:

- The Roman Empire: comparing the map of the area of the Roman Empire with the map of the European Union Expansion.
- The language: matching some English words with their Latin origin with the words in Latin and translating them into L1.
- Roman engineering and architecture: listening to some recordings and completing some activities to become familiar with some basic vocabulary and learn about some of the Roman buildings. After that, they had to decide upon one type to prepare an oral presentation about.
- Roman life: reading some information about Roman society finding out more about Roman daily life (they had to choose a role, e.g. senators, gladiators, or tavern-keepers and to research it).

In order to prepare their oral presentation about a Roman building the students:

- Looked for information in websites, analysing and summarising it and then rewriting the information into a presentation with a poster or PowerPoint as a visual aid.
- Prepared their oral presentation by planning and deciding the responsibilities of each group member. This meant deciding what each member was going to say, practising the introduction, the

conclusion, deciding which was the most appropriate body language,and the way they would present the information, etc.

Following their preparation, the students gave their oral presentations. This was video recorded so each group could then fill in an evaluation chart based on their own analysis of their final product. They also used the chart to analyse the process taken to get to the output. Additionally, the other classmates completed a chart with the most important information about each presentation, thus ensuring that they were listening carefully and would ask for clarification if necessary. Yet another chart was provided so the learners could take notes about the aspects they liked about their classmates' presentations and the aspects they felt the presenters needed to improve.

Following the same process as in step 3, students had to choose and develop one aspect about Roman life. To do so, students had to:

- Choose one role (e.g. senator, gladiator, wine-maker) and explain a typical day related to that role.
- Imagine themselves in their chosen role and write a diary about their everyday activities or a letter to a pen friend who lives in another Roman province.
- Decide how to best explain their information to classmates. This might be in the form of a dramatized presentation, a PowerPoint to give explanations, a movie (using Windows Movie Maker) or any other similar idea.

The final step aimed at reaching some conclusions. This phase included the following activities:

- Students had to put all the information together and think about how life is similar or different from Ancient Rome.
- Students analysed different items: housing, school, free time activities, food, etc.
- To finish students answered a quiz to see what they had learned about the Roman world.

Discussion

During the activities the group was enthusiastic and, broadly speaking, they tried to do their best to use the target language and to complete the activities to the best of their ability. Upon observing their learning process through the transcriptions and their own analysis of the transcriptions, all the students agreed that they had used English significantly more than they had originally anticipated. Moreover, the group's head teacher was pleasantly surprised by the amount of English used and the students' total engagement in the activities: "I saw that they were very content, very motivated, they were working very well, very quietly engrossed and I think they liked it a lot... I don't think it was difficult for them... The activities came with a lot of additional support material."

In relation to the initial questionnaires, 100% of the students stated that learning subjects in foreign language held many advantages for them, but many of them (45%) noted that they felt they had difficulties in expressing themselves in English: "It is difficult because I can't say in English what I'd like to say". "It is difficult because sometimes I didn't say anything because I wasn't sure how to say it in English". In comparison, following the CLIL experience, the reference group did not mention that they felt any limitations to speaking in English —perhaps due to new self-confidence stemming from the experience?

The students also stated that they had enjoyed the activities and 63.3% said they would choose an optional subject in English if they had the opportunity next school year. In their opinion: "I can learn more about other subjects and at the same time I get to practise English" and "It's definitely easier to speak English after doing these activities because we usually learn it writing. I think that if we did more tasks of this kind, although it's sometimes uncomfortable, people would end up learning more English than they learn now".

As for their assessment of their recordings, 64% of the learners said that they did better than they had thought they could and 55% said that they used more English that they thought they were capable of using. Using the recorder and then hearing their conversations helped them to talk more or better: "When there was the recorder I spoke English better than usual. After hearing it I could hear what I did wrong and I didn't usually make the same mistakes"; "I did better because I knew that we had to listen to it and I wanted to do the best I could".

Although more analysis and more work needs to be done, the experience points towards very positive and encouraging conclusions. It is apparent that students use English for interaction when they have opportunities to use it in real communicative situations, especially in a supportive environment. Clearly, they need some tools to help them and give them the confidence needed to take risks and use the foreign language, despite their limitations –particularly when they are worried that the quality of their speaking is lower than when they use their L1.

It also seems that explicit awareness of communicative strategies helped the learners increase their use of these strategies, in particular the cooperative strategies, which are extremely useful in "authentic" language-use situations the students may well encounter in the future. By providing the students with opportunities to use a foreign language in a Cultural Studies course, as well as scaffolding the learning process of contextualised language specific to the interaction taking placed, students used the target language more readily, and more competently than before starting the project.

Works Cited

Grenfell, Michael and Vee Harris. 1999. *Modern languages and learning strategies in theory and practice.* London: Routledge.
Harris, Vee., Alberto Gaspar, Barry Jones, Hafdís Ingvarsdóttir, Renate Neuburg, Ildikó Pálos, and Ilse Schindler. 2001. *Helping learners learn: exploring strategy instruction in language classrooms across Europe.* Strasbourg: Council of Europe Publishing. http://www.ecml.at/documentspub222harrisE.pdf [Last viewed 16 Jan 2007]
Macaro, Ernesto. 2003. *Teaching and learning a second language. A guide to recent research and its applications.* London: Continuum.
O'Malley, J.Michael and Anna Uhl Chamot. 1990. *Learning Strategies in second language Acquisition.* Cambridge: Cambridge University Press.

TALKING ENGLISH TO LEARN SCIENCE: A CLIL EXPERIENCE IN BARCELONA

CRISTINA ESCOBAR URMENETA

Introduction

A merely well-informed man is the most useless bore on God's earth.
—Whitehead 1932, in Nisbet 1993: 281

Despite an increase in general knowledge of foreign languages throughout Catalonia in the last ten years, compulsory education is still unable to produce exit levels that guarantee successful multilingual communication amongst graduates. With this in mind, in recent years a number of commendable experiences have been promoted by Educational authorities under the umbrella of innovation programmes carried out enthusiastically by a minority of language and content teachers (Escobar and Pérez-Vidal, 2004; Escobar, 2004; Figueras, 2005; Roquet, et.al. 2004). In particular, this article looks at innovation through CLIL being carried out in Catalonia.

Although there are programmes that support innovative initiatives such as the one discussed in this article, some sectors of parents, teachers, teacher-educators and administrators are sceptical about the capacity of the Catalan school system to generalize the CLIL approach and to still be able to cater to mixed ability students. In particular, they are worried because students will be asked to use a third language (L3)[1], not only as a target language in a foreign language classroom, but also as the vehicular language for subject learning. They are afraid that some students whose command of the foreign language is limited will not be able to cope with the demands of academic life, thus leading to a lowering of general standards. This fear holds especially true for late arrival students or for students with slower learning rates.

---

[1] Education in Catalonia is bilingual; Catalan and Spanish are the co-official school languages.

These views reveal a set of well established beliefs and prejudices about language learning in multilingual environments, such as:
- Languages are hard to learn. It is more sensible to tackle languages one at a time and only after the students are proficient in the first language (L1) should the second one (L2) be introduced, then the L3 and so on.
- Only privileged learners will be able to cope with the demands of a curriculum taught through the medium of an L3. The average student and, obviously the under-average one as well, is bound to experience serious difficulties in such a programme.
- It is more sensible for students to be proficient in the target foreign language before beginning content study in that language.
- A focus on content will not result in satisfactory language learning, which requires explicit instruction on the formals aspects of language.

In fact, early studies on immersion classes in the USA and Canada consistently report a huge gap between the learners' ability to understand written discourse, and to produce oral or written language. However, this mismatch has been attributed to the scarce number of opportunities that the students in those programmes were given to engage in extended oral discourse, as the majority of the lessons tended to be teacher-centred (Swain, 1988). Likewise, teacher-centred lessons are the preferred style in many of the schools in Catalonia. Even if it is generally accepted that small group-work is a "positive" strategy, teachers have their reservations about its efficacy in terms of learning outcomes. It is considered time-consuming (learners use up too much time to come up with a solution or information that would have been reached much more rapidly in a teacher-centred class) or a paradise for lazy students (they simply waste their time off-task). In the CLIL classroom, the benefits of peer work are even more of an issue as it is suspected that learners may be unable to use the foreign language to respond to the challenge of a cognitively demanding task.

Rationale for a teaching sequence

ArtICLE was a research project on CLIL, developed in collaboration with secondary teachers and teacher trainers from the Language Didactics Department from the Autonomous University of Barcelona. The tasks were implemented at three schools in 2005 and in two more schools in 2006; the sequence took between seven to ten lessons. The project revolved around three different focus points: materials design, classroom-based collaborative research and teacher development. In this chapter we will describe the process of materials design[2]. The need for learner-centred interaction was the starting point for the the development of the teaching material. It was felt that there must be authentic interaction (conversation) between learners, stemming from structured pedagogical tasks, thus shaping a favourable environment for both academic and linguistic learning in the CLIL classrooms.

Choice of topic, subject-matter content and materials

Rainforests was chosen as the topic since it was a core theme in both the primary and secondary Science curriculum and had strong links with cultural aspects. The availability of quality resources (e.g. webpages for young learners, adolescents and general readers) also played an important role in the selection, along with the fact that news about the Amazon regularly appears in the press. This made it easier to exemplify the main characteristics common to rainforests and also the main dangers that threaten them. Subject-matter target content was organised around four main areas:

- General characteristics: geographical situation, extension, climate, etc.
- Rainforests as biomes. A study of the Amazon.
- Main threats to rainforests and their consequences.
- Actions to protect rainforests.

Selection of target language content

The starting point was the identification of Content Obligatory Language (COL) needed for the subject-matter content. The term Content Obligatory Language was coined by Snow et al. (1989), who defined it as:

> the language required by students to develop, master and communicate about a given content material. For every topic or concept certain language is essential or obligatory for understanding and talking about the material. (205-206)

In the ArtICLE materials, COL included:
- Topic specific language: lexical items and language forms closely related to rainforests and the Amazon (e.g. biodiversity, deforestation, Yanomami, etc.).

---

[2] The materials can be retrieved from http://www.clil-si.org

- Genre specific language: terms, phrases, verb tenses, connectors or other language forms characteristic of the type of explanatory discourse that students were required to process for understanding and/or production in the academic situation. These might include expressing cause-effect relationships, explaining processes or formulating hypothesis (e.g. because; as a result; due to; etc.).
- Genre specific text types: explanatory texts of the academic type (e.g. science reports).

The vast amount of COL in the webpages was too demanding for the target students so some 50 target terms were short-listed as priority content obligatory language. Short-listed items were integrated into teaching materials.

Methodological approach

In recent decades, pedagogical interest has moved from "what" is learned to "how" it is learned, although both are in fact two sides of the same coin: the "how" determines the "what" to a great extent. Likewise, the type of learning activities in a teaching sequence will determine to a large extent whether the students will learn an "inert" list of facts, or rather will be able to use those facts to compare and contrast ideas and develop new critical ways of looking into those facts. Thus, in our sequence, we took into account the 4Cs that Coyle (2002) outlines for a balanced CLIL Curriculum, namely: Content, Communication, Cognition and Culture, and also integrated one more "C", standing for "Critical thinking" into our own requirements for planning CLIL tasks.

Research on tasks shows that they should favour the active processing of the input made available and foster productive communication among learners (see Task-Based Language Learning, in Chapter Two of this book). This meant the designed activities had to comply with all four criteria stated by Skehan's definition of task (1998:268):
1. Meaning is primary
2. There is a goal which needs to be worked towards
3. The activity is outcome-evaluated
4. There is a real-world relationship

We will try to briefly explain how ArtICLE understood and implemented these four traits:

Meaning is primary: Being a CLIL programme, instructional activities focused on subject matter content. Precisely because meaning is primary in content study, provision was made to present and familiarise students with indispensable specific lexical terms in contextualised purposeful activities (see description of the tasks below). Help was provided for problems the students encountered, be they grammatical, lexical or discursive. Students also got a short bilingual English-Catalan glossary with the more difficult words they would be needing.

Although the role of form-focused instruction in content-based programmes has been clearly stated by research (Genesee, 1987), in our sequence we discarded any type of explicit teaching of language and discourse rules as we wanted to focus exclusively on content —and subsequent language knowledge that emerged. However, one of the tasks (*Rainforest detectives*) was designed to centre students' attention —even if diffusely— on the linguistic features of texts. To do so, students were told that although they were working on science, language was to play a role in their work.

There is a goal which needs to be worked towards: Communicative or learning goals that transcend mere language practice are essential as they help students picture what is expected of them and to better grasp the learning targets. In this respect, Task 3 (academic presentations) acted as a "natural" final task, which justified from a scholarly point of view the students' efforts throughout the whole sequence. As this goal was a distant one (presentations were to be made at the end of a three-week sequence), intermediate closer sub-goals became necessary.

Goals, from the point of view of learners, can be of a very different nature and may or may not coincide with the teacher's goals. For example, the quiz competition described below in the task description was, in the eyes of the learners, the justification they needed for accurately exchanging information. In the teacher's eyes, it was no more than an artful device to get students engaged in purposeful (and hopefully fruitful) conversation. On the other hand, each single activity had an "inner" goal which was easily identifiable by the learners and which transcended language practice.

The activity is outcome-evaluated: This premise was included in the degree to which the student efficiently resolved a puzzle (see description of *Rainforest detectives* below), in the communication of a message to a peer (see jigsaw puzzle task) or to the rest of the class (see presentation). The level of competent communication indicated the degree of success in the task.

There is a real-world relationship: Science is not only a subject at school it is a reality students are confronted with outside of the school as well through news and documentaries about climate change. Rainforests as thermo-regulators are a frequent topic in mass media and this can be used to draw the attention of adolescents.

How the task sequence was designed

The entire Rainforest sequence was designed around three main tasks:
- Task 1. Jigsaw task (Become an "expert")
- Task 2. Problem solving task (Develop "expert" advice)
- Task 3. Academic presentation (Disseminate expertise)

While the three tasks were quite different in many aspects—thus maintaining student motivation by varying the tasks—all of the tasks were designed to be carried out collaboratively in student pairs. Globally, all the tasks involved:
- Interaction in the target language through listening, speaking, reading and writing.
- Rich varied oral and written input.
- The use of ICT as a source for information.
- A cyclical approach to subject-matter content presentation, wherein the content was presented, recycled, systematised and progressively extended through the different activities.
- Manipulative and visual skills had an important role, serving as a scaffold for the composition (Task 2) and delivery (Task 3) of the students' proposal.

The three main tasks had either a preliminary or follow-up task, or both, thus creating three-task cycles (described below). While the preliminary tasks aimed at equipping students with the essential linguistic and heuristic tools in order to succeed when carrying out the main tasks, the follow-up tasks sought to officialise the students' efforts and achievements through teachers' comments, points or grades and at the same time provide opportunities for reflection on learning.

Description and discussion of task-cycle 1

A cooperative learning technique (Kagan 1995) was developed for conventional content classes in L1; however its features make it a very useful method for CLIL classrooms. It "creates a real information gap, promotes authentic language use and encourages students to interact; in the process, they share their insights, test hypotheses and jointly construct knowledge" (Crandall 1993: 117). An example of a task designed for joint construction of knowledge can be seen in figure 3-2.

Fig. 3-2 Tasks for joint construction of knowledge

Sub-task	Task Features	Main challenges
Sub-Task 1-A	"Expert" phase in the jigsaw technique. Students in small groups read the assigned text in order to understand and memorize it.	Decoding, understanding the ideas and memorising an academic text.
Sub-Task 1-B	"Expert" phase in the jigsaw technique. Information swap in dyads through face to face interaction.	Recalling information. Being able to pass the message to partner and to understand partner's message. Cooperating efficiently in order to complement each other's gaps.

After the students had become familiar with the information (developed their expertise in phase A) they changed pairs and shared information (phase B) with their new partner. In the new pairs, each member is expert on a different set of information, as a result of the work carried out in phase A. In phase B, each expert teaches her part to her partner and learns her partner's part as well.

Importantly, this task was preceded by some preliminary tasks. The preliminary tasks for the jigsaw technique began with self-assessment tasks. Students were informed that in the upcoming weeks the classwork was going to revolve around a set of topics related to rainforests. Students were given a list of these topics and asked to self-assess their degree of familiarity about each topic by rating themselves from 1 to 4 (1 being I don't know anything about this topic; 4 being I can talk about this topic in English).

The self-assessment was followed by a task entitled "Rainforests Slide Show". The objective of this task was to activate the students' previous knowledge on the subject. Over ten to fifteen minutes students watched a set of twenty slides which showed photographs, maps and diagrams directly related with the content of the unit. During the slide show, the teacher elicited information from the learners about what they already knew. For instance, when a student was able to name an item in the L1, the teacher acknowledged it and then reframed it towards the target language by writing it on the chalkboard in English.

The slide show was followed by an activity called "Rainforest Detectives". In this activity, students were presented with a set of words and phrases marked in three different colours. They were then asked to find the common features of all the terms highlighted in the same colour—the common feature being word—classes (nouns, adjectives, verbs). This activity had a two-fold goal: to familiarize students with possibly problematic content language and to serve as a metalinguistic awareness-raising task.

The task sequence ended with a follow-up activity in the form of a quiz. Once the "experts" had shared and taught their information to their partners, students filled in a quiz individually about the content studied thus far. The answers were checked and each individual student's score was added to that of her partner. The pair with highest score was named the winners.

In "Rainforests detectives" it took some of the classes more than 10 minutes to "break the code". Students reported that they had been considering all sort of relationships between the "meanings" of the words. The "solution" to the problem proved to be a surprise. The task helped highlight the relationship between meaning and word-class. It also helped the students remember the content words. Video recordings show that Sub-Task 1-A experts put an incredible amount of effort into understanding and memorizing their texts, in order to pass their new knowledge on to their partners. Moreover, in order to understand the texts they used all kinds of strategies such as using the students' L1 as an aid for decoding and also for encoding their messages.

In the Phase B English virtually excluded L1 and L2 and the students remained "on-task" almost 100% of the time (Horrillo, 2006). The student pairs managed to adapt the task to their own capacities and student cooperation between pairs was the norm (Escobar & Nussbaum, 2008). Nonetheless, when the task was managed by student teachers (who also participated in the project), they found it very stressful and had the impression that students had been wasting their time. Only when confronted with the transcripts of their own students did these student teachers become aware of the pedagogical value of the task.

Brief description and discussion of Task-cycle 2

The problem-solving task was based on the assumption that learning through the resolution of problems promotes the use of higher order cognitive abilities (Sellwood 1989). The task was designed to scaffold students' critical thinking. This is outlined in Figure 3-3.

Fig. 3-3 Problem-solving task

Sub-task	Task Characterization	Main Challenges
T2-A	Pairs are assigned different areas of specialization within the common topic. Students try to find the required information on the Internet in order to answer questions. Students can take notes, but cannot use the "cut & paste" function.	ICT skills. Effective cooperation when working *side by side* with a partner. Reading skills: skim and scan for information. Writing skills: summarizing
T2-B	Pairs of students are asked to formulate a proposal of sustainable development for the Amazon in their respective *area of expertise*. The proposal must consist of five recommendations which are displayed on a poster, using photographs or drawings.	Emphasis on application and integration of knowledge in "original" ways. Composition skills: writing a report. Creative skills in the design of the poster.

For sake of brevity, this task cycle is not described as fully as task-cycle 1, however it is important to highlight the fact that students became fully engaged in the task during their Internet search and in the design of the poster. Moreover, the volume of students' use of English when searching for information was higher than expected and involved not only talk about the content but also task management and personally addressed utterances, such as jokes (Corredera, forthcoming).

On a more critical note, it was found that attention needs to be paid to the amount of information students have access to. Students had access to five or six selected webpages, which proved to be too many as they needed a lot of time simply to browse through the pages. Also, some of the pages were not available when needed. In the writing stage, some students experienced difficulties when writing the "recommendations". The complete absence of "model" language input was identified as the cause of the problem.

Interestingly, in the original planning of the tasks, making the poster was just an excuse to help students organize their ideas for the oral presentation. The students had a different perspective and wanted their posters to look nice, so they demanded an extra lesson to finish them. Many students asked for permission to take the posters home in order to have more time.

Brief Description and discussion of task-cycle 3

In this task, students were expected to give a presentation in front of the class of their previously prepared proposal. Students were encouraged to use their poster as visual support but were not allowed to use any sort of written text. From the students' perspective, the main challenges of the task laid in the recall of information and delivering the message effectively. The students took the task very seriously and made huge efforts to overcome the challenge of a face-risking task. This effort was supported by the teachers who reassured their students very professionally and suggested on-the-spot strategies to overcome their particular problems.

Nonetheless, attention needs to be paid to the overall performance as the students' competence in the presentations was very uneven. In some cases, students had little previous experience giving presentations in English or in their L1. For these students it was hard to understand exactly what the task demanded and they tended to concentrate on remembering the text and did not pay attention to the audience.

Conclusion

A quick look at several of the commendable experiences and projects involving CLIL demonstrates the interest and relevant institutional support this approach has enjoyed in the last eight years in Catalonia. Nevertheless, further implementation of innovative foreign language teaching and learning is still called for. The tension between innovation and prudence is understandable: clearly more CLIL experiences are needed, but it is probably sensible that these experiences are observed carefully to ensure that the appropriate pedagogical decisions are being taken and that learning, both in the domains of content and language, is actually taking place.

ArtICLE has tried to do its bit by designing teaching materials according to well established pedagogical principles, and then putting them into practice and evaluating the results. For instance, notable progress in formal linguistic and discourse features in students who had not undergone any type of previous instruction on those features has helped us to gain a better understanding of the type of benefits that students may get from CLIL instruction. It has also helped us to identify formal grammatical and discourse features that may become the target of form-focused instructional activities in complementary foreign language lessons.

Last, but not least, collaboration between teachers and researchers was beneficial for all of the participants involved. Researchers gained access into "authentic" classroom life and benefited from the expertise and wisdom of the practitioners involved. Practitioners benefited from the support of the university team during the preparation and implementation of the sequence. Also, the analysis of data allowed teachers to confirm empirically and systematically the outcomes of their teaching work; something extremely valuable for teachers, but which is rarely within reach. And best of all, together, everyone learned a lot.

Works Cited

Figueras, Neus. ed. 2005. *CLIL in Catalonia, from theory to Practice*. Barcelona, APAC Monographs, 6.

Corredera, A. (forthcoming) "Uso de la lengua extranjera en tareas para aprender ciencias en inglés: ¿hablan en inglés?" Actas del XXV Congreso Internacional AESLA; Murcia 19-21/04/2007.

Coyle, Do. 2002. "Against all Odds: lessons from CLIL in English Secondary Schools." In *Education and Society in Plurilingual Contexts*, ed. Daniel So and Gary Jones, , 37-55. Brussels: VUB Press.

Crandall, JoAnn. 1993. "Content-centered instruction in the United States". *Annual Review of Applied Linguistics* (13) 111-126.

Escobar Urmeneta, Cristina and Luci Nussbaum. (2008). "Tasques d'intercanvi de informació i processos d'aprenentatge en l'aula AICLE". In *I Jornades de recerca sobre l'educació lingüística i literària en entorns plurilingües*, ed. Anna Camps and Marta Milian, 147-167. Barcelona: Graó. Spanish version available at http:clil.si.org

Escobar Urmeneta, Cristina and Carme Pérez-Vidal. 2004. "Teacher education for the implementation of a Content and Language Integrating Learning approach (CLIL) in the school system". In *Integrating Content and Language. meeting the challenge of multilingual education*, R. Wilkinson, ed. 402-415. Maastricht: Universitaire Press.

Genesee, Fred. 1987. *Learning through two languages: Studies of immersion and bilingual education.* Rowley, MA: Newbury.

Horillo, Zoraida. 2006. *A Study of the On-task and Off-Task Activity.* Master Thesis UAB. Unpublished. Information available at: http://www.clil-si.org

Kagan, Spencer. 1995. "Dimensions of Cooperative Classroom Structures". In *Learning to Cooperate, Cooperate to Learn*, ed. Robert Slavin, Shlomo Sharan, Spencer Kagan, Rachel Hertz Lazarowitz, Clark Web and Richard Schmuck, 67-96. New York, Plenun Press:

Nisbet, John. 1993. "The thinking curriculum." *Educational Psychology* 13: 281-290.

Pérez Vidal, Carmy. 1998. "Towards Multilingualism and Content Language Integrated Learning in Spain." In *Future Scenarios in Content and Language Integrated Learning*, ed. David Marsh, Bruce Marsland and Anne Maljers, 45-61. Jyväskylä. University of Jyväskylä.

Sellwood, Peter. 1989. "The role of problem solving in developing thinking skills." *The Technology Teacher*, 49(3): 3-10.

Skehan, Peter. 1998. "Task-based Instruction."*Annual Review of Applied Linguistics*, 18: 268-286.

Snow, Marguerite, Myriam Met and Fred Genesse. 1989. "A conceptual framework for the integration of language and content in second/foreign language instruction". *TESOL Quarterly* 23: 201-218.

Swain, Merrill. 1988. "Manipulating and complementing content teaching to maximize second language learning." *TESL Canada Journal*, 6: 68-83.

ALONG THE CONTINUUM – AN EXPLORATION OF INTEGRATING LANGUAGE AND CONTENT LEARNING IN ENGLAND

DO COYLE

The central philosophy [is] that motivating students to learn [modern languages] will be the cornerstone to success and that the principle of "one size does not fit all" should apply to all developments
—Dearing Modern Languages Review 2007

Introduction: language learning in England

This chapter will describe the recent expansion of content and language integrated learning (CLIL) in England and discuss a range of models which respond to critical contextual national needs as well as regional and local demands. Whilst Baetens-Beardsmore (1993) acknowledged that "no model is for export", in order to build quality learning environments I argue that clear theoretical principles underlying and defining any CLIL model must be rigorous and transparent.

The United Kingdom is not monolingual. There are for example 600,000 speakers of Welsh and 60,000 speakers of Scottish Gaelic (2001 National Census). Over 300 different languages are used in London alone and over 10% of primary children do not have English as their first language. From a survey of 850,000 school children (Baker and Eversley, 2000), the most common languages spoken other than English are Bengali and Sylheti (40,400), Panjabi (29,800), Gujarati (28,600), and Hindi/Urdu (26,000), followed by Turkish (15,600) and Arabic (11,000). Such statistics however are in sharp contrast to the well-documented complacent attitudes towards learning languages prevalent in the UK, embodied in the "island mentality", a disincentive to learn languages - we can speak English anyway – along with a limited national capability for a plurilingual work force. The *National Nuffield Languages Report Languages*: *the next generation* not only recognised that

> English alone is no longer enough and that the advantage of speaking a global language is eroded daily as more and more people not only speak it as well as we do, but speak other languages too. (2000:38)

but also warned that

> It is also dangerous. In a world where bilingualism and plurilingualism are commonplace, monolingualism implies inflexibility, insensitivity and arrogance. Much that is essential to our society, its health and its interest, including effective choice in policy, realisation of citizenship, effective overseas links and openness to the inventions of other cultures, will not be achieved in one language alone. (2000:14)

Evidence suggested that current classroom foreign language experiences, often dominated by the demands of the national examination system do not motivate learners (Nuffield, 2002; Dearing, 2007). Moreover the use of these results as an evidential data source for measuring national standards is demoralising both for learners and teachers. The legacy of narrowly defined practices built on communicative approaches often resulted in formulaic irrelevant learning and led to the national inspectorate reporting that pupils in KS4 [after four years of language learning] are unable to express themselves in the target language in a wider range of contexts than in KS3 [after 3 years of language learning] (OFSTED, 1996).

Research carried out into motivation for language learning (Dornyei, 2005) highlights the need for relevant learner experiences to provide authentic opportunities for language using in a young people's world. The issue remained however that in terms of our English national curriculum the content of language learning is mainly irrelevant to young people and lags behind the realities of their everyday lives.

Promoting CLIL through national policy

A national languages strategy was set up in 2002 *Languages for All: Languages for Life* to "look at innovative ways of enabling language learning" and to implement the Nuffield recommendations. One such initiative focussed on the development of CLIL, *The Nuffield Report* (2000) had cited as an example of good practice the case of Hasland Hall Comprehensive School in the Midlands, where 11 year old beginner learners of French in secondary school were taught approximately half of their school curriculum through the medium of French - with very remarkable results.

11 year olds at an 11-16 comprehensive school [...], study geography, ICT, history and personal and social education through the medium of French......It was found that lower ability children who had followed the bilingual programme performed better in English than those who had not. Boys seemed to do especially well. (Nuffield Foundation, 2000: 46)

This "experiment" confirmed some of the results of the Canadian immersion programme findings (Cummins and Swain, 1986) by highlighting CLIL benefits for all learners but especially the less able who, it was discovered, had raised their mother tongue literacy levels alongside a motivational impetus for language learning which included boys as well as girls. A National Languages Strategy could build on findings such as these and for the first time CLIL initiatives were included in official documentation.

The government pledged to invest £115 million in language learning in 2002 and it seemed that a funded route for exploring CLIL was now possible. Whilst learning a subject through a foreign language was neither a new concept nor an untested one in England, a range of initiatives since the 1980s tended to focus on a model of "bilingual sections" in schools. Inspired by Canadian immersion programmes, in many cases, students learned their Geography through French, their History through German or their Business Studies in Spanish for example. Such bilingual initiatives, whilst highly successful in specific settings or in the pilot phase, were sometimes problematic in the longer term due to teacher supply and the absence of national examinations to recognise achievement. The question of who should teach these subjects – language teachers or subject teachers – remained unresolved. Native speaker teachers or language teachers were often targeted since having the language skills to teach in a language was considered a crucial starting point – leaving the implications for teaching through a language to emerge over time. Moreover in the majority of cases, the pilot work had been initiated by language teachers who were looking for alternatives to regular language learning to motivate their learners.

In 2002, the government funded a three year study "CLIP" (content and language integrated project) set up by CILT (the National Language Centre, London) to examine the potential of CLIL programmes at both primary and secondary level. Eight schools in England took part. Each school had to nominate a pair of teachers to work together: a language teacher and a subject teacher. The funding for pairs of teachers symbolised the Ministry's wish to encourage participation by subject teachers in what was considered a predominantly language promotion initiative. The range of participating schools from selective grammar schools to inner-city socially-deprived colleges reflected the broad appeal and variety of applications CLIL offers.

Subjects such as Geography, History and Citizenship were taught through French, German and Spanish in very different ways through modules of work for learners from 10 -16. In some cases the CLIL modules were taught by both the language and content teachers but in the majority of cases the modules were delivered by the language teachers. In some cases CLIL lessons took place throughout the year on a regular weekly basis but in most instances a CLIL module of work was organised for between 6-10 weeks. All CLIP schools reported gains in motivation and attitudes towards language learning by the majority of learners since the CLIL modules had transformed "language learning" into "language using" and had clear "added value". There were also reported gains in terms of raising learner and teacher expectations and a willingness to engage in risk-taking to actively promote classroom interaction. Extracts from learner-teacher interviews include (Wiesemes: 2005):

> Learner A7: It was cool learning our geography in French- it just didn't seem like language lessons... we forgot about the language even when it was hard.
>
> Learner B4: In some of the activities we had to do I thought we just can't do these in French but we found we could... it didn't matter and we learned lots of new words and stuff which we never wouldn't have if it had been in English.
>
> Learner C2: It's enjoyable coz we learn things that are more interesting... We learn things like history. It's better than normal French... we learn more.
>
> Teacher F: They are very enthusiastic not self-conscious or not to the same extent.

It seemed like a promising start towards mainstreaming CLIL.

Developing CLIL-beyond "a shell for language learning" (Stoller 2002)

CLIP had explored CLIL in terms of its potential to raise standards of attainment across the curriculum; improve pupils' foreign language capability; develop a more integrated approach to curriculum delivery; and take forward the citizenship agenda. Merging the goals of the CLIL projects across the different participating schools, revealed that over twenty of the collective aims were related to language learning (e.g. emphasising the need to improve motivation, attainment, confidence, competence and attitudes) whereas only seven related to subjects or content-usually expressed in terms of national curriculum requirements. In addition, eight further aims focussed on "delivering" global citizenship such as "developing the skills and knowledge to become active citizens in an ever expanding global community", with three targeting ICT.

The predominance of language learning goals for CLIL in the CLIP experience is not surprising. They reflect the national need to find ways of addressing the decline in attitudes towards language learning in secondary schools and its marginalisation as a core curriculum subject. They also reflect the lead taken by language teachers in delivering curriculum through the language. After all

> It is absurd to ignore the role of content in the language class, just as it is absurd to ignore the role of languages a medium of learning in the content class. Every language teacher has to organise content material to support language learning, and all language teachers have an interest in doing this more systematically (Mohan, 1986:iv)

Moreover, the link made to the global citizenship agenda also mirrors needs expressed by schools to respond pragmatically to a non-statutory but high profile citizenship agenda towards a more values-driven curriculum. A new national curriculum launched in England (2007) gives a clear steer towards more curricular linking in order

> to encourage schools to be innovative in the way that they plan the school timetable. Teaching subjects together, group projects or school visits can all help to make pupils more enthusiastic about learning. Through creating this kind of curriculum, we will achieve our objective of producing successful learners, confident individuals and responsible citizens. (Boston: 2007)

The national context moulds the CLIL vision in England towards potential gains in language learning (motivation, attitudes and competence) and responds to national policies such as those which measure and make schools accountable for raising national standards through the *National Literacy Strategy* or which take account of a personalised syllabus through closer curriculum linking. This raises an interesting issue - can initiatives which emphasise foreign language competence and wider cross-curricular issues be redefined as content and language integrated learning?

Marsh (2002) defines CLIL as

> [A] generic umbrella term encompassing a wide range of initiatives, in which learning of second/foreign languages and other subjects has a joint curricular role in education. Usage of this term allows us to consider the myriad variations....without imposing restrictions which might fail to take account of school or region-specific implementation characteristics. ..It does not give emphasis to either language teaching or learning, or to content teaching and learning, but sees both as integral parts of the whole.

However if interpretations of CLIL are so flexible, is this simply a new term replicating task-based (TBI) and content-based language instruction (CBI) - a case of rebranding 21st century communicative language teaching?

For Nunan (2004) TB learners engage in:

> comprehending, manipulating, producing or interacting in the target language while their attention is focussed on mobilising their grammatical knowledge in order to express meaning, and in which the intention is to convey meaning rather than to manipulate form. (Nunan 2004:4)

In TBI learners are encouraged to use grammatical knowledge to express meaning which is clearly not the same as using grammatical exercises to extend grammatical understanding. For Willis (1996) learners are involved in "an entirely different mental process as they compose what they want to say, expressing what they think or feel" (1996:18). In this sense applying grammatical knowledge enables the learner to express different meanings and encourages creative language use. Certainly Nunan's seven principles for TBI are closely related to general learning processing rather than focussing on language learning strategies. Whilst they also take account of integrating form, function and meaning in the language learning sense, they also consider wider learning processes such as scaffolding, task sequencing, recycling, active learning, integration, progression from reproduction to creating, reflecting (Nunan, 2004:37). At the same time it could be argued that content matter in TBI remains peripheral.

Content-based instruction (CBI) according to Brinton and Master (1997) grew out of immersion, language-across-the-curriculum and English for Special Purposes, where content encourages language learning and acquisition. Crandall and Tucker (1990) define it as "an approach to language instruction that integrates the presentation of topics or tasks from subject matter classes (e.g. math, social studies) within the context of teaching a second or foreign language" (1990:187). Genesee (1994:3) suggests that content ...need not be academic; it can include any topic, theme or non-language issue of interest or importance to the learners. Met (1998:150) suggests that ... "content ... is cognitively engaging and demanding for the learner", and is material that extends beyond the target language or target culture. Might CBI provide a bridge towards the development of CLIL from a language teacher's perspective?

Whilst CBI is open to wide interpretation, there is nonetheless a clear steer towards the cognitive challenge afforded to learners through the content which moves the focus on from language learning and TBI. On the one hand Stoller's (2002) point that CBI should offer a framework for language and content learning rather than using content simply as a "shell for language teaching" suggests there remain fundamental differences between approaches to language learning, which do not strategically integrate content and cognitive challenge, and CLIL. On the other hand, Marsh (2005) argues that language learning is also an integral part of CLIL:

> Formal language teaching is part of the CLIL approach, so language teachers who re-position their teaching philosophy according to the new demands could, in fact, become conductors of the orchestra within the new language learning framework.

It seems therefore that there may be developments based on TBI and CBI principles which could usefully pave the way for the development of CLIL. As new approaches to curriculum organisation, teaching and learning emerge, boundaries become fluid and terminlogy is open to wide interpretation. CLIL is no exception.

Articulating national CLIL principles and models

The CLIP case studies revealed very different types of CLIL teaching and learning which seem to point a way forward for more systematic and rigorous contextual variations in England (Wiesemes:2005). Two key issues emerged from the CLIP evaluation which underline

- An identified need for a shared understanding of fundamental principles, based on rigorous principles for promoting CLIL in different contexts.

- A need to articulate a range of models which share CLIL principles yet can be developed in different contexts to realise and describe effective learning environments

A useful starting point is to explore more closely the construct of integration. It could be argued for example that where language learning and content learning are integrated then the teaching will be planned to achieve learner progression through both content and language goals – not necessarily in equal measure. Shared understanding also implies the need for content and language teachers to work more closely together to realise the full potential of a given learning context.

> It is obvious that teaching a subject in a foreign language is not the same as an integration of language and content... language teachers and subject teachers need to work together... [to] formulate the new didactics needed for a real integration of form and function in language teaching. (de Bot 2002:32)

For learning to take place in a CLIL environment, then teachers

> must convey not only the subject content and disciplinary language but also the practical problem-solving, negotiations, discussions and classroom management in ways that characterise disciplinary pedagogic practices (Graddol, 2006:86).

This highlights the basic principles of quality learning around fundamental cognitive and metacognitive challenges which both content and language integration provide – again not necessarily in equal measure.

Holmes (2005), director of the CLIP initiative, believes that CLIL in England is best conceptualised along a continuum which will allow for contextual variation in terms of emphasis on content, language and cognitive challenge – thus making initial steps by adapting TBI and CBI approaches.

> An essential feature of CLIL is that it places both language and the non-language content on a continuum without implying preference or dominance of one over the other [...] recognising curriculum development as part of this continuum has allowed us to be inclusive of a variety of approaches, methods and curriculum models adapted to meet needs of the learners and flexible enough to match the readiness of the teaching force to provide appropriate and relevant learning programmes of a sufficiently high quality in both language and the non-language content subject. (Holmes, 2005:1)

In addition, considering the EU drive linking language learning and citizenship (Commission of the European Communities: 1995, 2005) and the well-documented interrelationship between language, culture and thinking, CLIL also has the potential to offer opportunities to integrate "intercultural learning" into the curriculum (Grenfell, 2004).

If CLIL provides a range of opportunities for integrating language, content, cognitive and meta-cognitive challenge and intercultural learning, then these principles might serve as a useful basis on which to build and explore shared principles (e.g. Coyle's 4Cs conceptual framework for CLIL, 2005). However defining and articulating a robust set of principles implies that these must be present across all CLIL contexts whilst allowing flexibility for different emphases according to the contexts. The CLIP case studies suggest that to maximise the potential of CLIL, then different models must incorporate content learning, language learning, cognitive challenge and intercultural learning objectives to different extents.

An analysis of CLIP case studies thus far (Hood, 2005: 33) indicates that there are four potential CLIL models emerging in England which could be placed along a continuum which contain elements of different approaches to language and content learning:

- Surface cross-curricular linking led by the language teacher which takes account of other curricular themes and incorporates them into language lessons (the languages approach) e.g extending a language topic on "house and home" to include lives of people living in Burkino Fasso to link with a geography study.
- Integrating language and recycling/deepening content usually led by the language teacher where content already covered in L1 is used as a confidence builder or revision aid in L2 – but is then explored further or deeper e.g. introducing the Viking invasion of England (already covered in L1) but extending the CLIL project to investigating the Viking influences in France.
- Integrating language and new content led by either the language teacher or the content teacher where new content is introduced and developed e.g. a study of a dictator (history syllabus) from a country where the CLIL language is spoken such as the study of Hitler in German, or Franco in Spanish.
- Immersion led by the subject teacher where the content learning determines the language learnt (content approach) e.g. photosynthesis as a new concept taught through the medium of French .

Pilot studies such as CLIP play a crucial role in helping construct an evidence base for successful CLIL, rooted in the national context and which take account of specific issues and define effective practice in situ.

Future thinking

In 2006 a subsequent national inquiry *The Languages Review* (2007) was tasked to address a worsening situation regarding the learning and teaching of modern languages in England as the number of students taking the first national examination in a modern language (such as French, German or Spanish) at the age of 16 had fallen from 80% in 2001 to 51% in 2006. Whilst national policy has changed to making the study of a foreign language compulsory at primary school level, the greatest challenge that remains is one of motivating young people in England to engage with language learning beyond their primary experiences and especially beyond the statutory age of 14. It is a national priority to find ways of motivating and encouraging young people to study languages. Pilot studies suggest that contexts which promote the integration of content and language learning alongside cognitive and intercultural challenges have a role to play in addressing future language learning in England.

There are, and will continue to be, many pioneering classrooms where "traditional" language learning is being transformed - from sterile scripts to interactive knowledge construction and from cognitively unchallenging content to motivating language using.

There are, however, no "quick-fix" solutions to England's language learning shortfall. As the *Languages Review* (2007) concluded, the way ahead is through exploring different routes to language learning since "one size does not fit all". The UK government agency, the DfES (2006), has now set up a National Steering Committee for CLIL and the Teacher Development Agency in England is currently piloting initial teacher training programmes for CLIL which unite learners, teachers and trainers. England can and will respond to the CLIL challenge as one possible route for changing language learning but its success will depend on sharing principles which are defined and made transparent to all stakeholders. Transforming and reconceptualising these principles into potentially rich CLIL scenarios based on clear learning goals and outcomes will require the development of contextual models which share the same agreed and robust principles yet are suited to match individual needs along the continuum – a case of "bespoke tailoring" rather than prêt-à-porter. The process has begun…….

Works Cited

Baetens-Beardsmore, Hugo. 1993. "Introduction." *In European Models of Bilingual Education*, ed. Hugo Baetens-Beardsmore, 1-5. Clevedon: MultiLingual Matters.

—. 1999. "La consolidation des expériences en éducation plurlingue/Consolidating experience in plurilingual education." In *CLIL Intiatives for the Millenium: Report on the CEILINK Think-Tank*, ed. David Marsh, Bruce Marsland, and Anne Maljers, 24-30. Jyvaskyla:University of Jyvaskyla.

Baker, Philip and John Eversley, eds, 2000. *Multilingual Capital*, London: Battlebridge.

Boston, Ken. 2007. *Qualifications and Curriculum* Agency Chief Executive. http://www.qca.org.uk/qca_10899.aspx

de Bot, Kees. 2002. "Relevance of CLIL to the European Commission's Language Learning Objectives". In *CLIL/EMILE- The European Dimension: Actions, Trends and Foresight Potential*, ed. David Marsh, 29-32. Public Services Contract DG EAC: European Commission, Strasbourg.

Brinton, Donna M. and Peter Master, eds. 1997. "New Ways in Content-Based Interaction," In *TESOL Series II Innovative Classroom Techniques*. Jack C. Richards Series Editor. Bloomington: Teachers of English to Speakers of Other Languages, Inc.

Chaput, Patricia. 1993. "Revitalizing the Traditional Program." In *Language and Content: Discipline- and Content-Based Approaches to Language Study*, ed. Merle Kreuger and Frank Ryan, 148-157. Lexington, MA: D.C. Heath.

CLIP: Content and Language Integrated project (CILT/DfES) Online: http://www.cilt.org.uk/clip/#toppage

Commission of the European Communities (1995) *White Paper: Teaching and Learning- Towards the Learning Society*, Objective IV, Council of Europe, DGV, Brussels.

Commission of the European Communities (2005) *A New Framework Strategy for Multilingualism* http://europa.eu.int/comm/education/policies/lang/doc/com596_en.pdf

Cook, Vivian. 2001. *Second Language Learning and Language Teaching 3rd edition* London: Arnold.

Coyle, Do. 2005. "Developing CLIL: Towards a Theory of Practice," *APAC Monograph* 6, APAC, Barcelona.

Crandall, JoAnn and G. Richard Tucker. 1990. "Content-based language instruction in second and foreign languages," *In Language teaching methodology for the nineties*, ed. Sarinee Anivan, 83-96. Singapore: SEAMEO Regional Language Centre. ED 366 187.

Cummins Jim and Merrill Swain. 1986. *Bilingualism in Education: Theory, Research and Policy.* London: Longman.

Dearing, Ron. 2007. *The Languages Review.* Nottingham: Department for Education and Skills Publications. http://www.teachernet.gov.uk/_doc/11124/LanguageReview.pdf (accessed 6 August 2007).

DfES (2002) *Languages for All: Languages for Life – A Strategy for England.* London: DfES.

Dörnyei, Zoltan. 2001. *Motivational Strategies in the Language Classroom.* Cambridge: Cambridge University Press.

Eurydice Report 2006 http://www.eurydice.org/

Genesee, Fred. 1994. *Educating Second Language Children.* New York: Cambridge University Press.

Graddol, David. 2006. *English Next* Plymouth: British Council

Grenfell, Michael, ed. 2002. *Modern Languages Across the Curriculum* London: Routledge Falmer

Holmes, Bernadette. 2005. *Language Learning for the 21st Century- the normalisation of Content and Language Integrated Learning (CLIL) within the curriculum for England Position Paper*: CILT

Hood, Philip. 2005. "Developing models for CLIL." In *The Final Report for the Content and Language Integrated Project*, ed. Rolf Wiesemes, 33. London: CILT

Krueger, Merle and Frank Ryan, eds. 1993. *Language and content: Discipline- and content-based approaches to language study*, 85-102. Lexington, MA: D.C. Heath.

Marsh, David. 2005. Guardian Weekly "Adding language without taking away". http://www.guardian.co.uk/guardianweekly/story/0,,1464367,00.html

—. ed. 2002. *CLIL/EMILE- The European Dimension: Actions, Trends and Foresight* Potential Public Services Contract DG EAC: European Commission.

Marsh, David, Bruce Marsland and Anne Maljers. 1999. *CLIL Initiatives for the Millenium: Report on the CEILINK Think-Tank*, Jyvaskyla: University Jyvaskyla.

Met, Myriam. 1998. "Curriculum decision-making in content-based language teaching." In *Beyond bilingualism: multilingualism and multilingual education*, ed. Carme Cenoz and Fred Genesee, 35-63. Clevedon: Multilingual Matters.

Mohan, Bernard. 1986. *Language and Content*, Reading, MA: Addison-Wesley.
The Office for National Statistics. "National Consensus 2001". http://www.statistics.gov.uk/census/default.asp (accessed 15 June, 2007).
Nuffield Language Inquiry. 2000. *The Final Report Nuffield Languages Enquiry Languages: the Next Generation*. London: Nuffield Foundation.
Nunan, David. 2004. *Task-Based Language Teaching*. Cambridge: Cambridge University Press.
OFSTED 1998 *Secondary Subject Reports 1996/1997 Modern Foreign Languages*. www.ofsted.gov.uk
Stoller, Fredricka, L. 2002. "Content-Based Instruction: A Shell for Language Teaching or a Framework for Strategic Language and Content Learning?" TESOL: Plenary Address, Salt Lake City, UT. http://www.carla.umn.edu/cobaltt/modules/index.html?curriculum/main.html (accessed 6 August 2007).
Wiesemes, Rolf. 2005. *The Final Report for the Content and Language Integrated Project*. London: CILT.
Willis, David and Jane R. Willis. 2001. "Task-based language learning." In *The Cambridge Guide to Teaching English to Speakers of Other Language*, ed. Ron Carter and David Nunan. Cambridge: Cambridge University Press.

RECOMMENDED READING: CONTENT LANGUAGE AND INTEGRATED LEARNING

Baetens Beardsmore, Hugo. 1993. *European Models of Bilingual Education.* Clevedon: Multilingual Matters.
Cenoz, Jasone and Fred Genesee, eds. 1998. *Beyond Bilingualism. Multilingualism and Multilingual Education.* Clevedon: Multilingual Matters.
Coyle, Do. 2005. *Developing CLIL: Towards a Theory of Practice*, APAC Monograph 6, APAC, Barcelona.
Coyle, Do. 2006 Motivation and CLIL *Scottish CILT* http://www.scilt.stir.ac.uk/SLR/Current%20Issue/SLR13%20Coyle.pdf
Dalton-Puffer, Christiane and Ute Smit, eds. 2007. *Empirical Perspectives on Clil Classroom Discourse (Sprache Im Kontext).* Pieterlen, Switzerland: Peter Lang.
Escobar, Cristina. 2002. "Attention and the processing of comprehensible input in communication tasks among secondary school learners." In *Beyond L2 Teaching. Research students in second language acquisition*, ed. A. Nizegorodcew, 45-52. Krakow: Jagiellonian University Press.
Fruhauf, Gianna, Do Coyle, and Ingeborg Christ, eds. 1996. *Teaching Content in a Foreign Language. Practice and Perspective in European Bilingual Education.* Stichting Europ des Platform voor het Nederlandse Onderwijs. Alkmaar.
Genesee, Fred. 1987. *Learning Through Two Languages.* Cambridge, MA: Newbury University Press.
Halliwell, Susan. 1992. *Teaching English in Primary School.* London & New York, Longman.
Marsh, David and Gisella Langé, eds. 2000. *Using Languages to Learn and Learning to Use Languages.* Jyväskylä, Finland: UniCOM, University of Jyväskylä.
Marsh, David, ed. 2002. *CLIL/EMILE— The European Dimension: Actions, Trends and Foresight Potential.* Strausbourg: Public Services Contract DG EAC: European Commission.

So, Daniel and Gary M. Jones, eds. 2002. *Education and Society in Plurilingual Contexts* Brussels: Vrije Universiteit Brussel Press.

Wilkinson, Robert, ed. 2004. *Integrating Content and Language. Meeting the Challenges of a Multilingual Higher Education.* Maastricht: Maastricht University Press.

PART II

NEW TEACHING AND LEARNING PARADIGMS FOR THE 21ST CENTURY

INTRODUCTION TO PART II

MELINDA DOOLY

I never teach my pupils; I only attempt to provide the conditions in which they can learn.
—Albert Einstein

In a fast changing global world, the needs and means for language learning are constantly evolving and these factors will influence the way languages are taught and learnt. Globalization is not only transforming many areas in terms of economy and commerce, but also in terms of education and culture. One relevant consequence of this is the rapid emergence of new resources and materials for language learning. The concept of resources, as explained earlier in the introduction to this book, should not be limited to the tangible, material concept of resources. New technologies, new scientific discoveries, new understandings of cognitive processes, new means of communication and travel, all of these factors contribute to the fact that time and space must be re-defined, new identities and new metaphors of understanding must be accepted as the norm inside the classroom. Thus, resources are best understood as the means or sources from which learning takes place –a wide definition which encompasses the many different ways in which language teaching strategies can emerge from a learner-centred environment.

Our world, our culture, our discourse practices and our literacy in those discourse practices are constantly being constructed and reconstructed by the tools (resources) we use (Bruner, 1985; Vygotsky, 1978). This implies that the way in which teachers employ the available resources or tools to orient and guide learners in constructing new knowledge will play a key role. Few will argue with the statement that literacy (indirectly brought about by printing) has had a dominant role in the Western culture for the last two or three hundred years. The importance of the written word is hardly ever questioned and the need, or better said, the expectancy to be literate (in the traditional sense of reading and writing) has dominated the educational scene since the inception of public schooling. The traditional tools (books, paper, pencil and pen) are not questioned either. Ironically, however, now confronted with a major shift from paper to digital, many stakeholders in the world of education question the relationship between education and "tools" emerging from this transformation and how knowledge is recovered, stored and passed on.

It can be argued that there is a need for more models of how to integrate emerging resources into the many variants of the language learning process. This may mean incorporating new findings into one's language teaching; or adding newly developed materials designed to enhance previously held theories about language learning into class materials (for instance, the use of the European Language Portfolio); or using hypermedia to create opportunities for purpose-based, authentic language learning. The focus in this section of the book is on the tool (portfolios, Internet, videocameras, drawings and so forth) as a support for learners to work together to construct knowledge. Within this innovative education paradigm even the learners themselves can and should be considered a resource –the human resource which is absolutely essential for integrative teaching strategies aiming to contextualize the learning process. Inevitably, this will generate different and more productive modes of discourse in the classroom. "Communication is not learned through language, but rather the reverse; language is learned through communicating" (Devitt, 1989: 7).

We begin with a section on Technology Integrated into Language Learning (TILL) which is an ever-growing sector of interest for language teachers. Following that, the next three articles are dedicated to the European Language Portfolio (ELP), a teaching resource that provides motivating possibilities for teachers and language learners alike. Our last chapter, entitled "Going beyond the parameters of the classroom" explains how "new paradigms" in language teaching and learning are helping to extend learning beyond the more traditional views of language education. Two of the articles discuss the move towards younger learners as potential resources themselves. As schools begin teaching students at younger ages, the teacher must look at each individual as a new and exciting source for learning in the language classroom. The last contribution looks at ways in which teachers are using language teaching as a resource for other development, such as the development of multiple intelligences. Despite this apparent diversity of the articles, all of the texts included in these sections have several points in common —not least of which is the fact that the authors have chosen to integrate different available resources into communicative, situated, meaningful language learning practices.

Works Cited

Bruner, Jerome. 1985. "Models of the Learner." *Educational Researcher* 14, 6: 5-8.

Devitt, Sean M. 1989. (Spring) "Classroom Discourse: its nature and its potential for language learning". *CLCS Occasional Paper N° 21*. Dublin (Ireland): Trinity College, Centre for Language and Communication Studies.

Vygotsky, Lev S. 1978. *Mind in society: The development of higher psychological processes.* Cambridge, MA: Harvard University Press.

Chapter Four

Technology Integrated into Language Learning: Introduction

Melinda Dooly

Materials used in language teaching have always been designed with the learner's needs in mind, however, the new opportunities brought about with the advent of diverse technologies have prompted many educators to rethink their approach to language teaching and to seek innovative ways of incorporating technological resources into their teaching. This may include using materials and tools that were not originally designed for language learning. Increasingly, language instructors are concerned with finding ways to ensure that their students have the opportunity to apply new knowledge acquired in the classroom to real communicative practice, as well as making sure that what students learn is relevant to their needs and many teachers are convinced that network-based communication fits this requirement nicely.

In the examination of learner needs it is becoming more and more apparent that language learning should simulate likely work conditions that students may face when they begin their professional lives, including using new technology to communicate in various languages. In today's world, this means an increase in the use of computer-mediated communication technologies to engage in either real-time (synchronous) or asynchronous communication among team members separated by great geographic distances. This might include business people working together on a trans-national project, doctors collaborating on research at a number of medical institutions around the world, or primary school teachers participating in an online conference. The possibilities seem infinite and students need to be prepared for these opportunities as much as possible.

Of course, technology is not new to the classroom. Beginning with the heavy use of audio equipment utilized by the audiolingual approach and moving to visual equipment, the use of cassettes and videos for "authentic" language exposure has become a common staple in most language classrooms. Spurred by the rapid inclusion of new technologies into everyday life, computer-assisted language learning (CALL) has also become a regular component in language classrooms, especially since the 1990s. Nonetheless, the ways in which technology is used as a language learning tool may differ considerably from context to context. For instance, in the case of computers, there is a growing movement to make use of Internet to engage in authentic communication with other speakers of the target language. This type of communication is often referred to as Computer-Mediated Communication (CMC) or Network-based Language Teaching (NBLT) and the emphasis is no longer on individual interaction between the student and the computer –the emphasis of the tool is upon facilitating interaction among learners, thus promoting collaboration and group participation.

As Sadler has indicated in his article "Computer-mediated communication and a cautionary tale of two cities" (2007), CMC and NBLT research in the field is abundant and the results of this research indicates that this type of learning framework enhances learner motivation (Paver, 2003; Samsonov, 2001; Warschauer, 1996). It has also been shown that networked learner interaction can reduce anxiety and produce more talk (Fanderclai, 1995); improve sociolinguistic proficiency (Belz and Kinginger, 2002, 2003; Meskill and Anthony, 2005); and increase self-confidence (Beauvois and Eledge, 1995; Ware, 2004). The importance this can have for students learning languages cannot be understated. A number of research studies have mentioned that CMC can strongly enhance participant motivation (Hofsoy, 2001) and also provide additional opportunities for authentic interaction and meaning negotiation (Kern, 1995; Smith et al., 2003). Other benefits include a reduction of anxiety accompanied by increased production of talk (Fanderclai, 1995) and an increase in self-confidence.

Perhaps even more importantly, research has found that the teacher's theoretical framework of learning has a direct link to the way in which teachers incorporate computer use into their teaching. A 1998 study of 655 American schools conducted by the National Science Foundation and the U.S. Department of Education found a relationship between teacher pedagogy and their use of computers in teaching –a socioconstructivist approach implied the use of computers for collaboration and communication (see Anderson and Ronnkvist, 1999). A later study conducted by Becker and Reil (2000) found that there was a clear relationship between teachers with constructivist principles and the way in which computers were used for facilitating knowledge. Not only were these teachers "more likely to have their students use computers on a regular basis during class time" they also engaged in more communicative, collaborative activities such as communicating with other people, analysing data or learning to work collaboratively.

Network-based language teaching can easily build upon constructive approaches which focus on content and task-based learning, learner autonomy and collaborative learning. The need for new strategies is not to simply re-do "old" educational practices; it is a requisite for preparing students for modern society. Students' future "employability" may well require knowledge of effective collaborative efforts as part of team work performance. As Gromik's chapter in this section indicates, the same can be said about learning to use digital filming and editing —it is fast becoming a valued skill both personally and professionally. Furthermore, the need for a storyboard (part of the planning period of movie-making) promotes collaboration and creativity as well as teaching project management skills and decision-making skills. As there are more and more outlets for video to be published online, this allows language learners to collaborate in video-making with other students throughout the world.

In today's world, there is high possibility that a language student living in a mountain village somewhere (in Estonia, for instance, which is one of the most advanced countries in Europe in providing wi-fi in public places) has, quite literally, the world at her keyboard (or perhaps webcam). She has access to thousands of potential language practice partners —both native and non-native speakers of the language she is studying. As computers and computer networks are becoming so widespread, especially in the younger generations, language teachers are obliged to reconsider the resources they use in their teaching. Just as no one could escape the so-called "print" culture of the last two centuries, there is now the inevitable evolution towards "new literacy" practices (a term coined in 1993 by Anderson to describe the changed literacy demands stemming from the new technologies in schools). And as the students become more technically "savvy", teachers often feel uncertain or uncomfortable about how to manage new technologies.

Sadler and Eröz' chapter highlights the fact that there is a need for more focus on teacher training in relation to network-based language environments —it is not infrequent to find the language teacher at a clear disadvantage compared to students who have much more knowledge about

ICT than the teacher. For many teachers, this can be a cause for anxiety, making them more reluctant to try new technological tools.

Inevitably, there are many issues which must be resolved before new technologies will be common-place within the classroom. Not least of these is the fact that access to technology is not egalitarian. (For a more in-depth discussion of this topic, see Warschauer's article "Electronic literacies: Language, culture, and power in online education" 1999). Many have argued that the insistence upon new technologies is driving in the wedge of inequality between already imbalanced societies and social classes even further. No matter how one stands on the issue, few can argue that advances in technology have now dramatically changed the way people live, work and play. However, these circumstances place many youth who do not have easy access to new technology at a disadvantage in the classroom, in the job market and they are then ill-equipped to take up some positions in society which will inevitably require these skills and knowledge. These conflicts have yet to be resolved; however we have three examples of language learning which converge with new technologies to offer highly challenging, but rewarding learning opportunities for all their students.

In the first article of this section, Gromik considers the way in which the increasing presence of inexpensive and easy to use video equipment with computers has allowed movie making to become a tangible learning strategy. Such technological combinations empower students to gain greater control over their ability to express their opinion and to share it with the wider online community. Based on this precept, the author describes how movie making has been integrated into the curriculum for advanced Japanese EFL learners at Tohoku University. The chapter focuses on three approaches which places learners in the production seat, consequently encouraging them to become more aware of how they use prior knowledge, thinking and learning skills to express their opinions to an audience.

In the second article, Dooly and Ellermann describe an online project between two schools, one in France and one in Germany that aimed to develop students' Intercultural Communicative Competence (ICC) within the framework of the two foreign language classes. The chapter outlines in detail the designing of the project, with emphasis on the way in which ICC was integrated into both the online activities and the face-to-face activities of the students.

In the final article, Sadler and Eröz describe a teacher training programme which endeavoured to cover the gap between teachers' competences in the use of ICT modes and current teaching practices. The

"How we're going about it": Teachers' Voices on Innovative Approaches to Teaching and Learning Languages

chapter describes a transnational programme coordinated between the University of Illinois at Urbana-Champaign (USA) and Middle East Turkey University. While the programme covered nine different ICT modes, the authors concentrate their attention on the electronic discussion board to explain the way the students explored the mode both theoretically and empirically and then designed teaching units to integrate forums into their curriculums.

Works Cited

Anderson, Jim. (April, 1993) *The New Literacy and Technology*. Keynote address to the 38th International Reading Association Convention, San Antonio, Texas.

Anderson, Ronald E. and Amy Ronnkvist. 1999 *The presence of computers in American schools (Report #2)*. Irvine, CA: Center for Research on Information Technology and Organizations, University of California, Irvine, and the University of Minnesota.

Beauvois, Margaret Healy and Jean Eledge. 1995. "Personality types and megabytes: Student attitudes toward computer mediated communication (CMC) in the language classroom." *CALICO journal, 13*(2&3), 27-45.

Becker, Henry Jay and Margaret M. Reil. 2000. *Teacher Professional Engagement and Constructivist-Compatible computer use (Report #7)*. Irvine, CA: Center for Research on Information Technology and Organizations, University of California, Irvine, and the University of Minnesota.

Belz, Julie A. and Celeste Kinginger. 2002. "The cross-linguistics development of address form use in telecollaborative language learning: Two case studies." *Canadian Modern Language Review/Revue canadienne des langues vivant, 59*(2), 189-214.

Belz, Julie A. and Celeste Kinginger. 2003. "Discourse options and the development of pragmatic competence by classroom learners of German: The case of address forms." *Language Learning, 53*(4), 591-647.

Fanderclai, Tari Lin. 1995. "MUDs in education: New environment, new pedagogies." *Computer-Mediated Communication Magazine, 2*, 8-10.

Hofsoy, Morten B. 2001. *Network-based EFL: Motivational aspects of using networked computers in the EFL classroom*. University of Bergen. Available at: [http://www.ub.uib.no/elpub/2001/h/501001/Hovedoppgave.pdf] Accessed 20 August 2007.

Kern, Richard. 1995. "Restructuring classroom interaction with networked computers: Effects on quantity and characteristics of language production." *The Modern Language Journal, 79*(4), 457-476.

Meskill, Carla and Natasha Anthony. 2005. "Foreign language learning with CMC: Forms of online instructional discourse in a hybrid Russian class." *System, 33*, 89-105.

Paver, Jennifer A. 2003. *The zone of proximal development in an online ESL composition course.* Unpublished Master's Thesis, University of Nevada, Las Vegas.

Sadler, Randall. 2007. "Computer-mediated communication and a cautionary tale of two cities." *CALICO Journal* 25(1). Available at [https://www.calico.org/a-667-Computermediated%20Communication%20and%20a%20Cautionary%20Tale%20of%20Two%20Cities.html]

Samsonov, Pavel. 2001. *Effectiveness of teaching a part of a foreign language course through computer-mediated communication as perceived by the students of Texas A&M university and military reservists: A case study.* Unpublished doctoral dissertation, Texas A&M University.

Smith, Bryan, Maria José Alvarez-Torres and Zhao Young. 2003. "Features of CMC technologies and their impact on language learners' online interaction." *Computer in Human Behavior, 19*(6), 703-729.

Ware, Paige D. 2004. "Confidence and competition online: ESL student perspectives on web-based discussions in the classroom." *Computer and Composition, 21*(4), 451-468.

Warschauer, Mark. 1996. "Motivational aspects of using computers for writing and communication." In *Telecollaboration in foreign language learning,* ed. Mark Warschauer, 29-46. Honolulu: University of Hawaii Press.

—. 1999. *Electronic literacies: Language, culture, and power in online education.* Mahwah, NJ, Lawrence Erlbaum Associates.

LIGHTS! CAMERA! ACTION! A VIDEO PROJECT FOR THE WEB 2.0 CLASSROOM

NICOLAS GROMIK

And for seizing the reins of the global media, for founding and framing the new digital democracy, for working for nothing and beating the pros at their own game, TIME's Person of the Year for 2006 is you.
—Grossman, 2006: 23

Audiovisual resources have been an important element in education to expose students to content, as well as to raise their cultural and linguistic awareness of the target language. However, such resources have constantly maintained students in the consumer seat. Whether students completed a worksheet or filled in a software comprehension activity, the task and the computer kept authentic communicative activities in the background. Such constraining learning environments are slowly changing, because as Warschauer (2005) notes, media literacy is empowering learners to become active agents in the construction of authentic artifacts which can become online resources. As Grossman states in the quote above, video production and Web 2.0 technology is giving a voice to individuals and these individuals are our students.

The aim of this article is to document the possibility of empowering language learners to create and edit their own video productions. The information reported in this article is based on three years of Action Research, student observation, discussion and feedback as well as data collected from end of term exams. Nonetheless, since providing evidence of the benefits of learning outcome is beyond the scope of this article, the focus is rather on exemplifying approaches that assist teachers prepare themselves to deliver, support and manage a video production project in the language classroom. The first part of the article focuses on; 1) sociocultural framework and video production, 2) learning development consideration, 3) equipment and resources organization, and 4) suitable project selection. The second begins with a detailed description of two on going projects at my university and it finishes with an explanation about publishing students' final productions online. To begin, the educational environment from which this article emerged is described.

Educational Environment

Video production is integrated in the EFL syllabus for advanced Japanese EFL learners at Tohoku University. This university located in Sendai welcomes students from various parts of Japan (for example, Hokkaido, Tokyo, Osaka and Fukuoka). The Advanced Communicative Language course is conducted in the university CALL lab which comprises thirty Windows XP computers. This is a ninety minutes elective course which meets once a week for an average of 15 classes per term. Students from various departments (such as Education or Law), with at least a "B" grade (80% or above) in their former English studies, or with a TOEIC score of 700 points or above participate in this course. Therefore student numbers are usually low, between 5 to 10 members.

Japanese students complete six years of formal English studies from junior high school to senior high school. Their studies of English are formal; they are primarily exposed to extensive drills and testing to improve their memorization of the target language. At the university level, students are required to complete two more years of English studies. While their first year continues to emphasize grammar and vocabulary exposure, the second year allows them to either extend their grammar cognizance or to experiment with native teacher led communicative classes.

With this knowledge in mind, while designing a suitable language learning syllabus in 2003, it was decided that a sociocultural teaching approach that gives prominence to prior knowledge, peer to peer scaffolding and independent studies to enhance lifelong learning skills was most suitable. Since students who enroll in the Advanced Communicative language course may have limited communicative experiences and technological exposure, a socioculturally-based video production project would provide them with an authentic and engaging learning environment.

Video production and the sociocultural framework

While defining the Zone of Proximal Development, Vygotsky (1978) explains that

> [t]he zone of proximal development defines those functions that have not yet matured but are in the process of maturation, functions that will mature tomorrow but are currently in an embryonic state. (p. 86)

As explained previously Japanese language learners who select to participate in the Advanced Communicative language course may have seven years of language learning experience. Therefore the premise of the Advanced Communicative syllabus is that these students have some prior knowledge of English and that some of this knowledge may not have been used to speak spontaneously but rather to read and appreciate grammatical structures. Thus the aim of the video production project is to give students a context for stimulating the embryonic state of their cognizance. Furthermore, Vygotsky (1978) states that "in play a child always behaves beyond his average age, above his daily behavior" (p.102). What ensues is a brief explanation about how the objectives of role play stimulate students in the creation of their production.

In terms of peer to peer scaffolding, students share the burden of writing their script. However, most importantly, during the writing stage students usually write their dialogues as if they were writing a report. The story generally does not flow and does not provide any information about cause and effect between characters, location or action. Also in this early stage students spend a lot of time writing their scenarios, but do not understand that it will be connected with the visual element. Therefore with teacher guidance students begin to think about the final film; how to explain an event, and reveal the intentions of the characters in a near native like relaxed conversation. At this stage, instead of correcting students' work, I provide them with examples of storyboards that they can use to connect the written with the visual elements (for examples of storyboards see Stempleski and Tomalin, 2001).

The pre-edited film performance evidence reveals the extent to which some students will prepare themselves to act like professional actors. Students usually either place cue cards in their field of reading vision or they remember segments of their speech and only film that segment until all the segments are filmed to the desired level. Some students may decide to re-film segments until they are satisfied with their performance. Evidence reveals that during the filming stage some students exchange acting tips and opinions, thus repeating a scene until both students are either satisfied or simply give up and move to the next scene.

The film editing stage reveals to students how they act and speak. It is usually a fun time because it challenges their perception about their use of the target language. Nonetheless, students need direction with this phase of the project. They need to understand how to: select their best performance (based on whether or not they break their dialogue with first language utterances or hesitation and interruptions, or if action or lighting are not used effectively); use the video effects and transitions effectively; insert and sync music and make pictures from their films. During classroom editing sessions, observations have revealed that most students will be able to recognize what makes a good film segment worth keeping and peer to peer collaboration will engage students in discussion as to their preference of one segment over another. In contrast, few students will have video editing expertise; once they understand the basic tools, students will be able to edit their film to a satisfactory level.

As can be deduced from the brief evidence above, during the whole process students are engaged in planning, monitoring and evaluating their contribution towards the full film construction until they achieve the final satisfactory production (Wenden, 2002). Finally, the whole process is governed by students' linguistic abilities, historical experiences with language learning, social maturity in working in teams and a connection with the objectives of the course (Lantolf and Pavlenko, 2001). Hence as Vygotsky (1978) explained, the Zone of Proximal Development is the gap between what the student is and is able to do at the beginning of the task without assistance and what she will become and be able to do given a learning environment which is mediated by tools, interaction and signs.

Success for integrating video projects in the language classroom depends on the teacher's access to the required equipment and facilities. The next part of the article discusses these issues.

Organizing the Course

For students to appreciate the benefits that a video production project can present, teachers need to be familiar with the software and have strategies in place to undertake such a project. Concerning the hardware, the projects outlined in this article use video editing software which are included in computer packages; for example Apple's iMovie (2005) and Microsoft's Windows Movie Maker (2004). This software is free, already installed, extremely user friendly and their manufacturers provide online tutorials. Other online services such as Atomic Learning (2006) also provide video tutorials.

In terms of equipment teachers will need to have access to:
- Digital video camera (with inbuilt microphone)
- Compatible computer and software
- Compatible cables (to transfer the film from camera to computer)
- Digital videotapes
- Batteries and battery charger
- CD or DVD recorder and CDs or DVDs to archive projects
- Tripod

- Attachable microphone (for better quality audio)
- Projector to display students' work to the class
- Portable Hard Drive

Finally, depending on the quantity of available equipment, teachers may need to organize a borrowing schedule and reserve the computer room in advance. Another important factor is that teachers need to discuss with their administration issues such as borrowing/lending process and insurance policies.

The assessment outline, Skehan (2003) and Hughes (2003) inform, should provide sufficient direction without constricting students' creative thinking and be achievable within the time assigned. An appropriate assessment engages students to consider and negotiate suitable topics or issues to be filmed. Gromik (2006) suggests using rubrics, as well as letting students assess peers' productions.

Once these matters are organized and the assessment criteria is designed, the teacher can either provide a list of suggested appropriate projects, or guide students to discuss and select topics that they think would be of interest to them.

Projects

Visits to Yahoo! Video (2006), youtube.com (2007) and other such video storage websites will reveal myriads of video projects that students could embark on. Sherman's (2003) text provides a variety of detailed projects categorized by genres that students could undertake. While Forrest's (1992) article explains the process of improvising video drama, Burston's (2005) investigates the possibility of video dubbing to incite students' verbal production. It is possible to undertake whole class projects (Ryan, 2003; Sharp, 2005), or as this article suggests, pair work productions.

Since it is possible that some of the Tohoku University students come from different areas of Japan, the documentary film genre is perceived to be suitable. Firstly, some students may not be familiar with Sendai's history, monuments and organizations, so documentary film making is an appropriate approach to encourage students to investigate their host city. Second, the aim of a documentary is to educate, to share one's view and opinion with others or as Ellis & McLane (2005) explain "to turn citizen's attention to … factors to be considered" (p.59). Furthermore, in terms of production, documentary film does not require many actors or a lot of staging. Dialogues are kept to a minimum and narration is the most preferred approach to describe the theme under focus. Finally, as Dufon

(2002) explains, filming and editing will come to play a stronger role in professional skills; for example, to provide future teachers with research data collection skills and improve the outcome of their research. Thus documentary film as a project-based activity is perceived as providing long term practical skills.

Movie Making Projects

Participants create and edit two video productions. These projects have identical requirements and objectives; i.e. to promote tourist areas and services available in Sendai city. For beginners with limited technical knowledge, editing can be a demanding creative task. It was observed that once students had some experience with the editing process and features, they would be better prepared to operate the English editing software equivalent. Therefore, these projects have one distinctive difference. The first film is edited with Japanese software on campus. The second film is edited with the teacher's English software and computer.

One minute project: For the one minute commercial project, I established contact with Non-Profit Organizations (NPO) located in Sendai. After explaining the purpose of the films and the time constraints set by the term schedule, I was able to find willing NPOs interested in participating in this project. Students are given the contact details and it is then their responsibility to arrange a suitable filming program and location with the NPO. Students are also fully responsible for editing and completing the films by the due date. Three weeks is allocated for this task.

Once students hand in their first project one lesson addresses the following topics. At the beginning of the class students view all the one minute films and they are encouraged to take notes about best filming strategies. Thereafter, a brief discussion ensues whereby class members comment on their editing experiences. Since students may not have commented on all the aspects of the editing process, they are then provided with an English editing guideline from mightycoach (ROOT, 2003). The purpose for providing this guideline is to begin another discussion which relates students' first video editing experience with professional suggestions and to highlight the differences. The final part of the lesson covers the issue of picture and music copyright law. Students peruse an article concerning Creative Commons licences (see Phillips 2006). Since music is a contentious topic, students are advised to access audio resources from either ccMixter.com or Jamendo.com as both of these websites provide access to Creative Commons licences based free music. The teacher explains that during the editing stage students need to attribute or recognize the work of the artist and the song retrieved as well as the location where the music was retrieved from. This process is very similar to academic referencing.

There are two reasons for establishing a small project before embarking students on a bigger video production project. First, it allows teachers to consider which students require assistance during the second project. This enables better team allocation judgments for the second project. For example with an odd number of students it might be possible to notice that one student has the necessary creativity and drive to undertake a project independently. The second reason is that it gives students confidence to manage their project. They become better able to recognize their abilities, to develop problem solving skills and to decide when they need assistance.

The general feedback gathered from students is that at first they imagine that making a one minute film will be extremely difficult and they feel unprepared for taking the responsibility of managing their film and contacting and organizing the NPO members. However since the aim of the first project is to experience film production and not the artistic and lexical performance, once they have completed the first project, students have a better understanding of the video editing process and are better equipped to deal with the five minute project.

With the five minute project, students select an original tourist spot in Sendai of interest to them. Then they contact the selected site and check that they are allowed to film certain parts of the facilities. For example, museums might not be favorable to having some of their major works filmed and broadcasted to the general public. Due to the length and format of the second project, students are encouraged to write a script, design storyboards, select and collect appropriate images, suitable music, as well as organize a filming schedule. Four weeks is allocated for filming and one week for editing.

Once students have completed filming a touristy location in Sendai, they are ready for editing. To do this, they make an appointment to use the English computer. Editing a five minute film may take up to four hours, especially since students use the English software. Therefore the teacher must ensure that enough time is available for students to access the computer.

The second editing project session requires that students explore the software further to complete a more semi-professional film. This may include overlaying a few audio tracks over one another, or it may require using certain editing effects to improve the flow of the film. During the editing stage of the second project, students have time to explore the artistic creation of video production, this may include creating pictures from the film, retrieving audio from certain parts of the film and moving it to another part, or it might involve matching lyrics of the audio track to particular visual acting.

Since the students use the teacher's English computer to edit their film, I have observed that when editing a video using the English software, Japanese students do not automatically converse in the target language. I have noticed that first students express their ideas and explore solutions in the L1. When they have either exhausted all solutions or they have reached an agreement, then they are ready to seek advice. Some students have commented that once they have discussed their problems in the first language, they feel more confident speaking in English about their editing strategy. Another approach is to ask students to give a progress report or to explain the tasks that remain to be completed for the next editing session.

During the editing process of the second project, I do not interfere with the work that students undertake in my office. Even when the computer is overworked and it crashes, I let the students solve their problem so that they can experience safely technical constraints and become familiar with the unpredictable idiosyncrasies of computers, for this is also part of learning about technology. This is why it is important for teachers to save students' original films.

Once the second projects are completed, consideration must be given to storing the final productions. The next section briefly explores firstly the issue of storing video productions and secondly video blogging which is a new form of online delivery of audiovisual productions.

Storing video productions

Storing video productions occurs at many stages. First, in case projects are accidentally lost, teachers need to save all students' pre-edited films. These are usually large files and a portable Hard Drive is recommended. Thereafter teachers have the option to delete or to save them on other storage devices. Edited films are usually smaller in file size and can be catalogued on DVDs.

Before contemplating using students' productions as potential teaching resources, teachers need students' consent to display their work. Third party participants' consent is also needed. Explaining how video productions will be used is a motivating component and makes a good topic of conversation with students.

There are a few options available for utilizing students' work. Videos can be delivered on the course's website. They can become part of teaching resources to be used by future students. They can be entered in competitions such as the Hometown Video Alliance (Alliance for Community Media, n.d.), or iLife Educator Award (Apple computer 2006a). Finally the best productions can be displayed to the general public via a school event or the local television network (Harding, 2001). Depending whether or not students can complete their project ahead of schedule, it may be possible to expose students to the process of embedding videos in blogs.

Online delivery: videoblogs

For teachers interested in creating and delivering students' video productions online, the internet is providing better and more reliable video storage services, such as dailymotion.com, blip.tv, ourmedia.org or youtube.com and myspace.com. Since these are generally free, subscribers are not confined to one product, instead they can use the service which provides the most useful feature for the task, and this section of the article explains how teachers can make use of these services (see Gromik, 2007a). For a virtual demonstration about uploading videos online go to Jason's (2007) video tutorial at:
http://www.teachertube.com/view_video.php?viewkey=3847419bb3de39a609af

The internet provides an increasing number of services which makes the process of storing and cataloguing videos feasible. While Campbell (2007) provides a checklist for selecting a blog service, Gromik (2007b) explains the process for embedding videos into a blog.

Conclusion

While explaining the whole process of video production as a project based learning approach, from script writing, to filming, editing, storing and delivering it online, this article provides evidence that such a project is manageable by both learners and educators. After investigating a few film genres, documentary film making was perceived to meet the needs of a transient student community. The article reveals that providing students with two projects allows them first to become familiar with the process of editing a film and second to consolidate and extend upon their newly acquired skill. The overall objective of this article was to demonstrate how sociocultural concepts such as mediation, the Zone of Proximal Development and socio-historical and cultural backgrounds assists learners utilize their prior knowledge of English in order to undertake an authentic project as well as provide them with the knowledge base to express their opinions about a selected theme.

Much remains to be discovered about the relationship between video production and students' learning development, linguistic gains, as well as best teaching strategies. Considering the constant technological developments, such as iPods and smart phones, educators and researchers can no longer ignore the opportunities that the internet and technological devices are offering to learners, who can now not only access global information at the click of a button, but who can also broadcast their self-generated news.

Works Cited

Burston, Jack. 2005. "Video dubbing projects in the foreign language curriculum." *Calico Journal*, 23(1), 79-92.

Campbell, Aaron. 2005. "Weblog applications for EFL/ESL classroom blogging: a comparative review." *TESL-EJ*, 9(3). http://www-writing.berkeley.edu/TESL-EJ/ej35/m1.html (accessed 7 August 2007).

DuFon, Margaret A. 2002. "Video recording in ethnographic SLA research: Some issues of validity in data collection." *Language Learning & Technology*, 6(1), 40-59.

Ellis, Jack C. and Betsy A. McLane. 2005. *A New History of Documentary Film*. London: Continuum Publishing Group.

Forrest, Tracey. 1992. "Shooting your class: The videodrama approach to language acquisition." In *Video in second language teaching: Using, selecting, and producing video for the classroom*, ed. Susan Stempleski and Paul Arcario, 316-318. Alexandria, VA: Teachers of English to Speakers of Other Languages, Inc.

Gromik, Nicolas. 2007a. "Video casting: what's in it for the teachers and students?" *The Language Teacher*, 31(2), 26-27.

—. 2007b. "From film editing to video blogging: what are the steps?" Paper presented at the IATEFL Wireless Ready 2007 conference, Nagoya, Japan, March 24 2007.

—. 2006. "Meaningful tasks with video in the ESOL classroom." In *Language Learning Through Technology*, ed. Elizabeth Hanson-Smith and Sarah Rilling, 109-123. Alexandria, VA: TESOL.

Grossman, Lev. 2006. "Person of the Year: You." *Times*, December, 20-23.

Harding, Thomas. 2001. *The Video Activist Handbook*. London: Pluto Press.
Hughes, Arthur. 2003. *Testing for Language Teachers*. Cambridge: Cambridge University Press.
Lantolf, James P. and Aneta Pavlenko. 2001. "(S)econd (L)anguage (A)ctivity theory: Understanding Second language learners as people." In *Learner Contributions to Language Learning: New Directions in Research,* ed. Michael P. Breen, 141- 158. Harlow, Essex: Pearson Education.
Phillips, Jonathan. 2006. "Licence to create." *Linux Format*, 81, 60-63. Retrieved from http://www.linuxformat.co.uk/mag/creativecommons.pfd
Ryan, Stephan. 2003. "Practical digital video in the language classroom." *C@lling Japan,* 11(1), 12-16.
Richardson, Will. 2005. "The educator's guide to the read/write Web." *Educational Leadership,* 24-27.
Sharp, Steven K. 2005. "A Blueprint for successful video projects." *Essential Teacher,* 2(1), 36-37.
Sherman, Jane. 2003. *Using Authentic Video in the Language Classroom.* Cambridge: Cambridge University Press.
Skehan, Peter. 2003. "Focus on form, tasks, and technology." *Computer-Assisted Language Learning,* 16(5), 391-411.
Stempleski, Susan and Barry Tomalin. 2001. *Film.* Oxford: Oxford University Press.
Vygotsky, Lev .S. 1978. *Mind in Society.* London: Harvard University Press.
Warschauer, Mark. 2005. "Sociocultural perspectives on CALL." In *CALL Research Perspectives,* ed. Joy L. Egbert and Gina Mikel Petrie, 41-51. Mahwah, New Jersey: Lawrence Erlbaum Associates.
Wenden, Anita L. 2002. "Learner development in language learning." *Applied Linguistics,* 23(1), 32-55.

Websites and Software for video editing

Atomic Learning, http://www.atomiclearning.com
Bliptv., http://blip.tv/
Blogger.com, https://www.blogger.com/start
CreativeCommon, http://creativecommons.org/about/licenses/meet-the-licenses
Google, http://video.google.com/
Hometown Video Alliance,

http://www.alliancecm.org/index.php?page_id=7
iMovie, http://www.apple.com/support/imovie
iLife Educator Award, http://www.apple.com/education/ilifeawards
Jason (2007), Uploading a video on teachertube, retrieved April 25, 2007 from http://www.teachertube.com/view_video.php?viewkey=3847419bb3de39a609af
Mightycoach, http://www.mightycoach.com/articles/mm2/index.html
Tohoku University blog, http://sendai-city-tourism-tohoku-university.blip.tv/
Videogrunt, http://gruntmedia.com/Welcome_to_gruntmedia.html
Windows Movie Maker, http://www.microsoft.com/windowsxp/using/moviemaker/default.mspx
Yahoo!, http://video.yahoo.com/
Youtube.com, http://youtube.com/
Education Service Center Region12 (2003) http://www.esc12.net/pitx/htm/storyboard.htm

ENGAGING YOUNG LEARNERS IN ONLINE INTERCULTURAL LEARNING: THE MICALL PROJECT

MELINDA DOOLY AND CARMEN ELLERMANN

The project described here was actually part of a larger European Union funded project, called MICaLL (Moderating Intercultural Communication and Language Learning)[1]. The two schools, Ecole elémentaire publique de L'Huisserie (Laval, France) and *Grund- und Hauptschule mit Werkrealschule* (Neckargemünd, Germany), were partnered within the wider MICaLL project. One of the MICaLL project's aims was to promote the development of teacher and teacher trainee competences in the area of online collaborative teaching, so the members of the project were necessarily involved in hands-on experiences of setting up and carrying out online international projects. Both of the schools mentioned had had previous experience with international, online projects, thus the partner members were aware of the responsibilities and opportunities which such experiences entail.

The two schools, while part of a wider project, had complete autonomy in decisions about the type of collaborative activities they would carry out and how to design and implement them. This "upped the ante" in the sense that the experience was empirical for all the stakeholders involved (teachers and students alike). As many teachers may have found out through previous experience in international projects, the planning, designing, developing and implementing of a project that encompasses partners from different countries requires a wide range of knowledge and skills, not least of which is Intercultural Communication Competences (ICC). This meant that the participants in the project were acquiring new technology *and* ICC skills, while teaching and learning languages in a motivating, meaningful environment.

---

[1] This was a Comenius 2.1 project (118762-CP-1-2004-NL-COMENIUS-C21) which ran from 2004 to 2007.

Before starting: Designing the project

Some principal aims established during the design phase of the project were to use the online activities to develop the pupils' Intercultural Communicative Competence (ICC), promote a positive evolution of the pupils' cultural and social perspectives, improve their media competence and, at the same time, expand their knowledge of the target language (English, although French and German were also used by the students in their exchanges).

Before involving the pupils, the partner teachers went through a preparatory stage at the "local" level which included clarifying the project details with the school administration, (for instance, arrangement of unlimited access to the computer room). The partners also had to discuss the timeframe for the project (the project went on for four months from February to June 2006.) It was also very important to fully inform the pupils' parents about all the different aspects of the project, especially the legal aspects concerning pupils' rights and privacy on the Internet. Signatures from the parents or legal guardians were gathered, in which they agreed to the posting of personal texts and pictures on the portal (note that the material on the portal was exclusive to portal users).

Next the teachers had to look at the organization and availability of technical tools in the school computer labs and request installation of any material lacking for the project. High-speed-internet access was required as well as other equipment such as individual head phones, scanners and webcams. Following this, the teachers tested the software they would be using (in this case, a portal made available through the MICaLL project) and the team members decided on how to most efficiently employ the available portal features.

When designing the tasks, it was important to keep in mind the age group and language levels of the pupils in the project. Both schools participated with a class of year 5 pupils, meaning that the students were between 10 and 11. Both classes had had basic lessons in computer skills and typing, however there were differences between the classes when it came to the amount of time they had spent studying English as a Foreign Language. The French students were in their third year of English while this was the first year for the German students. This meant designing the project so that the children were confident they could reach both the technical and linguistic goals of the project and not become frustrated in the process.

In the design of the project, the partners decided to have the pupils introduce themselves as a first task—using their previous knowledge of the target language to write simple introductions and to record themselves in a short oral presentation. The teachers were aware of the fact that there would be new vocabulary that the students would have to deal with during the project phase so it was then decided that it would be better to focus on the oral aspects of communicating online via audio-blogs and live chats.

Also, in order to avoid asking the pupils to create long difficult English texts which would require considerable in-class time to decode, the pupils were requested to illustrate their understanding of intercultural issues which came up during the project, which were then scanned and later posted in the project portal. This was more appropriate for their age and language level although admittedly for more advanced students the pictures could be accompanied by short texts suitable to the students' ages and language levels.

After agreeing upon all the activities to be covered during the project period, the partner teachers exchanged emails about their schedules in order to draw up a first complete outline for the project. This included an overview of the different vacations and national holidays in both countries during the project duration. This was an especially relevant part of the project design as it is often the "small" details that "trip up" an online project. As Warschauer, Schetzer and Meloni (2000: 41) point out, "usually, planning and implementing interclass projects requires a great deal of time and energy, and in some cases these projects achieve disappointing results because of logistical or coordination difficulties". Bearing that warning in mind, the teachers made sure that they had a fixed table of regular times when they contacted each other online (e-mails, blogging, text chatting or using skype for audio chatting) so that they could discuss any important issues of the project which came up. They also made sure that the activities fit both schools' timetables. This was one of the major components of making this telecollaboration work. Without having set this up the project could not have been successful.

Getting started: Integrating new technology and the textbooks

The first step of the project was to get the pupils to introduce themselves through an audio-blog. To further enhance a feeling that the students were getting to know each other and to give them a "virtual" space to add personal items, the pupils' set up individual homepages in the portal. This way the pupils could tell about their interests and hobbies, accompanied by images and links. They could then discover similar information about their partners.

Fig. 4-1 Part of a student's homepage

> **My name's Alexis.**
> *I'm ten years old.*
> *I was born on 21th of april 1995.*
> *I was born under the taurus sign.*
> *I have got a cat and a dog.*
> *I like playing badminton.*
> *Red is my favourite colour.*
> *I would like to become a fireman.*
> *My favourite car is ferrari.*
> *I've got blond hair.*
> *I've got blue eyes.*
> *My favourite meal is fish.*

An important part of the organisation of the project involved setting up "local" work groups, as suggested by Warschauer *et al.*:

> ..in the early stages of a project, students should develop teams ... and should be encouraged to engage in friendly introductions. Taking time for some personal communication will humanize the long-distance partners and establish better working relations, not to mention making the project a more enjoyable experience for everyone (Warschauer, Schetzer & Meloni 2000:43).

The teams were composed of four French pupils and two German pupils. Each team came up with a group name and a group logo for themselves. By using dictionaries, the German pupils wrote a first e-mail to their partner team introducing themselves shortly after finishing the audio-blog in which they referred to their individual homepages.

Following this, the activities began to link several units of the pupils' English textbook which both schools had in common. For instance, when the topic *Places in town* was taught, the German pupils created an English description of their home town and in the following lesson they came up with a useful text to show their partner class where they lived. Each pupil was assigned one line and the lines were audio-recorded with a digital

MP3-recorder. The file was then uploaded to the MICaLL portal (see figure 4.2). The French pupils presented their hometown through a computer slide-show of their town, with an accompanying "narrative soundtrack", produced by the pupils.

In order to integrate listening and speaking skills, both classes wrote and recorded a class song (the German students created a "rap"). The lyrics were uploaded as word-files for the partner schools to follow along. The pupils at first found it slightly embarrassing to hear their own voices using English, but later were proud of their achievements and moreover, the pupils discovered that other learners of English make similar mistakes in pronunciation as well. From then on, they were less inhibited to speak in the target language.

Fig. 4-2 Students' rap songs

listen to the text, because we recorded it.

Click here to read the text "Our town"!

Click here to listen to the audio file "Our town"!

We also created a rap song.

The name of *our rap song is "Class Five Rap"*.

You can again read the text of the rap song, then click here.

Or you can listen to our rap song, then click here.

Focusing on the Intercultural aspect: The children's book "Das Land der Ecken"

The project did not just focus on language learning. The students at each school were introduced to the book "Das Land der Ecken" by Irene Ulitzka and Gerhard Gepp[2]. This enhanced the intercultural aspect of the exchange through discussion of the book and the connections the pupils could see between the book and the project itself. Because the book deals with two characters who are from different countries and who eventually become friends, the students could identify the parallelisms in the story and the activities they had carried out, e.g. the characters in the book talk about their hometowns and describe their way of life to each other. The pupils talked about their experiences of going abroad and were able to identify situations when they felt foreign and misunderstood.

As part of the online activities, the pupils drew their own version of a "Das Land der Ecken" (which evokes an imaginary country). The pictures of each group were scanned and posted in the portal, along with descriptions written by the pupils. The partner school had to share their opinions about whether they agreed with these interpretations and then the students drew the country a second time, with further clarification of the drawings. In the outline of the project design, a third picture, created by the teams, was intended however this could not be carried out (see the next section).

Difficulties and how they were resolved

One of the first difficulties encountered within the partnership was the difference in number of students involved. There were 29 French students and 16 German students (one of whom left during the year), which meant that they had to form teams of two to four members (ideally, it would have been partners of two on each side). Nonetheless, the groups were matched age-wise and the teachers ensured that the group members had similar hobbies and could thus "identify" with each other. This helped create a positive attitude about the partner groups. As a final step towards group consolidation after the group partners had introduced themselves they exchanged pictures through their homepages, which further aided the

---

[2] This book is part of the European Picture Book Collection (EPBC). The collection was designed to help pupils to find out more about their European neighbours through reading the visual narratives of carefully chosen picture books. You can visit the site at http://www.ncrcl.ac.uk/epbc/EN/index.asp

sense of group solidarity. It was considered optimal that the students have opportunities to hear and see their partners, otherwise they would have remained anonymous to each other and they may not become personally interested and engaged in the project and in the collaboration.

Also, as often happens in online projects, the student profiles of the partners did not coincide completely. As was mentioned earlier, the German students had more class time in the target language per week (five hours) than the French students (one hour). On top of that, this was the first year of English as a Foreign Language for the German students (in their year 5) and the third year for the French. This undercut considerably the original idea of establishing a synchronous, communicative approach in the project since the French students did not have enough time to "stay in touch" with their German counterparts and the teachers were worried that the students would become frustrated by their very basic knowledge of both the target language and typing skills. (Often, the importance of this skill is overlooked when planning online collaborative projects).

Timing and work schedules were also inhibiting factors in the outcome of the project. The project did not really get off the ground as soon as had been anticipated, largely due to the overlapping of other projects in the French school, thus taking away time and effort by that teacher. Inevitably, if such collaborative efforts are spearheaded by only one person in a school, it is easier for extenuating circumstances to affect the entire project. The German partnership did incorporate more members into their local team before the end of the term and this helped distribute the tasks and spread the responsibilities. To compensate for the lesser amount of exposure to the partner culture, the teachers incorporated extra information about the partner culture into the regular class material (reviews of television shows, films, discussions, etc.).

As mentioned above, it was meant by the partner teachers to finish the project by creating a third picture by each group with the theme of "Our Dream School" (relating this to the work they had done previously on the book "Das Land der Ecken"). The third picture should have been a combination of elements of both German and French schools. Unfortunately, due to problems in scheduling, the collaboration went slower than anticipated and the original plans did not get finished. The German pupils became frustrated because the collaboration seemed one-sided to them and they became less motivated to finish the project as they could not see the objective for finishing the "fictional picture" when they knew that the French students would not see it. It became apparent that besides carefully planning the schedule of a telecollaborative project, it is necessary to stick to the schedule or make adjustments in the activities and objectives immediately if the timing must change.

Another problem which became apparent towards the end of the project was the lack of personal exchange. The curiosity the students demonstrated about their partners waned as the amount of exchange and communication diminished (mainly due to end-of-term pressures). This could have been avoided by a class blog where the students posted their questions and answers about each other. With the teachers monitoring the amount and quality of information exchanges, interest might have been maintained throughout the project. For instance when a German student wondered whether the French friends were wearing uniforms to school or not, it could have been answered easily in a blog instead of relying on one-to-one communication, which can often fail.

The last phase of the project "saying good bye" to the partners team did take place via web-blog. Nonetheless a problem occurred which Kreeft Peyton (in Egbert &Hanson-Smith 1999:22) explains as the consequences of "anonymity". The online partners can become impertinent because they are not face-to-face in their interactions and sometimes even offend others and hurt their feelings (ibid.). In this project, one German team got frustrated with the partnered French team and sent a blog entry stating their (low) opinion of the French. In fact, this occurred twice and had to be dealt with on a personal level by the teachers involved.

Project results

The two partner teachers agreed that there was a need to move away from more static interaction with computers to a dynamic interaction wherein the students see a real reason for using the language—because there is someone "on the other side" interested in knowing about them and what they are doing[3]. The students, both in France and Germany, were used to a "compartmentalised" approach to new technologies in their lives. In other words, computers at school were principally engaged as a mechanized tutor designed to deliver instructional materials to the student without much interactive feedback, if any at all. Outside the school, technology played an important role in the lives of most of the students, from interactive videogames to digital cameras. The two teachers decided

---

[3] This exchange continued with two more classes the following academic year and ended with an actual visit of the entire French class to the German school. The German parents, teachers and local dignitaries (e.g. town mayor) arranged a local party for everyone involved. The event was recorded in the town newspaper and featured on a local television station.

to try to integrate different aspects of the language learning process with features from the students' personal lives in order to create opportunities for more authentic (and at the same time scaffolded) learning experiences.

The learners were quite young and had very basic technical skills (typing or online publishing) and were beginners in the target language. However, they were able to collaborate in the tasks by drawing and sharing pictures as well as helping to make the audio-blogs in the early stage of the project. The German students produced a text and audio-file called "Our Hometown" and a rap-song entitled "Class 5 Rap". The French students produced a text with digital pictures of their hometown and audio files explaining the pictures. Using this approach certainly allowed for intercultural learning and also intercultural communication.

The project itself was embedded in a communicative approach in the classroom, wherein the students were afforded as many authentic language encounters as possible (for example, inviting English native speakers in the first few weeks, watching parts of movies, and communicating with other speakers of English in the MICaLL portal). Thus, the students were motivated to use the target language as much as possible, to take risks, and to experiment with the foreign language. Upon reflection, both teachers involved in this project agreed on the findings of several researchers who claim that it is not the use of new media in the modern classroom that leads to successful foreign language learning, rather it is the way in which the media is used. The media does not replace a special teaching method but offers technical possibilities that allow different approaches and means for applying pedagogical beliefs.

In this project, the use of the children's book "Das Land der Ecken", along with all the ICT modes that were described, helped the students carry out an intercultural exchange, based on high standards of social and academic interaction. They were then able to achieve the technical, linguistic and intercultural objectives of the project. Within only a few months the pupils learned the technical aspects of typing, e-mailing, scanning in pictures as well as creating their own individual homepages to be seen worldwide. At the same time, intercultural learning took place on a learner-oriented level while affording them the chance to build on their language knowledge and use it to communicate with their partners.

One of the big advantages of this project was that the media activities (such as uploading songs and pictures) were aimed at certain outcomes in each phase of the project which were linked to other project phases and outcomes. For instance, in order to introduce themselves to their partners individually, the pupils had to start by posting their individual profiles online in their homepages. This was followed by web-blogging which allowed them to get to know their partners better and formed the basis for the drawing later on, which in turn was connected to the book, "Das Land der Ecken". By tying together each phase and outcome, the pupils saw cohesion and purpose in their project. The project also engaged the students affectively, as indicated in a final opinion survey (affective learning is an important element for intrinsic motivation; Rogoff, 1995; Simonson and Maushak, 2001). While the participating pupils admitted that at times the technical challenges were hard to face, they all agreed that the project had been fun and everyone recognised the need of knowing how to handle new media tools for the future.

Works Cited

Kreeft Peyton, Joy. 1999. "Theory and Research: Interaction via Computers." In *CALL Environments.Research, Practice and Critical Issues,* ed. Joy Egbert and Elizabeth Hanson-Smith, 17-26. Alexandria: Teachers of English to Speakers of Other Languages.

Rogoff, Barbara. 1995. "Observing sociocultural activity on three planes: participatory appropriation, guided participation and apprencticeship." In *Sociocultural Studies of the Mind,* ed. James V. Wertsch J V, Pablo del Rio and Amelia Alvarez, 139-164. Cambridge: Cambridge University Press.

Ulitzka, Irene and Gerhard Gepp. 1993. *Das Land der Ecken.* European Picture Book Collection (EPBC). http://www.ncrcl.ac.uk/epbc/EN/index.asp

Simonson, Michael and Nancy Maushak. 2001. "Instructional technology and attitude change." In *Handbook of research for educational communications and technology,* ed. David H. Jonassen, 984-1016. Mahway, NJ: Lawrence Erlbaum Associates.

Warschauer, Mark, Heidi Schetzer, and Christine Meloni. 2000. *Internet for English Teaching*. Alexandria, VA: Teachers of English to Speakers of Other Languages, Inc.

GETTING THE MESSAGE: TRAINING LANGUAGE TEACHERS IN THE THEORETICAL AND PRACTICAL APPLICATIONS OF FORUMS

RANDALL SADLER AND BETIL ERÖZ

In order to fully take advantage of the potentials of Computer-Mediated Communication (CMC) in language learning, it is becoming increasingly important that future teachers are trained in the appropriate ways to utilize this technology since, as with any other teaching tool, adequate knowledge and strong pedagogical training are essential. The results of such a training program and some ideas for integrating message boards into language classes are outlined in this chapter.

Matching participants and course objectives

The CMC teacher training project discussed in this chapter involved two graduate level TESL/TEFL classes, one located at the University of Illinois at Urbana-Champaign (UIUC) in the United States and the other at Middle East Technical University (METU) in Ankara, Turkey. The METU students were enrolled in a course titled "Instructional Technology in English Language Teaching" while their UIUC counterparts were taking "Computer-Mediated Communication for Language Learning."

There were a total of 18 student participants between the two classes, 8 from METU and 10 from UIUC. The UIUC students included 5 males and 5 females representing 6 different countries, while the 5 female and 3 male METU students were all Turkish nationals. It was relevant that all of the student participants had experience teaching in either ESL or EFL environments, with experience ranging from 1 to over 15 years; this meant that the students would be able to collaboratively construct new knowledge based on their combined previous knowledge of language teaching. Their experience in teaching did not extend to the integration of CMC modes into teaching —although all of the participants were familiar with some aspects of CMC, none had used all of the tools discussed in the course. All of the participants had high levels of English proficiency and did not have problems in expressing themselves in either oral or written formats.

Although the course titles differed, these were, essentially, the same course—with the same syllabus, daily schedule and reading —focusing on training future teachers to use CMC for language teaching and learning. Although the courses had slightly different schedules, they did "meet" online at the "same" time every Wednesday throughout the semester (8:30 AM at UIUC and 4:30 PM at METU, with the 8 hour time difference resulting in a synchronous meeting time). The fact that the courses were similarly designed (this was done beforehand by the course instructors) was important for ensuring that the students felt there was a purpose in their online collaboration, beyond simply "practicing the language". It also meant that the course instructors were not adapting the online activities to "fit" an already established course curriculum, which can often create conflict in scheduling and overall aims of the course. In the case of the combined course, the agreed aims were to give the participants the following:

- A solid theoretical foundation in the field of CMC and language learning.
- An overview of nine CMC modes that they might use in future language teaching. (Email, message boards, blogs, podcasting, wikis, text, audio and video chat).
- The opportunity to engage in interaction via those modes.
- Practical activities for each of these modes that participants might use in their future teaching.

Providing a theoretical basis for students' knowledge

Both professors began their respective classes with several class meetings that prompted the students to explore the connections between CMC and general learning theory as well as between CMC and sociolinguistics (i.e., Barnes, 2003; Julie A. Belz, 2002; Chism, 2000; Egbert, Chao & Hanson-Smith, 1999; Murray, 2000; Warschauer & Meskill, 2000). These readings were meant to give the students a foundation that would enable them to better understand future readings in the course —readings that focused on more specific CMC modes. (For a complete list of the readings, syllabus, and daily schedule, you may visit: www.eslweb.org/587.htm).

After this stage, the remainder of the course was spent examining/experimenting with the CMC modes listed above. For each mode, at least one article was read illustrating research done on that mode.

Exploring message boards

Rather than attempting to provide detailed information on what was discussed for all nine modes, this chapter will focus on message boards to illustrate the nature of the class.[1] One of the activities included the compilation of innovative teaching ideas using this mode and some examples are provided for the readers.

While studying this particular CMC mode, the students read two research studies which examined the effectiveness of Message Boards for language learning (Hanna & de Nooy, 2003; Kamhi-Stein, 2000), followed by more empirical activities.

First, students were introduced to a number of pre-existing message boards that might be useful to language learners. There is a large number of pre-existing message boards that may be of interest for language learning/teaching (for an extended list of such sites go to http://www.eslweb.org/cmcforum/index.php?topic=24.0). Some of these boards are specifically designed for language teachers (e.g., the forum at TEFL.net: http://www.tefl.net/forums/index.php), while others are not specifically designed for language learning, but may be useful nonetheless (e.g., the travel talk board at frommers.com: http://www.frommers.com/cgi-bin/WebX), as shown in figure 4.4.

During this phase of the course the students examined these types of boards and discussed how they might be useful for language teaching. While this was sometimes obvious, as with the tefl.net site, with its focus on teaching, the participants also discussed how to use message boards like the one at frommers.com. In this case, we suggested that language learners might go to the section of the travel talk board that focused on their own country and answer questions posted by travelers. For example, a native speaker of Spanish from Mexico learning English might go to the board and answer questions from someone considering a trip to the Yucatan. In this case, even if the Mexican student has somewhat limited English ability, his expertise on his own country will help to shift his role from a "learner looking for help" to an expert on his own country willing to share his expertise with those less knowledgeable.

---

[1] While some differentiate between *message boards* and *forums*, these two terms will be used as synonyms in this report.

Fig. 4-3 Frommer's Travel Board

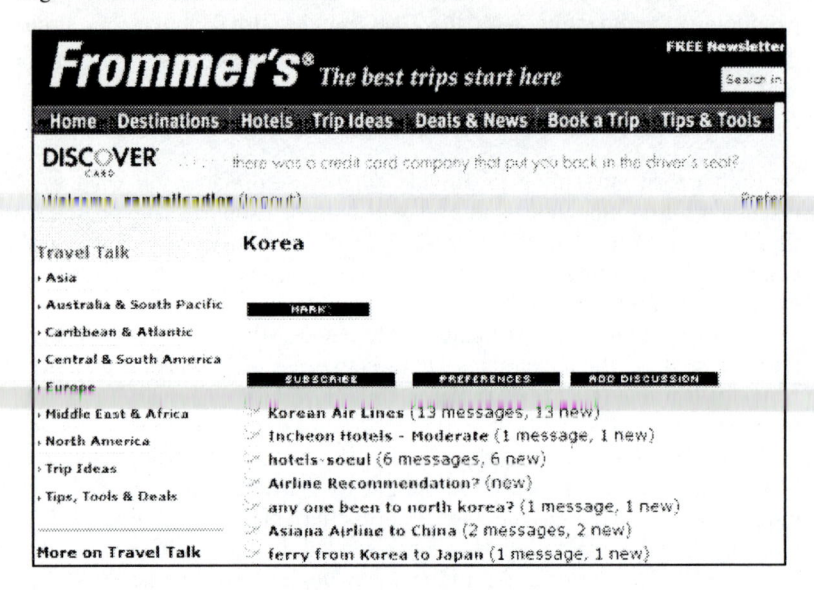

Next the students examined a number of free sites where they could either join an already existing group or create their own message board using a pre-existing service (E.g., MSN: http://groups.msn.com/ or Google Groups: http://groups.google.com/grphp?hl=en&tab=wg&q=). Both of these sites have a number of pre-existing forums focusing either on teaching or learning ESL. For example, at the time this article was written, there were 1,472 boards listed under "Teaching Groups" and 44 boards listed related to "ESL." In addition, these types of sites allow users to set up their own custom boards.

Finally, the students explored how to set up their own customized message boards on their own server space using *Simple Machines* open source software. This is the same software used to create the board utilized in the course, as shown in Illustration 2 (http://www.eslweb.org/cmcforum):

Fig. 4-4 The CMC Forum

	General Topics	
	General Questions A place to post your general questions related to CMC	10 Posts 3 Topics
	General Links Use this section to post CMC-related links--post the link and a bit about it. What is it? How could you use it? PLEASE NOTE--there is also a message for links in each of the sub-categories below; so you might post in both places.	9 Posts 5 Topics
	Language Exchange Site Links Please post links here for language exchange sites. Please also provide a short description/evaluation of the site. What is the focus (email, chat, audio?)? how is the website to use? Can you find partners or is it not too useful? Etc.	1 Posts 1 Topics
	Email for Computer-Mediated Language Learning Please post your ideas here for how email might be used for language learning. This would include any aspect of language or culture.	111 Posts 24 Topics
	Message Boards for Computer-Mediated Language Learning Please post your ideas here for how Message Boards might be used for language learning. This would include any aspect of language or culture.	134 Posts 23 Topics
	MUDS, MOOs, and WOOs for Computer-Mediated Language Learning Please post your ideas here for how MUDS, MOOs, and WOOs might be used for	113 Posts

We first discussed the advantages of setting up such a customized board, including total teacher control over membership, appearance, and technical aspects of the forum (e.g., whether or not to allow attachments, member privileges, etc.). We also created four videos for this section of this course that took the students step-by-step through this process, including how to get their own server space, choose their message board software, set up their database, and manage/administer the board. (These videos may be found at: http://www.eslweb.org/cmcforum/index.php?topic=33.0).

During this section of the course the students were required to design their own activities to illustrate how message boards could be used for language learning/teaching. The full list of their ideas can be found on the board (http://www.eslweb.org/cmcforum/index.php?board=5.0), but in the following section we will present a few of their ideas.

Focusing on message boards: Teaching Ideas from Students

The students were really creative and varied in their suggestions pertaining to how to use message boards in their own language teaching. The students' comments and suggestions can be grouped in two categories: those with a focus on integrating reading and writing skills and those with a focus on speaking and discussion skills. In both cases, the examples have a focus on encouraging "real" interaction with participants outside the classroom, via the use of authentic materials.

Integrating reading and writing: In this group, the students suggested activities that would enhance EFL learners' reading and writing skills, sometimes integrating speaking into the lesson.

Işıl: This student proposed a writing lesson in which the teacher takes the initiative and posts a sentence on the message board to start an electronically-enhanced story chain activity. Each student then takes this sentence and writes up a story with that sentence as the first line of the text. The teacher provides a new sentence each week, and the students find a way to work that into their stories. When the individual stories are finished, the students post these on the message board, read each others' stories, and write responses to a pre-determined number of entries. The student also recommended having a story competition at the end in which all students vote for their favorite story.

In her own words: "One good thing about using message boards is that the students will be able to make use of the language learned in the classroom and check their language output before sending out their messages. Message boards also give the students the opportunity to check their spelling and grammar and revise their own work. Furthermore, the teacher can also follow how his/her students are proceeding with their writing and give help when necessary."

Penny: Penny proposed an introduction to an argumentative writing unit in which the teacher introduces a topic of her choice and gives the class five minutes to do free writing on that topic. The students then post these writings on the message board for others to read later on. After this, the teacher divides the class into small groups and assigns a reading text about that topic to each group. Groups read their assigned article and post the main ideas and their personal responses to these readings on the message board. The teacher may provide questions for guidance at this stage. The groups view each others' posts and do a Q&A session online. This lesson is followed by the drafting of an argumentative essay.

In her own words: "I think message boards can be effectively used in ESL writing for …brain storming and accumulating ideas. [I]n a traditional class, not all students contribute equally at this stage for various reasons; however, everybody should be able to contribute something because definitely we all have our own opinions on [a variety of topics.]"

Lisa & Babürhan: Another suggestion for integrating reading and writing in a class via the use of a message board came from a student from UIUC who argued that her idea could be applicable in a variety of teaching situations. This student's proposal involved having EFL students read a popular novel (E.g., *Harry Potter*, *Lord of the Rings*, or *the Narnia Chronicles*) that has a number of web sites for their fans to have online discussions. She suggests directing advanced level learners to join the listservs, online chat rooms, or message boards that have discussions on various aspects of these novels (characters, plot, movie versions, etc.) and report their findings or experiences on the class message board. For intermediate level learners, she suggests reading articles on current issues published on web sites of news sources such as the BBC. The learners sign up for discussion rooms of these news agencies and join in the chats, later reporting what other people say about the issues on the classroom message board. Web sites she suggested were www.encompassculture.com (The Global Book Club);
http://boards.oprah.com (Oprah Winfrey's book club). This lesson idea was supported by Baburhan, who added that students need to be openly directed towards online chat rooms of the BBC because of its continuing discussions about a variety of current issues that may be of interest to the learners. This student maintains that learners should initially be quiet observers that only read other people's ideas and post summaries of these exchanges on the class message board. The learners may join in the conversations when they feel confident enough about participating. When learners do feel confident enough to begin contributing to the discussions in these groups, they will be interacting with a real audience and participating in authentic debates, which help them with their writing skills, argumentation skills, and acquisition of netiquette.

Improving speaking and discussion skills: Some of the students came up with EFL lesson ideas that focused on improving the speaking and listening skills of language learners, in addition to enhancing discussion skills.

Mete: Mete emphasized the importance of using technology in meaningful activities which make the use of certain innovations a necessity, rather than a requirement for the students. Mete highlighted the fact that language teachers should help their learners understand the use and function of technology in the classroom. He suggested a unit based on a television series in which the students are shown (or are requested to watch at home) an episode of a television show, such as *Friends*. After this, the students are encouraged to join an already set up message board with an ongoing discussion about this show (e.g., http://www.tv.com/friends/show/71/forums.html). The classroom forum will then be used for follow-up writing activities in which the students exchange their observations regarding the responses and comments of other people on the discussion board. In some ways Mete's suggestion is similar to that of Lisa, but watching a television series helps improve listening comprehension while reading a novel enhances reading comprehension and vocabulary knowledge.

In his own words: "By referring our students to forums built for authentic purposes where the main aim is not learning the language, their communication can be purposeful and authentic. However, "authentic" forums have their own culture, which may not welcome a language learner sometimes... So, while referring our students to online discussions we need to keep in mind that web discussions are genres as well, and the participation in them requires some kind of culture. In these forums the intention is not to teach the language but to use it while discussing some important matters."

Samphas: In his lesson proposal Samphas focuses on the use of authentic materials to encourage speaking and discussion and which integrate both face-to-face activities and message boards. In his lesson, the teacher tells the learners to bring to class some brochures from a neighborhood travel agency. In the first classroom session, the teacher gets them into groups based on their preferred agencies or travel destinations. In their groups, students brainstorm about why they have chosen that particular tour company or destination. Each group composes a persuasive essay and posts it on the message board for the other class members to read, with each reader adding at least one comment. In the next class session, the teacher prints out the comments from everyone and distributes them to the related groups for a debate on travel agencies and destinations.

In his own words: "This task can be conducted with higher intermediate EFL students to improve their critical thinking via speaking and writing. This class can be conducted in two sessions (90 minutes each) with an additional homework assignment."

Final comments

These suggestions are the results of a semester-long project that focused on training language teachers in the theoretical and practical applications of CMC in language teaching. Although we examined nine different CMC modes over the course of the semester, in this article we focused primarily on message boards as we feel that this is a CMC mode that is easily accessible to most teachers throughout the world. Just as our students came up with many creative, practical, and useful ideas about how to use message boards in the language classroom, we are confident that other teachers will find other interesting and engaging ways to use message boards in their lesson plans. A caveat is in order, however. As this brief description illustrates, utilizing even a single CMC tool like a message board is not as simple as it may at first seem. If teachers wish to make the best use of these powerful tools, they must have the appropriate training and hands-on practice with the technology in order to find their approach to integrating ICT modes into their teaching.

Works Cited

Barnes, Susan. B. 2003. *Computer-mediated communication: Human-to-human communication across the internet*. Boston, MA: Pearson Education.

Beauvois, Margaret Healy and Jean Eledge. 1995. "Personality types and megabytes: Student attitudes toward computer mediated communication (CMC) in the language classroom." *CALICO journal, 13*(2&3), 27-45.

Belcher, Diane. 1999. "Authentic interaction in a virtual classroom: Leveling the playing field in a graduate seminar." *Computers and Composition, 16*, 253-267.

Belz, Julie A. 2002. "Social dimensions of telecollaborative foreign language study." *Language learning & Technology, 6*(1), 60-81.

Belz, Julie A and Celeste Kinginger. 2002. "The cross-linguistics development of address form use in telecollaborative language learning: Two case studies." *Canadian Modern Language Review/Revue canadienne des langues vivant, 59*(2), 189-214.

Belz, Julie A. and Celeste Kinginger. 2003. "Discourse options and the development of pragmatic competence by classroom learners of German: The case of address forms." *Language Learning, 53*(4), 591-647.

Chism, Rebecca L. 2000. *A Vygotskian perspective on electronic bulletin boards: An exploratory study (Lev Vygotsky)*. Unpublished doctoral dissertation, Florida State University Press.

Chun, Dorothy. 1994. "Using computer networking to facilitate the acquisition of interactive competence." *System, 22*(1), 17-31.

Egbert, Joy, Chin-Chi Chao, and Elizabeth Hanson-Smith. 1999. "Computer-enhanced language learning environments: An overview."

In *CALL environments: Research, practice, and critical issues,* ed. Joy Egbert and Elizabeth Hanson-Smith, 1-13. Alexandra, Virginia: Teachers of English to Speakers of Other Language, Inc.

Egbert, Joy and Elizabeth Hanson-Smith, eds. 1999. *CALL environments: Research, practice, and critical issues.* Alexandria, Virginia: Teachers of English to Speakers of Other Languages.

Fanderclai, Tari Lin. 1995. "MUDs in education: New environment, new pedagogies." *Computer-Mediated Communication Magazine, 2,* 8-10.

Hanna, Barbara and Juliana de Nooy. 2003. "A funny thing happened on the way to the forum: Electronic discussion and foreign language learning." *Language Learning & Technology, 7*(1), 71-85.

Hofsoy, Morton B. 2001. *Network-based EFL: Motivational aspects of using networked computers in the EFL classroom.* Bergen: University of Bergen.

Kamhi-Stein, Lia D. 2000. "Looking to the future of TESOL teacher education: Web-based bulletin board discussion in a methods course." *TESOL QUARTERLY, 34*(3), 423-455.

Kelm, Orlando René. 1996. "The application of computer networking in foreign language education: Focusing on principles of second language acquisition." In *Telecollaboration in foreign language learning,* ed. Mark Warschauer, 19-28. Honolulu: University of Hawai'i Press.

Kern, Richard. 1995. "Restructuring classroom interaction with networked computers: Effects on quantity and characteristics of language production." *The Modern Language Journal, 79*(4), 457-476.

Kern, Richard and Mark Warschauer. 2000. "Introduction: Theory and practice of network-based language teaching." In *Networked-based language teaching: Concepts and practice,* ed. Mark Warschauer and Richard Kern, 1-19. Cambridge, UK: Cambridge University Press.

Meskill, Carla and Natasha Anthony. 2005. "Foreign language learning with CMC: Forms of online instructional discourse in a hybrid Russian class." *System, 33,* 89-105.

Murray, Denise E. 2000. "Protean communication: The language of computer-mediated communication." *TESOL Quarterly, 34*(3), 397-421.

Paver, Jennifer A. 2003. *The zone of proximal development in an online ESL composition course.* University of Nevada, Las Vegas.

Pellettieri, Jill. 2000. "Negotiation in cyberspace: The role of chatting in the developing of grammatical competence." In *Network-based language teaching: Concepts and practice,* ed. Mark Warschauer Richard Kern, 59-86. Cambridge, UK: Cambridge University Press.

Reid, Elizabeth. 1994. *Cultural formations in text-based virtual realities.* Unpublished Thesis, University of Melbourne.

Samsonov, Pavel. 2001. *Effectiveness of teaching a part of a foreign language course through computer-mediated communication as perceived by the students of Texas A&M university and military reservists: A case study.* Unpublished doctoral dissertation, Texas A&M University.

Smith, Bryan, Maria Jose Alvarez-Torres and Zhao Young. 2003. "Features of CMC technologies and their impact on language learners' online interaction." *Computer in Human Behavior, 19*(6), 703-729.

Ware, Paige D. 2004. "Confidence and competition online: ESL student perspectives on web-based discussions in the classroom." *Computer and Composition, 21*(4), 451-468.

Warschauer, Mark. 1996. "Comparing face-to-face and electronic discussion in the second language classroom." *CALICO journal, 13*(2), 7-26.

Warschauer, Mark and Carla Meskill. 2000. "Technology and second language teaching and learning." In *Handbook of undergraduate second language education,* ed. Judith W. Rosenthal, 303-318. Mahwah, NJ: Lawrence Erlbaum.

RECOMMENDED READING:
TECHNOLOGY INTO LANGUAGE LEARNING

Alexander, Jonathan and Marcia Dickson. 2006. *Role Play: Distance Learning And the Teaching of Writing (New Dimensions in Computers and Composition)*. Cresskill, Broadway: Hampton Press.
Barr, David. 2004. *ICT — Integrating Computers in Teaching*. Frankfurt: Peter Lang.
Chambers, Angela, Jean Conacher and Jeannette Littlemore, eds. 2004. *ICT and Language Learning: Integrating Pedagogy and Practice*, Birmingham: University of Birmingham Press.
Crane, Beverley E. *Teaching with the Internet: Strategies and Models for K-12 Curricula*. New York: Neal-Schuman, 2000.
Dudney, Gavin. 2007. *The Internet and the Language Classroom. (Cambridge Handbooks for Language Teachers)*. Cambridge, UK: Cambridge University Press.
Fotos, Sandra and Charles Browne, eds. 2004. *New Perspectives on Call for Second Language Classrooms*. Mahwah, NJ: Lawrence Erlbaum Associates, Inc.
Kötter, Markus. 2002. *Tandem learning on the Internet. Learner interactions in virtual online environments (MOOs)*, Frankfurt: Peter Lang.
Leask, Marilyn and Norbert Pachler, eds. 2005. *Learning to Teach Using ICT in the Secondary School* (2nd ed.). London: Routledge
Lewis, Paul. 2002. *The Changing Face of CALL: A Japanese Perspective*, Lisse, NL: Swets & Zeitlinger.
O'Dowd, Robert, ed. 2007. *Online Intercultural Exchange. An Introduction for Foreign Language Teachers*. Clevedon: Multilingual Matters.
Rösler, Dietmar. 2004. *E-Learning Fremdsprachen — eine kritische Einführung*, Tübingen: Stauffenburg Narr.
Seiz Ortiz, Rafael. 2006 *Análisis metodológico de cursos y recursos para el aprendizaje de inglés como secunda lengua a través de la World Wide Web*. Valencia: Editorial UPV.

Warschauer, Mark and Richard Kern. 2000. *Network-Based Language Teaching: Concepts and Practice.* Cambridge, UK: Cambridge University Press.

Warschauer, Mark. 2006. *Laptops and Literacy: Learning in the Wireless Classroom.* New York: Teachers College Press.

Windeatt, Scott, David Hardisty and David Eastment. 2000. *The Internet*, Oxford: Oxford University Press.

Webpages

European Association for Computer-Assisted Language Learning. CALL Bibliography: online articles. http://www.eurocalllanguages.org/resources/bibliography/articles.html [accessed 4 October 2007]

Online Bibliography and resources maintained by Teresa Almeida d'Eça. http://64.71.48.37/teresadeca/webheads/online-learningenvironments.htm [accessed 4 October 2007]

Information and Communication Technology for Language Teaching http://www.ict4lt.org/ [accessed 4 October 2007]

Chapter Five

Passport to Pluralism – European Language Portfolio: Introduction

Melinda Dooly

Devised by the Council of Europe's Language Policy Division, the *European Language Portfolio* (ELP) was officially launched in 2001. It has a much longer history than that, however. It is directly linked to *The Common European Framework of Reference: Learning, Teaching, Assessment* (CEFR); indeed for many language teachers throughout the EU, the two are interchangeable, as the reference levels in particular have become more and more consistently used by language teachers throughout the EU. The idea of a common framework for learning, teaching and assessment was initiated by the Council of Europe (CoE) as early as the 1970's, but it received a significant impulse with the CoE project "Language Learning for European Citizenship".

While there are national, regional and even institutional variations to the ELP, the versions should have three obligatory components (a language passport, a language biography and a dossier) and require compliance with the Council of Europe's Common Reference Levels in order to be accredited. The educational framework behind the ELP shifts the focus of language learning from decontextualised classrooms, organized by ages or language levels, towards recognition of multiple language competencies acquired through different lifelong learning experiences and across a range of sites and venues. The ELP encourages more transparency in the language learning process and subsequently, empowerment of the language learner by making him or her more aware of the learning process and placing more emphasis on self-established goals, learner autonomy and self-assessment.

Politically, ELP can be considered a tool for facilitating individual mobility within the European Union as it aims to provide a means of profiling individual language skills through portfolios as well as establishing "across-the-board" reference levels for language competencies and skills. The referencing includes six levels, ranging from: A1 – (Breakthrough) to C2 – (Mastery); all of which are related to the five skills of listening, reading, spoken interaction, spoken production, and writing. Typically this referencing is used for self-evaluation as well as collaborative evaluation (between peers or student-teacher, for instance) and often takes the form of a grid or chart. It usually includes "can do" statements or other descriptive statements by the learner which are aimed at explicitly outlining the learner's current competency levels in many different areas of language use.

These descriptions can be directly linked to the learner's aims in order to show progress throughout the language learning process as well as providing a means of supportive monitoring by the teacher. One of the more important features of this referencing system is the fact that it has created a recognized referencing framework which is comparable wherever the ELP is adopted, thus eliminating the need for showing the correlation between different (often local or regional) qualifications (or other assessment references) throughout the European Union.

The ELP is not devised exclusively for institutional use only; however it is arguably more easily and readily applicable to education institutions than for individual use, simply due to the fact that members of the education community have more practice in planning language teaching programmes and in assessing them. Most individuals, on the other hand, are not as readily prepared to embark on a solitary programme for validation of their language competence(s).

As mentioned earlier, in order for an ELP model to be validated by the CoE, it must consist of a language passport, a language biography and a dossier. The language passport (available through the CoE) allows the passport owner to outline their "linguistic identity, language learning achievement, and intercultural experience" (CoE). The passport also includes an assessment of the holder's language competence, based on the Council of Europe's Common Reference Levels, ostensibly providing easily transferable referencing for education or employment opportunities across Europe. The language biography also provides a record of relevant language learning and intercultural experiences. This biography is an ongoing record kept by the ELP owner and includes learning goals, learning milestones and review of progress. This can be a dossier or portfolio in which the owner includes significant samples of work, progress, achievements and experiences in language learning.

As with any resource for language learning and teaching, the ELP and CEFR are not without issues. For one, immediate adoption of ELP is not always feasible as it requires an overall commitment of teachers, students and administration which goes beyond simple changes within the classroom. Reports indicate that the more completely integrated the ELP is into the curriculum, the higher the possibility of success of the ELP (Nováková and Davidová, 2001; Schärer, 2000). Without proper planning and commitment, use of the ELP may run into problems due to time and curriculum constraints. This, in turn, necessitates a clear understanding of the purpose and content of the ELP by all the stakeholders: students, teachers, administrators and parents. Studies also indicate the need for explicit student and teacher training in the use of ELP (Scharer, Op. Cit). This prerequisite is echoed by Bruen in her assessment of the pilot project which she describes in this chapter. Self-assessment requires previous training and experience by the students and unfortunately not all educational experiences help students develop this level of reflection and analysis. Expecting students to use the ELP autonomously, without training or without a clear link to the class content is not very realistic and may prove to be demotivating for the students.

One of the more polemical areas of the ELP seems to lie in the reference levels. Arguably, the CEFR lacks theoretical basis for setting the levels and their cut-off points. The established levels are based on a widespread study into European language teachers' *perceptions* of language proficiency (Fulcher, 2004), not theoretical understandings of proficiency. In effect, this means that referencing is based on descriptors of proficiency levels which may seem ambiguous and difficult to interpret. And as descriptors, the levels should not be understood by the teachers as hierarchical or sequential language acquisition levels; multiple language competencies are not hierarchical, they are more directly related to individual use and experience. This means that the language learner's biography may prove to be a more efficient tool for assessing multiple language competencies than the passport and should not be overshadowed by the referencing system. Moreover, lack of immediate milestones in the different levels may not provide enough input for students to readily see their progress as they go along, thus resulting in learner demotivation.

Of course, the resource itself does not necessarily constitute the problem; the efficiency of a resource as a learning tool will depend on the way in which it is used. Indeed, the CEFR promotes plurilingual competence(s) and recognises that language learning is a lifelong task. "The responsibilities of educational authorities, qualifying examining bodies and teachers cannot simply be confined to the attainment of a given level of proficiency in a particular language at a particular moment in time…" (CEFR, 2001:5). The different components of the ELP can help highlight the different aspects of language learning –and highlight the fact that no language speaker is equally competent in all aspects of the first language, much less additional languages. Therefore balanced competences should not be an expectation for the learning process of other languages; nor should hierarchical acquisition be involved. Additionally, the ELP aims to help make the language learner more aware of his/her own language learning process and progress, thus promoting more learner autonomy. Contingent to this is the learner's understanding of the actual learning process. This can be more efficient if all the stakeholders are aware of the existence of plurilingual competence(s), without becoming too hung up on "obtaining" sequential levels. The following examples in this chapter demonstrate ways in which this has been promoted in actual learning environments.

This section provides descriptions of how the European Language Portfolio (ELP) is being used in Ireland, Portugal and Romania. Jennifer Bruen (Ireland) explains the development of an ongoing project to develop an online version of the ELP for higher education students. Her descriptive case looks at the use of ELP in the development of presentation skills for business students who are studying German. Moving to Portugal, authors Cristina Avelino and Francine Arroyo describe the development and implementation of a French portfolio for University level students at the University of Lisbon. They outline the dificulties encountered in trying to convince not only their students, but other faculty members that using the ELP would be beneficial to language teaching and learning. The article finishes with a discussion of the advantages and limitations of ELP, based on the authors' experience. To round off this section, Lilliana Dellevoet and Laura Mureşan describe a country-wide promotion of the European Language Portfolio (ELP) in Romania, a process which, in large part, was stimulated through an ELP dissemination project developed between ten European countries. Dellevoet and Mureşan provide examples of the pan-European version for adults being used in Romania and then go on to discuss teachers' and students' reactions to the ELP.

Works Cited

Fulcher, Glenn. "Are Europe's tests being built on an "unsafe" framework?" *Guardian Weekly TEFL Supplement*. March 18, 2004.

Nováková, Sylva and Jana Davidová. 2001. "The ELP pilot project in the Czech Republic." In *The European Language Portfolio in use: nine examples,* ed. David Little, 2-6. Strasbourg: Council of Europe.

Schärer, Rolf. 2000. *Final Report A European Language Portfolio Pilot Project Phase 1998– 2000*, DGIV/EDU/LANG (2000) 31rev, Strasbourg, Council of Europe.

THE EUROPEAN LANGUAGE PORTFOLIO: DEVELOPING PRESENTATION SKILLS AMONG UNIVERSITY STUDENTS OF GERMAN FOR BUSINESS

JENNIFER BRUEN

The School of Applied Language and Intercultural Studies at Dublin City University in Ireland is currently developing an on-line version of the European Language Portfolio (ELP) in partnership with a range of higher education institutions across Europe[1]. It is proposed that this on-line version of the portfolio will support the development of learner autonomy as well as the processes of self-assessment and reflection on language learning in a higher education context.

This on-line version of the ELP will retain the basic concepts and structure of the more traditional ELP but will at the same time seek to harness the potential of e-learning in order to improve the quality of language teaching and learning both inside and outside of the classroom. One important potential stemming from this fusion is a more dynamic engagement with the ELP through, for example, the creation of a Dossier section which can contain not merely examples of written work but also allow for the up-loading of video and audio files containing examples of oral and aural work. Another relevant aspect of the combination of e-learning with the ELP is the possibility of direct links from the ELP owner's "Biography section" to online exercises and materials – both directly linked to the learning priorities previously selected by the user. There are, of course, a wide range of other features which emerge with the online ELP but the scope of this article does not allow further details. A final proposition is that this version of the ELP should feature an enhanced

---

[1] The project, known as the "Language On-line Portfolio Project", (LOLIPOP) 2004-2007, is funded by the Socrates Lingua 2 progamme and the countries involved are Ireland, Germany, Spain, France, Austria, Norway, Latvia and Poland. Dublin City University (Ireland) is the lead partner institution.

intercultural dimension and the connection between the Internet and the ELP can help facilitate this.

The material used for the study described in this chapter[2] is taken from an initial prototype for the on-line ELP described above. This initial hardcopy version, put together by a team of lecturers at Dublin City University (DCU) in 2002[3], drew in particular on the portfolios designed by EQUALS (The European Association for Quality Language Services) and ALTE (The Association of Language Teachers in Europe) as well as on the checklists or "can-do statements" developed by Guenther Schneider and Brian North for the Common European Framework (CEF) and the Portfolio in the Swiss National Foundation Project, *Fremdsprachen koennen – was heist das?* (2000). The two sections entitled *Profile of Language Skills* contained in the Passport and *My Current Language Learning Priorities* were of particular relevance to the prototype of this study.

Case-study

The purpose of this particular study was to gather some initial insights into whether and how the ELP could be used to assist in the development of presentation skills. Such skills are key for students of business and experience has shown that they can pose a particular problem when it is required that the presentations be delivered in a foreign language. Furthermore, the development of such "transferable skills" as presentation skills can give an additional value to foreign language degrees, the popularity of which is waning in countries such as Ireland, where English is not only one of the official languages, it is a predominant international language. Arguably, many language courses are ideally suited to the development of transferable skills or "skills developed in one context which can be transferred to another" (Transferable Skills in Third Level

---

[2] Some of the material contained in this section was discussed during an oral presentation given by Bruen J. (with V. Crosbie and J. Péchenart) in 2003 entitled "The European Language Portfolio and the Business World" at *The Cutting Edge: Training to Communicate*, ENCODE Conference, University of Applied Sciences, Chur, Switzerland (25th-27th September).

[3] Project Director: Ms Veronica Crosbie. Team Leaders: Dr. Jennifer Bruen (German), Ms Juliette Pechenart (French) and Ms Veronica Crosbie (English). Layout and Design: Pink Design. Funding: Teaching and Learning Fellowship Scheme of the Dublin City University Office of the Dean of Teaching and Learning.

Modern Languages Curricula Project 2002-5). Other such skills include negotiation skills, critical thinking and problem solving.

The ELP and business students: getting introduced

The 12 students selected for involvement in the study were second-year intermediate students, meaning they had all achieved a higher level grade in German in the Irish Leaving Certificate[4] and had successfully completed their first year university exams in German. They were enrolled on the Irish/German strand of the BA in European Business. In this strand, students must study both language and business as core elements of their programme so they spend their first two years at university studying business at Dublin City University and their final two years at the *Fachhochschule Reutlingen*. The *Fachhochschule Reutlingen*, which is located in Germany, is a higher level educational institution focussing on business. Students must complete their studies at both Dublin City University and *Fachhochschule Reutlingen* before being awarded a dual degree from the two institutions.

The module selected for the study was "German for Academic Purposes: Business". This is a core, intermediate German language module offered in the fourth semester of the BA in European Business. One of the primary goals of the module is the development of the learner's competence in both spoken and written production in preparation for the study of business in a German-speaking country. In particular, the module aims to develop presentation and report-writing skills. (This study focuses particularly on the development of presentation skills). The course consists of three contact hours per week over eight weeks, one taking the form of a plenary lecture and shared with students on the BAs in International Business/Marketing and Languages, and the remaining two given in the form of small-group seminars. It was proposed that the ELP be used during the small-group seminars.

In their first seminar, the students were introduced in general terms to the concept of the European Language Portfolio and to its primary aims and objectives (Council of Europe Portal / European Language Portfolio, 2006). Each student was presented with a copy of the Dublin City University ELP in the form of a hard-backed ring binder into which pages could be inserted. They were then introduced more particularly to the Language Passport component of the ELP with emphasis being placed on

---

[4] The Leaving Certificate examination takes place at the end of secondary schooling when students are approximately 17 or 18 years of age. It is a requirement for university study.

the *Profile of Language Skills*. In line with the Council of Europe requirements for all ELPs, this profile consists of a series of tables similar to that shown below in figure 5-1 which the learners are required to complete for each language in which they have some level of competence.

Fig. 5-1 Extract from the Profile of Language Skills (Passport)

Deutsch	A1	A2	B1	B2	C1	C2
Listening						
Reading						
Spoken Interaction						
Spoken Production	S	A	M	P	L	E
Writing						

Using the self-assessment grid which contains descriptors ranging from A1 to C2 based on the Common European Framework of Reference for Languages (CEF) scales for each of the five skills, i.e. reading, writing, listening, spoken interaction and spoken production, they completed the German version of the Profile of Language Skills (*Raster zur Selbstbeurteilung*) for spoken production. To do so, the students selected the descriptor that they felt best described their level for spoken production. (A sample answer is contained Figure 5-2). In the case of this student, the selected descriptors outline their individual proficiency levels as ranging from B1 to C1 (Fig. 5-2).

"How we're going about it": Teachers' Voices on Innovative Approaches   209
to Teaching and Learning Languages

Fig. 5-2 Extract from the Self-Assessment Grid (Passport)

CEF Level/ Skill	B1	B2	C1
Spoken Production	I can connect phrases in a simple way in order to describe experiences and events, my dreams, hopes and ambitions. I can briefly give reasons and explanations for opinions and plans. I can narrate a store or explain the plot of a book or film and describe my reactions.	I can present clear, detailed descriptions on a wide range of subjects related to my field of interest. I can explain a viewpoint on a topical issue giving the advantages and disadvantages of various options.	I can present clear, detailed descriptions of complex subjects, integrating sub-themes, developing particular points and rounding off with an appropriate conclusion.

In the second seminar, the students were introduced to the Biography section of the portfolio and more specifically to the section entitled *My Current Language Learning Priorities*. This section contains "can do" statements for the CEF levels A1 to C2 for each of the five skills. Learners are required to indicate whether particular statements, corresponding to their current CEF level, represent something that they have already mastered or something that is a priority for them. For example, the figure 5.3 below contains the "can-do" statements for level C1.

Fig. 5-3 Can-do Statements for Level C1

> *I can give clear, detailed descriptions of complex subjects.*
> *I can orally summarise long, demanding texts.*
> *I can give an extended description or account of something, integrating themes, developing particular points and concluding appropriately.*
> *I can give a clearly developed presentation on a subject in my fields of personal or professional interest, departing when necessary from the prepared text and following up spontaneously points raised by members of the audience.*

The students identified individually their priorities for their chosen level (B1, B2 or C1). Working in pairs they then identified common priorities which they felt were also of relevance to the module in question. In a whole-class discussion, finally, several common priorities were identified as follows:

1. I can paraphrase short written passages orally in a simple fashion, using the original text wording and ordering.
2. I can give clear, detailed descriptions on a wide range of subjects related to my field of interest.
3. I can give a clearly developed presentation on a subject in my fields of personal or professional interest, departing when necessary from the prepared text and following up spontaneously points raised by members of the audience.

Using the ELP to set course objectives and activities

Possible strategies for the achievement of these objectives were also discussed in this forum. At this point in the study, the lecturer (who was also the "module coordinator" or course designer) was in a position to design activities and/or materials which could facilitate the achievement of the above objectives by the students. The activities designed and engaged in over the next eight seminars included the following:

- 2 minutes free speech by individual students on a general topic

This activity was designed to help the learners overcome initial inhibitions about speaking German in public. The lecturer provided topics which were of a general nature and included, for example, free-time, sport, university life, part-time jobs etc. Feedback on the presentation style was provided by the lecturer and as part of a general class discussion. All discussion took place through the target language, i.e. German.

- 2 minutes free speech on a commercial topic

The purpose of this activity was to habituate the students to public speaking using more specialised vocabulary. Possible topics included shop opening hours, Sunday working, the role of trade-unions in Germany etc. Topics were selected by both lecturer and students.

- 4 minutes free speech on a commercial topic using a short German article as a basis for the "presentation".

The first time this activity was engaged in, the students were provided with a short article in German on a relevant topic. They then paraphrased this article in the form of a short presentation. The second and subsequent time(s), they were asked to provide suitable materials themselves. They sourced these from the Dublin City University library and from the Internet. Gradually students were encouraged to incorporate more than one article on suitable topics. Articles containing alternative viewpoints on particular topics were encouraged. Presentations were given both individually and in groups of three to four students. Again, feedback was provided in class.

- A longer presentation using support materials such as transparencies and PowerPoint projectors and hand-outs containing for example glossaries of key terms.

These presentations mirrored the formal assessment type in this module[5] and also the type of presentations the students would be required to give at the *FH-Reutlingen*. They were given time to prepare and presented on such topics as aspects of the Irish economy (the recent economic boom, house prices, the influence of EU membership etc.), Germany and Ireland as export partners etc. As well as presenting the material to their classmates and the lecturer, the students presenting were required to elicit responses from their colleagues and to respond to comments and queries from them. At the end of the presentation, they were required to lead a discussion on the material. This exercise was repeated a number of times and feedback on both content and presentation skills was provided in class. The presentations were also peer-assessed through constructive feedback by the students' colleagues.

Finally, in the eighth and final week of the semester, the students once again determined their CEF level for spoken production using the self-assessment grid contained in the Passport and discussed the success or otherwise of the course. In particular, the emphasis was on whether or not their own personal priorities for the semester had been achieved and whether the group priorities, listed above, had been achieved. This was followed by a discussion of reasons for the achievement or otherwise of objectives.

---

[5] This module was assessed on the basis of an oral presentation worth 50% of the final mark and a written report also worth 50%.

Student response to the experience with the ELP

In general, students responded positively to this pilot study. They described engagement with the *Profile of Language Skills* as providing a useful basis for a discussion about what they needed to achieve in order to improve their language learning and progress within the framework. The "can-do" statements in the section on *Learning Priorities* contained in the Biography also helped them to break down these broader objectives into more manageable goals. Many of the students involved described these tools as having a positive impact on their motivation levels and giving them a clearer idea of the objectives of the particular module.

Some difficulties arose, however, over the course of the semester. Initially, many of these were associated with the process of self-assessment. A number of students found it difficult to determine their level using the descriptors provided in the self-assessment grid in the Passport. This difficulty arose both at the beginning and the end of the semester. Clearly, students require some form of training and support in the area of self-assessment. This process seems to require skills which are not currently developed to any great extent within the Irish education system.

Furthermore, the relatively broad nature of the CEF descriptors meant that few students could determine a progression from one CEF level to the next over the course of an eight week semester. This proved somewhat demoralising for them. It may be possible in the future to further break down the current six levels, particularly perhaps the "intermediate" levels, B1 and B2.

The students also described the ELP folder itself as being somewhat unwieldy and at times confusing with many different sections in different languages contained in the one document. This is a difficulty which the development of an on-line version of the ELP should address. For example, students will be able to select one language only to begin with, thus eliminating the need to trawl through a number of translations of the same section.

Teacher response to the ELP experience

In terms of course design, the ELP was useful in helping to operationalise a module with broad objectives contained in the course descriptor such as "developing presentation and report-writing skills in German". The ELP was also useful in encouraging students to think about exactly what their levels and skills were and how they could go about raising the level and developing their skills themselves. Thus, the ELP demonstrated itself to be capable of achieving one of its key objectives, i.e. the development of learner autonomy (Council of Europe Portal / European Language Portfolio, 2006). However, a difficulty associated with this apparent advantage of using an ELP as an aid in course design was the fact that it highlighted the presence in the student group of a range of different proficiency levels and correspondingly a number of different priorities. Obviously, therefore, there are issues around the development of one module and one assessment type for students with differing levels of competence in the target language.

This study was somewhat unusual because it attempted to use the ELP in the development of one particular skill, i.e. spoken production. In order to do so, it defined spoken production very specifically as presentation skills. This required the learners to focus on particular sections of the portfolio and on a specific skill within those sections. This meant, firstly, that the descriptors for spoken production did not necessarily relate directly to the giving of presentations— particularly at the lower levels of the CEF scale. Secondly, it meant that students in the course used only a small amount of the portfolio. As these students had not engaged with the portfolio before, they therefore found it difficult to get an overview of the learning tool as a whole. Nonetheless, all of the participants found that using even a small portion of the adapted ELP was useful for their long-term language learning.

If the ELP is to function effectively as a learning tool it is important that the learner be introduced to it at a very early stage in the language learning process, indeed when they first begin to learn language(s). Of course this was not possible at this stage for the German business students as the ELP is a relatively new language learning tool. Early introduction to the European Language Portfolio will allow learners to become highly familiar with the ELP so that they can dip in and out of it as the need arises. Secondly, it would ensure that the processes of self-assessment together with goal-setting and monitoring are introduced at a very early stage and therefore, hopefully, applied with greater ease and effectiveness throughout the language learning process during school and, in some cases, university years and hopefully beyond into the realm of lifelong learning (see also Pedagogical implications of the approach).

Pedagogical implications of the case study

The broad conclusions which can be drawn from the above case-study are that the ELP is capable of facilitating the development of presentation skills in a foreign language. Further studies have demonstrated that it is also effective in the development of related but more abstract and overarching skills such as self-assessment and goal-setting (Bruen, 2005; Little, 2002). Nonetheless, there are a still number of criteria which, should they be fulfilled, would further enhance the effectiveness of language learners' work with an ELP.

Firstly, the ELP should ideally accompany the language learner throughout their life from the moment they consciously begin learning languages. In other words, the ELP should not be tied to any one language course or module but instead should be used as an independent tool capable of supporting the language learning process throughout first and second level schooling, into third level and beyond.

If the ELP is used in such a way, it will encourage an approach to language learning wherein the learner maintains a more holistic view of themselves as a "multicompetent" learner of many languages. With support, the learner should also gradually develop the ability to assess their level at any one time in a given language and to determine their language learning needs and set their goals and objectives accordingly.

The development of such metacognitive awareness and the related skills in the learner will most likely result in a demand for more flexible courses which can be tailored to suit the individual needs and priorities of the learner. These courses will also be expected to allow scope and support for independent learning, perhaps parallel to a more formal course structure. For example, if a learner determines that an improvement in their ability to process specialist vocabulary is a key priority for them, it should be possible to integrate activities and materials capable of assisting them in achieving this goal into the relevant module or course. Not withstanding the need for guidance, in the words of Bruen and Sherry (2006), "the interests and particular needs of the learner will become increasingly central in such an approach. As well as impacting on curriculum design, such a shift in perspective will necessitate the revisiting of the processes of assessment and evaluation, in particular". For example, it may be possible to have a number of alternative assessment types from which the learner can choose depending on the priorities determined in conjunction with their lecturer at the beginning of a particular course. Clearly, such an approach is not without its challenges and a great deal of research and curriculum development is still required if it is to be successfully implemented, and what is described as a "portfolio attitude" (L'Hotellier and Troisgros, 2002) to be developed among language learners.

Works Cited

Bruen, Jennifer and Rhona Sherry. 2007. "New Perspectives in Language Learning: Transferable Skills and the Language On-line Portfolio Project," In *New Learning Environments for Language Learning, moving beyond the classroom*, eds. Jean E. Conacher and Helen Kelly-Holmes. 115-126. Frankfurt am Main: Peter Lang.

Bruen, Jennifer. 2005. "How good am I really at German and how good would I like to be? Some initial attempts to integrate self-assessment and goal-setting skills into a German language module using the European Language Portfolio," In *Developing Students Transferable Skills in the Language Classroom*, 7-21. Published by the Transferable Skills Project, 7-21. (Dublin City University, Trinity College Dublin and Waterford Institute of Technology).

Common European Framework of Reference for Languages: Learning, Teaching and Assessment: http://www.coe.int/t/dg4/linguistic/CADRE_EN.asp [accessed 15th July 2006]

Council of Europe Portal / *European Language Portfolio*. 2006. http://www.coe.int/T/DG4/Portfolio/ [accessed 15th July 2006]

Fremdsprachen koennen – was heisst das? 2000. Zurich, Swiss National Foundation: Ruegger.

L'Hotellier, Therese and Elisabet Troisgrois. 2002. "The "Portfolio attitude": using the ELP in a French technical secondary school." In *The European Language Portfolio in Use: Nine Examples*, ed. David Little, 13-18.
http://www.tcd.ie/CLCS/portfolio/ELP_network/ELPInUse_NineExamples.pdf [accessed 16th July 2006]

Little, David, Ed. 2002. *The European Language Portfolio in Use: Nine Examples*,
http://www.tcd.ie/CLCS/portfolio/ELP_network/ELPInUse_NineExamples.pdf [accessed 16th July 2006]

Transferable Skills in Third Level Modern Languages Curricula Project (2002-5) http://www.skillsproject.ie [accessed 14th July 2006]

The Portfolio: Challenges and Experiences in the Portuguese Context

Cristina Avelino and Francine Arroyo

The Council of Europe, which plays a key role in democratising language learning, has in recent decades been involved in a process aiming at the creation of common reference instruments for the promotion of multilingualism. The European Union has taken up this cause and is making use of these instruments to encourage the various member states to develop plurilingualism and pluriculturalism among all of their citizens. The European Year of Languages in 2001 represented the outcome of this work, with the publication of the Common European Framework of Reference for Languages (CEFR) and the proposed European Language Portfolio (ELP).

Portugal, which has been a member of the Council of Europe since 1978, has signed up to these initiatives and agents involved in education have participated in a number of seminars and symposiums on the fine-tuning of these instruments. Consequently, reform of the educational system has brought with it a reformulation of the various curricula, including those for foreign languages, on the basis of the provisional versions of the CEFR. In parallel with this work, a national team was set up to construct a portfolio suited to the Portuguese context.

We shall present the experience of creating and implementing a portfolio for the students of the Faculty of Arts at Lisbon University. Finally, we shall evaluate this experience and reflect on the advantages and limitations of this instrument in institutional learning pathways.

The Portuguese Context

The Portuguese school system is structured into a series of "cycles", with compulsory schooling ending at the 9th school year. Following compulsory education, secondary education offers pupils a diverse range of educational pathways, leading either to access to higher education or to the labour market. Within this framework, the place given to foreign languages has changed substantially over the course of the last decade. Indeed, since the latest reform of the curriculum[1], the study of two foreign languages has been made compulsory between the ages of 6 and 15. In the 1st cycle, the presence of foreign languages is limited to an extracurricular component, depending on the availability of human resources. Nevertheless, from the 2005 school year onwards, it became compulsory to study English in the 3rd and 4th school years, thus contradicting a number of the principles stated in the reform. In statistical terms, it was observed that 87% of primary school pupils started studying English in 2005/2006 under widely varying conditions, including the frequent use of temporary staff. This would hardly appear to provide favourable conditions for the construction of a coherent and well-planned learning process.

At secondary level (10th, 11th and 12th school years), the possibility of studying two languages is more limited, as the pupils must only continue one of their languages compulsorily, and can, in some subject combinations, choose to start another. Studies show that English is the most common language studied, while French stands out among the language options started at secondary level.

The European Language Portfolio (ELP) and language teaching in Portugal

The Office of European Affairs and International Relations (GAERI), the Ministry of Education and language teachers' associations have joined the initiative and have made efforts to produce three model portfolios which have been tested with around 2000 pupils. Two of these, accredited in 2001, are destined for basic education (10-15 years of age) and secondary education (15-18 years of age). The Ministry of Education has subsequently undertaken initiatives to disseminate the portfolio and train teachers in its classroom use, and has organised its printing. The portfolio for the first cycle (6-10 years of age) is currently being tested.

Despite the publicity and training campaigns, introduction of the ELP in the classroom has come up against a number of difficulties and has been slow to catch on. The first difficulty is economic: it represents an additional expense for families who are not convinced of its usefulness. In

---

[1] Legal Decree nº 6/2001 defines the reform of the 1st, 2nd and 3rd cycles and came into force in 2001/2002. Legal Decree nº 7/2001 on the secondary level was suspended in 2002 and subsequently modified by Legal Decree nº 74/2004, which entered force in the school year 2004/2005.

addition, publishers sometimes include a portfolio in school textbooks, which makes it appear all the more superfluous. The second difficulty is of a practical nature. In classes with an average of twenty five pupils, it is difficult for the teacher to find time to monitor individual progress and use the portfolio to improve learning quality. The third difficulty is of an institutional nature, as the Ministry has not made the portfolio compulsory nor even published instructions on its implementation.

Indeed, if there is a genuine will to give the portfolio a role in promoting better language learning, it will be necessary to:

- Include the use of the portfolio in the School Project[2].
- Inform parents and explain to them how the portfolio is to be used, and of their role in filling out the Language Biography.
- Implement a common procedure among language teachers, along with training in using the portfolio.
- Find ways to get pupils to take possession of an instrument which will accompany them throughout their school career.

In addition, general principles must be followed up in the teacher's day-to-day activities. Teachers should:

- Relate the stated aims of the textbook to the descriptors and make them understandable for the pupils.
- Present the instrument and explain the procedure to the pupils.

The pupils should then:

- Fill out the individual sections.
- Read and explain the descriptors.
- Carry out the self-assessment, taking the time to read the descriptors.
- Complete the Language Biography once per term and hand the Passport in to the teacher once annually.
- Organise the storage of portfolios to facilitate their use in class.

These fundamental conditions should make it possible to genuinely help pupils to "learn", to participate more actively and assess their own progress; to encourage pupils by placing value on their achievements; to support teachers in implementing curricula; and also to involve parents in language learning – as this is a process which takes place out of school.

---

[2] In Portugal, all schools are required to negotiate a yearly School Project that consists of statements of content to be covered in all subjects, along with other yearly objectives.

The experience of creating and using a portfolio at the Faculty of Arts of the University of Lisbon (FLUL)

The difficulties students had with language-learning and the absence of reflective attitudes observed among students called for an attempt to implement an instrument which would allow them to become more aware of the process of learning a foreign language and of managing this process better in order to facilitate learning. At the time, a working group had been preparing a national version for university teaching staff, which was never approved nor published. We therefore decided to draft a portfolio that responded to our needs.

We analysed a number of models for the portfolio, particularly the Swiss[3] and Canadian models[4] available online, as well as the French versions of the ELP published by Didier Publishing, all of which influenced our approach. The Language Portfolio – Higher Education', published in 2002, was designed to cover the length of a degree course – 8 semesters – and 3 foreign languages. The portfolio allowed the learner to analyse their own progress in each language and compare their skills in the various languages, thus becoming aware of their plurilingualism. The portfolio was written in Portuguese, the students' native language, to make it easy to read. The introduction, explaining what the portfolio is and relating it to the work of the Council of Europe, is followed by a list of instructions and practical guidance, and four further parts:

1) The first part, entitled *Perfil do aprendente* (Learner Profile) contains a series of questionnaires allowing the learner to better discern their profile. The first, inspired by the work of Paul Cyr (1998), was designed to help define the learner's cognitive profile, which is a decisive factor in choosing which type of activities will best promote learning. The others – dealing with learning habits, attitudes to assessment, and strengths and weaknesses in the foreign language – complete this profile.

2) The second part, *Auto-avaliação das competências em línguas estrangeiras* (Self-Assessment of Foreign Language Skills) contains self-assessment grids classifying skills into six levels (from A1 to C2) – identical to the levels of the CEFR: overall competence, the five communicative competences (listening, reading, spoken interaction, spoken production and writing) and the two linguistic competences

---

[3] Available at http://www.portfoliolangues.ch/esp_e/esp15plus/index.htm (Last accessed 9 October 2007).

[4] Available at http://www.language.ca/display_page.asp?page_id=1 (Last accessed 9 October 2007).

(vocabulary and grammar). A summary table and semester-by-semester target-setting tables complete this part.

3) The third part, *Trabalho em regime de autonomia* (Working Autonomously), contains a series of activities selected for independent work: reading original texts, contact with French-language media (television, radio, press, internet) or cultural and scientific products (cinema, songs, plays, exhibitions, conferences, colloquia, etc.) A double page spread per semester shows the activities recorded. The final table is for self-regulation of the learning processes, where the student should indicate the problems identified in language production and the measures taken to remedy the problem.

4) This portfolio should be completed by the dossier, where the most important pieces of coursework are to be kept, alongside regular progress reports on learning of the foreign language.

Use of the portfolio is compulsory for our students and in order to enhance its credibility at the institutional level it was decided to include it in assessment. The mark given counts for 25% of the final mark, including two compulsory pieces of coursework. These may be based either on curricular activities defined at the beginning of the semester by the teacher, or on autonomous extra-curricular activities: reviews of films, plays, exhibitions etc; reports on experiences in the foreign language; summaries of books; website analyses, etc… In addition, a written statement is requested from each student per semester, allowing assessment of students' reflective abilities. An interview at the end of the semester allows an exchange of opinions between student and teacher on the work they have put in and the progress the learner has achieved.

Evaluating the experience: data and commentaries

The overall balance to be drawn from the experience is rather mixed. Reception on the part of teachers and students at our faculty was not enthusiastic. The few colleagues who did use the portfolio subsequently abandoned it, giving the excuse that it required a lot of work without being particularly useful. Students did not always understand how the portfolio worked and did not really recognise its usefulness. They saw it as a supplementary constraint which many of their classmates did not have to share, and did not understand the philosophy behind it. For example, they had considerable difficulties filling out the self-assessment grids and some only filled out the tables on autonomous activities the night before the interview to "please the teacher" – or simply to receive a good grade. The students who already had good study habits used it well, while the others did not really improve or acquire a more methodical approach by using the portfolio.

In order to give an objective basis to our impressions of four years of using the portfolio in class, we have carried out a survey of the students who took part in the experience. The format, readability and structure received good scores, while lower scores were given for functionality and the relevance of some sections, such as the learner profile and working autonomously. These results are characteristic of the reception of the portfolio: the students are more sensitive to form than content, and they respond negatively to aspects which are new to them.

Indeed, the results of the questionnaire on usage are somewhat contradictory. On the one hand, the students state that the portfolio allowed them to become aware of their profile, to identify the level of their competences, and to develop their autonomy and their reflective attitude. On the other hand, they did not manage to follow their own progress or set new objectives. It did not increase their motivation, they did not use it for languages other than French, and then only because it was compulsory.

In fact, the results of this questionnaire are surprising because they do not correspond to our own observations. The students had no difficulties in using the various descriptors, whereas in reality they had to be told repeatedly how to fill in the grids, and the competence summary tables were often filled in with marks out of 20 rather than their level in the various competences. It also appears that the students did not understand the questionnaire, as it was, bizarrely, the competences where they were weakest (spoken interaction and grammatical competence) which were indicated as those where they had the least difficulties.

The students commented that they found the range of autonomous activities to be too detailed, and that there was a lack of space for the correction of errors, indicating that they considered the portfolio to be an instrument for summative assessment rather than formative assessment. This shows the fundamental role of learning cultures and the difficulties of making such learning environments familiar and comfortable for the students.

Discussion: Advantages and limitations of the ELP

The use of the ELP in the learning process for foreign languages reflects a positive idea of European integration and is based upon socio-affective, cognitive, linguistic and cultural dimensions. The socio-affective dimension involves the relationship with oneself and confidence in one's own competences. It explains different learning pathways and attributes to this learning process a fundamental social role. The legitimacy and value given to non-school languages by the ELP helps avoid the stigmatisation of certain languages, such as Arabic in France, and takes account of the multicultural composition of modern societies and the intercultural dimension implicit in all learning processes.

In the cognitive dimension, the ELP is an instrument which allows knowledge to be mobilised and transferred, but above all it allows the development of analytical skills to be applied to the learning process by enabling an awareness of individual procedures and strategies and the guiding role of the teacher. The linguistic and cultural elements are inherent to the task-based approach advocated by the CEFR. This approach facilitates the mobilisation of both knowledge and know-how in carrying out contextualised communicative activities, thus illustrating the diversity of social customs.

The versatility of the ELP is another undeniable advantage, as it can provide benefits to learning in other subjects, such as the mother tongue; it can be used in all learning contexts (Basic and Higher Education, bilingual classes, CLIL, language schools etc.); and can take a number of physical forms: paper or electronic format. The electronic ELP would be an advantage, both for the process of individual learning management and teacher guidance and for the social validation of experience and competences.

Still, there are certain difficulties involved, one of the main ones being the definition of an overall level of competence. Basically, it is easier to understand than to produce language and this is not made transparent in the CEFR descriptors. Learning a language in a school environment accentuates understanding over production because it is more natural to expose the learner to a range of "productions", particularly with the introduction of new technologies, than it is to encourage the learner to express herself in the foreign language to communicate in her everyday life, as she would in the foreign country.

Progress in the various competences will vary as a function of numerous factors, depending on the time given over to learning each competence, the methodology used by the teacher, the personality of each learner–who will tend to prefer certain activities over others–but also upon the different thresholds that must be crossed. For a beginner learning a language from the same family as her mother tongue, rapid progress is made in the early stages across all competences–she will arrive without too much difficulty at an overall A2 level and will feel satisfied by her learning abilities. The transition from the A levels to the B levels, particularly in terms of production, is much more difficult, and the qualitative leap between B1 and B2 often causes the learner to feel as if she were at a dead end and were unable to go beyond a certain stage.

A further difficulty resides in the self-assessment element, which remains somewhat subjective, especially when the difference between descriptors comes down to small nuances–for example, in the area of spoken interaction: "I can communicate with a degree of spontaneity and ease that makes normal interaction possible with a native speaker" (B2) and "I can express myself spontaneously and fluently without obviously having to search for words" (C1). The self-assessment also reflects the self-esteem and self-confidence of the person concerned, often linked to educational backgrounds: it is not unusual to see good students underestimating themselves and bad students being over-confident.

The ELP, in the form it was conceived, is rather an unwieldy instrument that sometimes lacks uniformity, as each country has adopted different models and, furthermore, it is not widely recognised in the labour market, which continues to prefer diplomas over competences acquired in other circumstances. Still, the Europass portfolio, adopted in 2005, is gaining currency. This "provides a detailed summary of the contents and results, expressed in terms of competences or academic results, obtained by an individual–whatever their age, level of education or professional situation–during the course of a structured stay in another European country for the purpose of learning, education or training." It is made up of five documents: the Europass CV, the Diploma Supplement, the Certificate Supplement, the European Language Portfolio and Europass Mobility, with standardised forms available in the languages spoken in the 31 countries involved in this mobility initiative.

In sum, the portfolio, in whichever form it is presented, is an instrument which enables quantitative and qualitative improvements in language learning to be achieved. Our own experience underlines the importance of the affective and psychological dimensions inherent to all learning processes, and the results can be explained by the fact that individual affirmation and autonomy are not highly valued in Portuguese society in general and in the education system in particular. The resistance shown by students and teachers to the introduction of this instrument in higher education could be overcome if the ELP were introduced as early as possible in pupils' school careers.

The restructuring of higher education in the framework of the Bologna Process is the ideal opportunity to implement the portfolio, at least in foreign languages. Ultimately, how can we assess the work put in by each student on an individual basis – which represents an increasing percentage of the hours taken into account by the ECTS – and the acquisition of competences, given that the number of teaching hours is to fall? This consideration is at the heart of the new educational paradigm, as can be seen from the many meetings of higher education language teachers taking place in a number of countries on this very issue, and the portfolio may provide part of the answer.

Works Cited

Arroyo, Francine and Cristina Avelino. 2002. *Portfólio das Línguas Estrangeiras – Ensino Superior*, Lisboa: Edições Colibri.
Council of Europe. 2000. *European Language Portfolio (ELP): Principles and Guidelines*, Strasbourg: Council of Europe.
Conseil de l'Europe. 2001. *Portfolio européen des langues pour jeunes et adultes*. Paris. Didier.
—. 2001. *Un Cadre européen commun de référence pour les langues: Apprendre, enseigner, évaluer: Guide général d'utilisation.* Strasbourg: Conseil de l'Europe.
—. 2001.*Un Cadre européen commun de référence pour les langues: Apprendre, enseigner, évaluer.* Paris: Didier.
Conselho da Europa. 2001. *Portfolio Europeu de Línguas. Educação Básica. 10-15 anos.* Lisbon: Ministério da Educação.
—. 2001. *Portfolio Europeu de Línguas. Ensino Secundário. 15-18 anos.* Lisbon: Ministério da Educação.
—. 2001. *Quadro Europeu Comum de Referência para as Línguas: Aprendizagem, Ensino, Avaliação.* Porto: Asa Edições.
Cyr, Paul. 1998. *Les stratégies d'apprentissage.* Paris: CLE International.
Scharer, Rolf. 2001. *Un Portfolio européen des langues: Rapport final du projet pilote (1998 – 2000)*, Strasbourg: Conseil de l'Europe.
Schneider, Gunther and Peter Lenz. 2001. *Un Portfolio européen des langues: Guide pour l'élaboration du Portfolio européen des langues.* Strasbourg: Conseil de l'Europe.

THE EUROPEAN LANGUAGE PORTFOLIO IN ROMANIA AND THE EUROINTEGRELP PROJECT

LILIANA DELLEVOET AND LAURA MUREŞAN

The aim of this article is to illustrate the implementation of the European Language Portfolio (ELP) in Romania, as well as to give an example of an ELP dissemination project[1] developed between ten European countries. A special focus will be on the EAQUALS–ALTE European Language Portfolio (2000), the pan-European version for adults[2]. For illustration purposes, reference will be made to the foreign language learning context within the Romanian Association for Quality Language Services (QUEST Romania), at the PROSPER-ASE Language Centre, and at the Academy of Economic Studies in Bucharest.

History and context of the EAQUALS-ALTE ELP in Romania

The introduction of the European Language Portfolio (the EAQUALS-ALTE version for adults) in Romania began in 1999 when it was piloted at several language centres, all of which were founding members of QUEST Romania (an Associate Member of EAQUALS—The European Association for Quality Language Services). As Schärer (2001) points out, QUEST Romania piloted the pre-final version of the EAQUALS-ALTE ELP with a number of adult language learners taking English courses as part of a lifelong learning process. Within the context of Romania's

---

[1] Lingua 1 Project "EuroIntegrELP-Equal Chances to European Integration through the use of the European Language Portfolio" (2004-2007), co-ordinated by PROSPER-ASE Language Centre, Bucharest, Romania, with partners in ten countries: Austria, Belgium, Estonia, Greece, Italy, Lithuania, Poland, Romania, Slovakia, and Croatia. www.prosper.ro/EuroIntegrELP/EurointegrELP.htm

[2] The EAQUALS-ALTE European Language Portfolio, validation number 6/2000, available in 19 languages.

declared intention to join the European Union, QUEST Romania wanted to mark the European Year of Languages 2001 by officially launching the European Language Portfolio —the EAQUALS-ALTE version— under the auspices of the President of Romania. This was carried out in partnership with other European Cultural Institutes in Romania (e.g. the British Council, Goethe-Institut, l'Institut Français, Instituto Cervantes, and the Italian Institute) and consisted of a pilot version of the Language Passport —comprising English, French and Romanian— and the translation of the Biography and Dossier for revision and consultation on Romanian key-terminology. The event was widely covered by the media.

Because this new approach to language learning has been supported and promoted by all the above-mentioned institutions, the idea of self-evaluation of one's language competencies began to gain ground, as did the conceptual shift in focus from teaching to learning. This implies empowering the learner as the responsibility for language learning shifts from teacher to learner and language user. Moreover, due to the wide school networks involved, this change covered not only the capital city Bucharest, but all the other major towns in Romania as well.

The translation of the three portfolio components into Romanian went through several stages, including revision, piloting, and consultation with FL teachers and teacher-trainers. Upon completion of this process, the Romanian version of the EAQUALS-ALTE Portfolio was approved by the National Board responsible for the validation of ELPs in Romania. 5000 copies of the EAQUALS-ALTE Portfolio—the version for Romania (made up of English, French, German and Romanian) were published by QUEST Romania (an NGO) in partnership with government and non-governmental organisations. In October 2004, the portfolio received a high profile launch at the annual national QUEST conference, presided by Dr. Peter Brown, Founding Chair of the European Association EAQUALS, and attended by representatives of ministries, European cultural institutes, embassies and other dignitaries.

Activities aimed at promoting the ELP in Romania were initiated mainly by QUEST Romania and QUEST language centres, as well as by cultural institutes such as Goethe-Institut Bukarest and l'Institut Français de Bucarest, often in partnership with the Romanian Ministry of Education and Research. Dissemination methods and materials have been adapted to the different target audiences: FL teachers, teacher trainers, inspectors, the media, and student organisations. The most frequent types of activities include conference presentations, teacher training workshops, meetings with representatives of ministries and other authorities, participation in educational fairs, and press conferences.

As a result of these activities, by the end of 2006 approximately 300 institutions were using the ELP, ranging from high schools, universities, language centres, European cultural institutes, to a number of corporate clients. Currently there are approximately 4500 ELP copies in use, as shown also in the *ELP: Interim Report 2006* (Schärer, 2007: 42-43). Still, the number of language learners and ELP users such as high school pupils, university students, and adults in companies who have come into contact with the portfolio is significantly higher, since there are users who have downloaded the electronic version of the EAQUALS-ALTE eELP.

Teacher Training and Development

The introduction of the new concepts and instruments can only be achieved with the full participation of its proponents, among whom teachers have a key role. Therefore, during the last few years, QUEST Romania—in cooperation with PROSPER-ASE Language Centre and other member schools—has been actively involved in running teacher training sessions. These are very often held in association with the Romanian Ministry of Education, teachers' associations and the European cultural institutions. The aim of such sessions is to familiarize the trainees, foreign language teachers and university faculty members with the concepts and instruments introduced by the Council of Europe and the European Union. These training sessions are also aimed at teachers of Romanian as a mother tongue. One goal is to instil an understanding of standardised language competencies for all these groups. Along these lines, the EAQUALS-ALTE version of the European Language Portfolio and the Europass Passport are presented to them as self-evaluation tools, encouraging them to use the checklists in the Language Biography and the self-assessment grid in the Language Passport, so as to experience ELP-based self-assessment as FL-language learners and users themselves.

For the success of such an activity, the participants in the training session are invited to think of a language that they have learned (either as a foreign language or a second language, not necessarily in a school-environment) but which they do *not* teach. They have to select one skill area they want to focus on and to reflect on the language level they might have in that particular area (e.g. listening comprehension or spoken interaction). They are then invited to go through the "can-do" descriptors in the relevant section of the Language Biography, to see which of the descriptors reflect their language competencies and which might become their "priorities" for further language learning. The next step consists of cross-checking with the "can-do" statements in the relevant section of the self-assessment grid in the Language Passport, to see if these reflect their language profile. In most cases, even without the trainer prompting it, the participants start sharing with peers the outcomes of self-assessment, as well as reflections on how they have learned a language, how their competencies in one field or one language compare with those in another, in what contexts they get to use their FLs and what benefits they derive from this. Experience of facilitating this reflective, self-assessment activity with numerous groups in various teacher training contexts has confirmed that language teachers are the most enthusiastic language learners.

Teacher development sessions for teachers already familiar with the ELP include illustrations of how the ELP can be correlated with the more detailed CEFR reference levels for specific communication contexts. These provide the basis for practical activities, engaging the participants in drawing the language profile of their groups of students for course planning purposes, for materials selection and writing, for standardising test design and evaluation. Among the materials used to this effect more recently are video recordings illustrating the European reference levels (Council of Europe & Cambridge ESOL, 2005), as well as a selection of activities from CEFR-related materials (North & Hughes, 2003; North, 2006) and the *EAQUALS (h)ELP Manual* (Blakey, 2007).

Participants in the training sessions appreciated the practical ELP-related activities, which convinced them of the usefulness of the EAQUALS-ALTE ELP as a self-assessment tool and enhanced their confidence in implementing the CEFR reference levels for course and test design purposes. To ensure the multiplying effect of this training, action plans have been drawn up for disseminating good practice among teaching staff in various educational institutions, and for promoting the CEFR and ELP as key-elements of "a conceptual framework for teaching, learning and assessment" (Heyworth, 2007). In addition, since 2001, all QUEST Romania conferences and seminars have focused on the CEFR, the ELP and quality assurance, as inter-related, transversal areas in language education, bringing together teacher trainers and teachers of all languages, fostering cooperation and networking among them.

Examples of Implementing the ELP in the Context of European Integration

Romania's entry into the European Union was a dream come true for many Romanians, but full integration requires a lot of preparation. With this purpose in mind, several English language teachers at the Academy of Economic Studies in Bucharest (a prestigious higher education institution) produced textbooks that included units meant to raise the young undergraduates' awareness of the existence and usefulness of European language learning tools such as the European Language Portfolio and Europass. Its usefulness for them was emphasised by pointing out how it could be helpful in case they should decide to study or work in other countries in the European Union.

Example One: ELP and Europass for European Integration

A case study of how students are introduced to the importance of the ELP for future job perspectives can be found in "Learning and Growing" (Codreanu *et al*, 2005) with a unit entitled "Citizens of Europe" (Dellevoet, 2005). The main aim of this activity is to introduce the students to the European instruments (Europass and the ELP) and the idea of self-evaluation through examples and reflective activities.

The unit starts by inviting the students to answer a key question: whether they are ready for European integration, considering that once a country accedes to the European Union, its language becomes an official language. In order to highlight the importance of learning foreign languages even under these circumstances, the students are invited to ask each other questions such as:

- Why do people learn foreign languages?
- Do you need to know foreign languages? Why?
- How many foreign languages do you know?
- When and how did you learn them? Etc.

The next step is to ask the students to read two short texts, the first one is an excerpt from "Language learning" (Cook, 1991) and the second one is taken from "Europe —a wealth of languages" (CoE, 2005). Students are asked to try to compare their own reasons for learning foreign languages with the objectives identified by the Council of Europe. The third step introduces the idea of learning foreign languages in order to study or to work abroad. Students are asked to identify the advantages and disadvantages of such situations and then to finalise the task by drawing up a list (working in pairs or small groups) that describes the main strengths needed by someone who wants to study or work in the EU and also, very importantly, how to prove to the respective educational institutions or employers that they have these competencies.

Inevitably, this activity prepares the ground for introducing information about the Europass: its aim "to encourage mobility and lifelong learning in an enlarged Europe and how it helps millions of citizens to make their qualifications and skills easily understood throughout Europe by 2010"[3].

Further on, the students are presented with two model CVs, the traditional one and the Europass CV, and asked to compare them and identify the elements of novelty introduced in the Europass CV. Finally, the students discuss how many of the new elements in the Europass are related to communication in foreign languages and intercultural skills.

The presentation of the Europass continues with the introduction of the Europass Language Passport. The teachers mention its importance for describing one's language skills—and as the students have already discussed—these are vital when working or studying in Europe. The fact that the European Language Passport was developed by the Council of Europe as one of the three parts of the European Language Portfolio is highlighted.

This is followed by a short reading activity that provides basic information about the EAQUALS-ALTE ELP, namely the Language Passport, the Language Biography and the Dossier. This leads into the next activity in which the students are guided, by means of a reflective activity, to understand how they can fill in the Language Passport (Dellevoet, 2005). This is the moment when the idea of self-evaluation is introduced. Students are made aware of how objective or subjective we are when assessing our own activity, as well as of the need to be true to oneself and as objective as possible when filling in this document. Using the self-assessment grid in the Language Passport, the students are then asked to fill in their own language profile (for English or any other foreign language), as shown in the example below.

---

[3] http://europass.cedefop.eu.int

Fig. 5-4 Example of self-assessment activity

Instructions: Look at the self-assessment grid—which is included in the Language Passport (see below)—and evaluate your present language level for the five skills in the grid. Some people may have different levels in the different skills. Don't worry; this may be due to your past or current priorities in language learning. You may want, depending on your future plans, to insist more on some skills than on the others.

The levels in the self-assessment grid stand for:

A1 and A2 – Basic User
B1 and B2 – Independent User
C1 and C2 – Proficient User

	A1	A2	B1	B2	C1	C2
Understanding Listening						
Reading						
Speaking Spoken interaction						
Spoken production						
Writing Writing						

Drawing from the authors' experience with hundreds of students who were presented the EAQUALS-ALTE ELP for adults, it can be assumed that students demonstrate a positive attitude toward self-assessment and that they are not inclined to overestimate their language skills. Indeed they tend to be quite objective and produce reliable self-evaluations.

Example Two: Preparing students for effective participation in business meetings

This is an example of integrating self- and peer-evaluation in the business English course both at the Academy of Economic Studies and the adult courses at the PROSPER-ASE Language Centre. The main aim is that of improving the students' overall performance in professional meetings, with a special focus on

- spoken interaction, communication strategies and the quality of verbal and non-verbal communication
- improving self- and peer-assessment competencies of performance in real-life like situations of professional communication.

The unfolding of this complex process takes up a series of sessions and comprises several stages, e.g.:

Warm-up activity: Students are asked to reflect for a few moments on (a) the most successful meeting they have participated in and to note down 3 aspects that, in their view, contributed to its success, and (b) the least successful meeting they can remember, trying to identify 3 aspects that might have caused problems in the meeting. This is followed by a brief sharing of impressions in pairs or small groups and elicitation of a few comments in plenary, so as to start drawing up a list of communication aspects of relevance in meetings.

Self-assessment activities: These focus on communication skills that are relevant for meetings. By the time students get to participate in these sessions on "business meetings", they are already familiar with the EAQUALS-ALTE ELP. They are, therefore, asked to re-visit the checklists in the Language Biography from a new perspective, with a special focus on the "can-do" statements for spoken interaction, strategies and language quality, so as to identify those that can be of particular relevance for communication in meetings, as shown in the excerpts taken from The EAQUALS-ALTE European Language Portfolio, the Language Biography (p. E-17)[4].

---

[4] The descriptors in the EAQUALS-ALTE Language Biography were developed for the CEFR and the ELP in a Swiss National Science Foundation project: (Günther Schneider & Brian North, 2000, *Fremdsprachen können - was heisst das?* Chur and Zürich: Rüegger).

Fig. 5-5 "Can-do statements"

C1 - Spoken Interaction (*excerpts*)
I can use the language fluently, accurately and effectively on a wide range of general, professional or academic topics.
I can express my ideas and opinions clearly and precisely, and can present and respond to complex lines of reasoning convincingly.

C1 - Strategies (*excerpts*)
I can use fluently a variety of appropriate expressions to preface my remarks in order to get the floor, or to gain time and keep the floor while thinking.
I can relate own contribution skilfully to those of other speakers.

Additionally, in order to help students establish their priorities and learning targets with more accuracy—for instance, specific sub-skills necessary in a professional communication context—the more detailed level descriptors for "Formal Discussion and Meetings" (CEFR, 2001: 78) are introduced as an awareness-raising activity. However, instead of presenting the scale as such, it has been turned into a matching and sequencing exercise, with the descriptors for C2 and A2.1 in their correct place and all the others (from A2.2 to C1) jumbled up. The students (individually or in pairs) re-order and match the descriptors with the corresponding reference levels.

Students are encouraged to compare the outcome of their selection and sequencing exercise with that of their peer(s) and discuss the specific elements that contributed to their decision-making. Next they are invited to reflect on their communicative competencies for participation in a professional meeting and to set their priorities for this particular communication context. (An illustration of this activity is included in Appendix E). Depending on the focus of the lesson or course, other CEFR scales (e.g. "Interviewing and Being Interviewed" CEFR, 2001: 82) can be turned into similar activities, in order to raise the students' awareness of the more detailed "can-do" descriptors for communication in specific situations (Mureşan, 2005).

One such awareness-raising activity is the use of a video session, illustrating effective and ineffective meetings, combined with practice in evaluating the observed meeting samples. This is based on the video course *Effective Meetings* (Confort, 1998) and includes a selection of relevant pre-, while- and post-viewing activities. In addition, it offers the opportunity to take further elements from previous stages, e.g. the discussion of positive and negative aspects responsible for success and failure in meetings. The teacher can also integrate the evaluation checklists provided in the video course with the discussion of the CEFR "can-do" descriptors. This allows students to start using the descriptors for the evaluation of the meeting samples observed and to make comparisons with their own perceptions of what counts as good and bad communication. In this way, students can gradually work towards standardising and improving their self- and peer-assessment skills.

Another awareness-raising activity is role play based on case studies. In this activity, students are presented with case studies selected from *Business Interactions* (Matthews, 1987) or *Professional Interactions* (Matthews and Marino, 1990). Students are invited to decide in groups of 5 – 7 on the "meeting" they would like to participate in and the role they would like to take on. It is best to allow the students to choose their roles. Experience of facilitating this process with numerous groups over the years has shown that it is counter-productive to impose a case study on a group of (young) adults or to prescribe the roles that individual students should play. By giving students the freedom to make their own choices, a more "real-life" environment is created and students are provided opportunities to engage in the speaking activities that they feel most comfortable with.

During the course of the activity, there is always also at least one observer, if possible, preferably two observers. If there are two or three observers, they can be asked to focus on different aspects of the meeting or on the performance of different teams participating in the meeting.

The role play or simulation of the meeting is followed by the participants' self-evaluation of their performance, using the self-evaluation sheets in *Business Interactions* (Matthews, 1987). These, combined with the CEFR "can-do" descriptors for communication in meetings not only help them recognise their language competencies, but also guide them for setting their next language learning priorities. At the same time, the self-evaluation sheets can be helpful for personalised remedial work. Language learners are also invited to assess their progress over one semester or at the end of an academic year or language course/module using the self-evaluation grid and to collect evidence of their language learning activity in the Dossier. In this way, most of them are more motivated because they can chart their own progress.

Example Three: Relevance of Self-Evaluation for BEC Preparation

This is an example of a class at the PROSPER-ASE Language Centre[5] with a group of 8 students (young adults) preparing to take the Cambridge BEC Vantage exam. The aim of this activity was to help students correlate ELP-based self-assessment with assessment guidelines used by international examiners.

The skills on which the lesson was focused were Reading in accordance with the specific requirements of the BEC exam and Interactive communication through problem solving (based on ideas included in the reading text "Starting a Business: service and manufacturing sectors compare" (Allsop and Aspinall, 2004). The purpose of the lesson was to help the course participants understand the usefulness of self-evaluation and to learn how to do so with the help of the descriptors in the Language Biography.

The course participants were already familiar with the European Language Portfolio, which had been introduced to them three months before, at the beginning of the module, as well as with the specific requirements of the BEC Vantage exam for all the skills to be tested: Reading, Writing, Listening and Speaking.

The activity used during the lesson was meant to give the students the opportunity to identify the similarities between the descriptors for level B2 in the ELP and the necessary skills for taking the BEC Vantage exam (also requiring the B2 language level). To begin with, the students received the lists of descriptors in the Language Biography of the EAQUALS-ALTE ELP for level B2 ("My current language learning priorities"). However, the teacher adapted the format of the checklist —after the two columns entitled "My priorities" and "I can" respectively, the teacher added a third column with the heading "I need this skill for BEC Vantage".

Then, working individually, the students analysed the "can-do" descriptors they had been presented with for the Reading comprehension part. They had to identify the descriptors they felt were relevant for passing the BEC Vantage exam. After individual reflection, conclusions were drawn as a group and it became clear for the students that the competencies they needed in order to pass the BEC Vantage exam were included in those listed in the Language Biography for Level B2. Having defined the necessary competence for Reading (e.g. "I can understand in

---

[5] This case study was included in a Report of the Romanian Institute for the Sciences of Education (2005): *Introducing the Europass Language Passport in the Romanian Education System – Opportunities, Challenges, Solutions* (unpublished).

detail texts within my field of interest or the area of my academic or professional speciality"), the students were asked to solve a variety of reading exercises with multiple choice questions at BEC Vantage level.

At the end of the lesson, the course participants expressed their appreciation of the usefulness of the ELP when learning a foreign language—business English in particular—since it provides them the opportunity of placing themselves on a standardised scale of competence levels, using descriptors related to actual situations in which they must be able to communicate.

Feedback on the ELP

Ever since the EAQUALS-ALTE ELP was introduced in 2001, there has been a constant concern to obtain feedback both from teachers and from learners, in various ways such as surveys, questionnaires, focus groups, informal interviews and discussions. An example of such a questionnaire can be found on the CD ROM *Quality Management in Language Education* (Mureşan *et al*, 2003).[6] Another example was developed for a specific group of teachers—Business English teachers at the Academy of Economic Studies participating in a professional development and mentoring programme. The questionnaire is included in Appendix F. The overview below comprises the most frequent responses obtained in the period 2004-2006[7].

Teachers' feedback: The experience accumulated by Romanian teachers regarding the use of the ELP in class has revealed clear benefits, as well as a number of constraints and challenges. On the one hand, teachers appreciate that the ELP is a very good evaluation and self-evaluation tool, which:
- can be used by a wide public.

---

[6] This CD ROM was the outcome of an ECML project *Quality Assurance and Self-assessment for Schools and Teachers* (Mureşan, Heyworth, Matheidesz & Rose, 2000-2003). It includes CEFR and ELP-related materials and is available on-line on the ECML web site: http://www.ecml.at/html/quality/index.htm

[7] Action research on ELP-implementation was carried out at PROSPER-ASE within projects such as
REFINE: Recognising Formal, Informal and Non-formal Education (EC, DGEAC Joint Action Programme, 2004-2006) - http://www.eucen.org/REFINE/All.html, and the Romanian Educational Sciences Institute research project on *Introducing the Europass Language Passport* (2005).

- is clear and accurate, since minimal differences were noticed between the evaluation made by the teacher and the results of the students' self-evaluation.
- the language used in the ELP is accessible, since it refers to real, daily situations.
- when students fill in the ELP, the language learning priorities and objectives become clearer to them and they can identify their learning style.
- it is a good method to become aware of one's personal strengths and weaknesses related to language learning. Consequently language learners become more aware of their role and responsibilities in the educational process.
- the way in which the items are structured raises the students' awareness of their level and their priorities in language learning and makes it easier for them to establish personal aims in language learning.

On the other hand, teachers also highlighted some challenges they encountered when using the ELP. The main ones mentioned by teachers include:
- some of the questions are too general and consequently some of the answers may be incomplete.
- some of the items contain more than one competency descriptors for competencies the students might be able to assess better separately.
- peer-teachers who had not participated in relevant teacher training may lack confidence and expertise.
- there aren't enough support materials and teaching activities linked to the ELP.
- the students had difficulties in evaluating what they could already do.
- students filling in the ELP need to receive clear instructions in order to do so correctly.

Students' feedback: Most of the students who came into contact with the ELP considered it an interesting experience and confirmed its usefulness for setting learning objectives, for measuring progress and identifying areas that still needed their attention. They also considered that becoming familiar with the ELP and self-assessment criteria made it easier for them to fill in the European CV and to prepare for job interviews. While there seems to be agreement on the main areas, there were also different views expressed regarding some aspects, e.g. some students thought that the ELP was too complex and that it took too long to complete.

They also felt that the ELP could have a more attractive design in order to keep the learners' attention focused. According to the students, there is too much information on the same page; the letters should be bigger and the blank spaces larger. Other students were worried that assessment results could be influenced by the subjectivity of the self-assessment and may be influenced by the learner's mood at the time of assessment. Also, for a self-assessment tool, they felt it is a bit too elaborate, and it might, therefore, be more difficult to use by people who had not been properly introduced to it.

Within QUEST Romania, there has been on-going interest in participating in national and international events focusing on the ELP and the CEFR and at the same time in finding out how teacher feedback on the ELP and the implementation of self-assessment in Romania compares with that expressed by teachers in other countries. Project meetings and surveys carried out within the EuroIntegrELP project have revealed that there are a lot of similarities as far as ELP-related challenges and opportunities go. In response to these, Council of Europe, EAQUALS, ALTE and ECML experts have produced very useful CEFR and ELP-related training materials. At the same time, EAQUALS members have produced and/or translated teacher training materials for their local context. Through the EuroIntegrELP project, teacher training was organised in all partner countries and a variety of support and dissemination materials have been produced and/or translated, so as to ensure the ELP's sustainability also after the project's end. It can, therefore, be assumed that as a result of the latest developments in the field, the implementation of the Common Reference Levels and of the ELP will gain a new impetus and that this will be reflected differently in the next round of surveys carried out among teachers and learners.

Concluding Remarks

As a conclusion regarding the ELP in Romania, we could definitely say that over the last 7 years people have become more familiar with the idea of self-evaluation and are more aware of the necessity to self-evaluate their competencies. The appearance of the Europass has given more visibility to this concept and the importance placed on self-evaluation has increased in many different sectors —both private and public—given its connection to employability.

At a national level, the growing interest in the relationship between education and employment can be observed, as is proven by a project initiated by the Romanian National Agency for Community Programmes in the Field of Education and Training, entitled "Education, labour market and employability in Minerva, Grundtvig and Lingua projects". Through the conferences organised as part of this transversal project, members of selected projects coordinated by various institutions in Lithuania, Bulgaria, Portugal and Romania offered project members, including the EuroIntegrELP team, the opportunity to share some of their expertise gleaned from their experiences in this area. This seems to portend an even more wide-spread integration of the ELP as education policy-makers are made more aware of the need to introduce changes that correspond to the future labour market.

Works Cited

Allsop, Jake and Tricia Aspinall. 2004. *BEC Testbuilders*. Oxford, UK: Macmillan Education.

Blakey, Rebecca. 2007. *Practical (h)ELP, The EAQUALS-ALTE European Language Portfolio: A Self-Help Manual for Schools and Teachers*, Trieste: EAQUALS.

Confort, Jeremy. 1998. *Effective Meetings*, video course, Oxford, UK: Oxford University Press.

Cook, Vivian. 1991. *Second Language Learning and Language Teaching*, London: Routledge.

Council of Europe. 2001. *Common European Framework of Reference for Languages: learning, teaching, assessment*, Cambridge: Cambridge University Press & Council of Europe (www.coe.int/portfolio and www.coe.int/lang)

Council of Europe. 2005. "The Celebration of Linguistic Diversity", Strasbourg: Council of Europe. Available at www.coe.int/EDL.

Dellevoet, Liliana. 2005. "Citizens of Europe." In *Learning and Growing*, ed. Anca Codreanu, Liliana Dellevoet, Tania Măgureanu, and Valentina Robu, 38-45. Bucharest: Cavaliotti.

EAQUALS & ALTE. 2000. *The European Language Portfolio, version for adults*, Council of Europe accreditation 6/2000, Milan: Editione Lang (for the eELP: http://www.eelp.org/eportfolio/index.html)

Heyworth, Frank. 2007. "Quality Principles and Basic Concepts". In *QualiTraining – A Training Guide for Quality Assurance in Language Education*. eds. Laura Mureșan, Frank Heyworth, Galya Mateva, and Mary Rose, 4-16, Graz/Strasbourg: European Centre for Modern

Languages and Council of Europe Publishing. Available at http://www.ecml.at/mtp2/QualiTraining/Default.htm

Matthews, Candace and Joanne Marino. 1990. *Professional Interactions,* Englewood Cliffs, New Jersey: Prentice Hall.

Matthews, Candace. 1987. *Business Interactions,* Englewood Cliffs, New Jersey: Prentice Hall.

Mureşan, Laura, Frank Heyworth, Maria Matheidesz, and Mary Rose, eds. 2003. *Quality Management in Language Education,* Graz/Strasbourg: European Centre for Modern Languages and Council of Europe Publishing (CD ROM, accessible also on-line at http://www.ecml.at/html/quality/index.htm).

Muresan, Laura. 2005. "Self-assessment of Communication Competencies with the Help of the European Language Portfolio". In *First Steps into Marketing,* eds. Monica Marin, Laura Muresan, Iulia Rășcanu, and Raluca Şerban, pp 31-43, Bucharest: Editura Uranus.

North, Brian and Gareth Hughes. 2003. *CEF Performance Samples: for relating Language Examinations to the European Framework of Reference for Languages: Learning, Teaching, Assessment,* Strasbourg: Council of Europe, Language Policy Division.

Schärer, Rolf. 2001. *European Language Portfolio: Final Report on the Pilot Project (1998-2000),* Strasbourg, Council of Europe

—. 2007. *European Language Portfolio: Interim Report 2006,* Strasbourg: Council of Europe, Language Policy Division.

Schneider, Günther and Brian North. 2000. *Fremdsprachen können — was heisst das?* Chur and Zürich: Rüegger.

Recommended Reading: European Language Portfolio

Dickenson, Leslie. 1992. *Learner training for language learning*, Dublin: Authentik.

Kohonen, Viljo and Gerard Westhoff. 2001. *Enhancing the Pedagogical Aspects of the European Language Portfolio*. Strasbourg: Council of Europe.

Little, David and Radka Perclová. 2001. *European Language Portfolio: guide for teachers and teacher trainers*. Strasbourg: Council of Europe.

Little, David and Radka Perclova. 2001. *The European Language Portfolio: A guide for teachers and teacher trainers*, Strasbourg: Council of Europe.

Little, David. 2005. "The Common European Framework of Reference for Languages and the European Language Portfolio: Involving learners and their judgements in the assessment process," *Language Testing*, 22: 321-336.

—. 2006. "The Common European Framework of Reference for Languages: Content, purpose, origin, reception and impact," *Language Teaching*, 39: 167-190.

Schärer, Rolf. 2000. *European Language Portfolio: final report on the pilot project*. Strasbourg: Council of Europe.

Schneider, Günther and Brian North. 2000. *"Dans d'autres langues, je suis capable de ...". Echelles pour la descript, l'évaluation et l'auto-évaluation des competences en langues estrangères*. Berne and Aarau: Direction du Programme national de recherche 33, en collaboration avec le Centre suisse de coordination pour la recherche en éducation.

Schneider, Günther and Brian North. 2000. *Fremdsprachen können – was heisst das?* Chur and Zurich: Rüegger.

Schneider, Günther and Peter Lenz. 2001. *A Guide for Developers of European Language Portfolios*. Strasbourg: Council of Europe.

Slavík, Jan. 1999. *Hodnocení v soucasné skole*. Prague: Portál.

Ushioda, Ema and Jennifer Ridley. 2002. *Working with the European Language Portfolio in Irish post-primary schools: report on an evaluation project.* CLCS Occasional Paper No.61. Dublin: Trinity College, Centre for Language and Communication Studies.

Chapter Six

Exploring New Horizons – Young Learners and Multiple Intelligences: Introduction

Melinda Dooly

In many ways, language plays a key role in all learning processes and language teachers can explore different means of expanding that process to encompass areas outside of the traditional language classroom. For instance, there is a growing trend across Europe, as well as in other parts of the world, to introduce foreign languages at early ages. This is based on the understanding that learning foreign languages in elementary and preschool education promotes the achievement of higher levels of language proficiency not only in the initial target language but also in multiple languages. The average age for beginning foreign language instruction is around 8 years old in most European countries, although there are many countries which are beginning "experimental" lessons (sometimes called "language tasting") as early as preschool. This contrasts quite sharply with foreign language teaching in the United States of America, for example, where foreign language instruction is not introduced until secondary levels, usually around the age of fourteen.

Many government policies which promote early language learning are based on research which indicates that early language learning may have a very positive effect on students with respect to fostering language skills (Garfinkel and Tabor, 1991), along with promoting other types of development. Research also implies that early language instruction can promote a positive attitude toward other languages and cultures, and may lead to increased self-esteem and intercultural awareness (Deardorff, 2004).

Furthermore, there are indications of academic and cognitive benefits, such as increased creativity and better problem-solving abilities, which may accrue from learning other languages (Bamford and Mizokawa, 1991). A study of the reading ability of bilingual children indicated that bilingual children had better reading comprehension than monolingual children (Bialystok, 1997). Of course, it is not our intention to imply that bilingual cases such as those studied by Bialystok are identical to cases of foreign language learning –which is usually limited to one to three hours per week. However, several studies have found better achievement test results from students who had participated in foreign language instruction compared to students who had not (Cooper, 1987; Thomas, Collier, and Abbott, 1993). (It should be noted that achievement tests tend to be comprehensive and cover areas of language, mathematics, and science. The comparisons were based on overall scores, not individual areas.)

Of course, this does not mean that language learning must necessarily begin at an early age —it is not an all or nothing situation. Nonetheless, research does support the notion that young learners have a more innate ability to attain near-native pronunciation (Patkowski, 1990) and of course, starting early language instruction probably means that, over time, the language learner will have more opportunities to use the target language in different situations, leading to greater proficiency in the long run (Curtain, 1997).

Notwithstanding research results, certain conditions, in terms of both pedagogy and resources, need to be created to achieve early language learning success. One of the most relevant conditions is the need for commitment at the administrative level, not only in the school but on a local, regional and national level. This may include specialized and enhanced teacher training, incentives for schools that offer early language instruction, and development and distribution of special teaching materials. Assessment may also be an issue when dealing with young language learners, considering the fact that the more frequent areas of language assessment often deal with competencies that young learners do not necessarily have; e.g. reading and writing skills.

Young language learners are often perceived as being prodigiously fast learners. An approach which attempts to introduce young learners to foreign languages may seem intuitively obvious, however it is not always as straightforward and automatic as it is often portrayed. Firstly, young learners must be understood within their context and limitations – their age, mental development and attitude toward learning do play an important role. Generally, young learners tend to be curious – and their interest in learning about the world around them provides a positive attitude towards learning and this attitude must be maintained and above all, they should not become afraid of making mistakes. At the same time, young learners must be taught to handle failure and be proactive about the learning process. In other words, learners must not be over-confident nor plagued by self-doubts. Inevitably, this requires special comprehension and planning by the teacher.

Language learning materials which take into consideration the special characteristics of young learners are not always readily available, although admittedly there are more and more available resources as the teaching of languages to young learners begins to gain more acceptance. For example, language learning materials which incorporate modern technology is a growing area for language teaching materials. And yet, for the young learner it is one area with inherent difficulties – they may not have the necessary skills to use a mouse and keyboard. Additionally, limited or slow typing skills can be a source of frustration and the use of online resources may prove to be too dense or be uninteresting for young learners. Online collaboration, while quite stimulating for most language learners due to its communicative potential (the use of the target language with another language user) may prove to be a source of frustration for young learners who are not able to deal with the sophisticated level of language necessary for Internet collaboration. They may not have had any exposure at all to the language needed, since most young language learners' texts probably do not provide the language structures needed for this type of collaboration (Milton & Vassiliu, 2000).

According to McGlothlin (1997), there are some key factors of a child's first language learning environment which might make the learning of other languages more efficient if these characteristics become part of the learning environment. Some of these factors are:

- Lack of pressure to learn the language.
- There are no time limits (learning is not contextualized into certain hours of the day).
- Language input is always there. In many cases, the input is simplified to meet the child's level of understanding.
- The target language is not sequenced or separated into specific areas (e.g., lexicon or syntax).
- Repetition of input is constant. This is combined with new input for learning.
- Language input is contextualized by the world around the child.
- Ample opportunities for attempts to communicate in the target language.

In order to incorporate these features into the young foreign language pupil's learning environment, the strategies which the child typically uses for first language learning should be kept in mind, beginning with the fact that the child is not necessarily interested in learning the language for its own sake –their interest lies in the contextualization of the concepts the child is learning (Op. Cit). Moreover, the young language learner is not bothered by the language he does not understand – as long as the gist and content are clear. The child's attention will be directed towards things which interest him and he will be more likely to learn things which help him participate in the world around him. Since the young learner is not interested in language learning for its own sake, it is important to make sure that the language learning process itself is enjoyable and that it satisfies the child's basic needs, such as the need for physical activity or emotional security (Vilke and Vrhovac 2003, 2005).

As far as introducing an early start to language learning, it is interesting to see how school systems respond to social and cultural needs on the one hand and to educational and political recommendations on the other. Throughout the European Union, formal education shows the popularity of English, French or German as the first foreign language taught at the primary level. According to Key Data on Teaching Languages at School in Europe, in the European primary schools 46.4% of children learn English, 6.5% learn German and 3.2% learn French. Other languages occupy much lower percentage positions —mainly Spanish, Italian and Russian, though a growing interest in the learning of Chinese and Japanese can be noted.

The role of particular foreign languages in the primary school does not, however, reflect their popularity (or lack of popularity) across the educational system. In the European lower secondary school context, 87.4% of the students learning a foreign language have chosen English although there is an indication of growing popularity of other languages (mainly French, German and Italian), although the demand is still much lower. The situation improves somewhat in upper secondary level. While most students still choose English as their first foreign language the percentage of students who choose a different foreign language is higher (French, German and Spanish, respectively). It can be argued that a programme of language learning that starts early in the primary school has a positive influence on the proportion of students leaving school with knowledge of two or three foreign languages.

Whichever language is being introduced in primary education and for whatever reasons, the starting age is usually determined by two factors: the educational budget and the perceived value or importance of language education in the school system. A foreign language may be introduced to children by the age of 5. To give a few examples of when a foreign language is introduced across Europe:

- Age 5 in the Netherlands,
- Age 6 in Norway and Luxembourg,
- Age 7 in Finland, Sweden, Estonia, Greece and Italy,
- Age 8 in Belgium, Austria and Spain
- Age 9 in Hungary, Slovenia, Lithuania, Latvia, the Czech Republic and Bulgaria,
- Age 10 in Estonia, Poland, Slovakia, France, Belgium, Denmark, Portugal and Iceland.

The data above shows, however, only obligatory language education for all the children in a given country which is paid for with taxpayers' money. A huge number of special projects take place in many countries bringing the starting age down for vast numbers of children in kindergarten and in early primary schooling (Komorowska, 2005).

Young learners are not the only area language teachers are exploring in their search for enhancement of the language learning process. They are also looking to expand their language teaching into other areas of childhood development. For instance, many teachers recognise the importance of new learning theories as foundations for engaging their students according to their individual learning styles and abilities. One theory which has had a profound impact on classroom teaching is Howard Gardner's idea of multiple intelligences. According to Gardner, human intelligence can be described as a "unique blend" (1999:34) or combination of different fields of human knowledge. No combination is exactly the same in any two people and genetic and environmental factors will play important roles in how these combinations are shaped in each individual (Melo Cabrita, this volume). Significant for teaching is the fact that these multiple intelligences are potentials which will be activated by the educational, cultural, social and personal opportunities and resources available to each individual. As Melo Cabrita points out in this volume, these intelligences have been used to pinpoint eight different types of learning styles that generally correspond to the eight categories of intelligence outlined by Gardner. These are:
- The logical-mathematical intelligence
- The verbal-linguistic intelligence
- The spatial intelligence
- The musical intelligence

- The bodily-kinesthetic intelligence
- The interpersonal intelligence
- The intrapersonal intelligence
- The naturalist intelligence. (Gardner, 1999: 41-43; 48)

Looking to go beyond traditional paradigms of what it means to teach a language, the theory of multiple intelligences provides language teachers with a radical new perspective on learning goals. Ideally, the learning process in the language classroom should aim at activating all intelligences, not just the verbal-linguistic intelligence. This theory also helps teachers recognise different "entry points" (Melo Cabrita, this volume) which can be exploited for engaging students with diverse learning styles and ensuring a more complete, well-rounded learning process. These entry points can provide a theoretical framework for greater coordination of learner-centred theory and practice.

So, in the spirit of extending the parameters of the learning process in the language classroom, this last chapter includes two that look at how the issue of initial age for language learning is being expanded to include young language learners and the opportunities which accompany an "early start" followed by an article that explore new conceptual frontiers in relation to language teaching and learning: the integration of multiple intelligences into foreign language learning.

We begin in Poland with an article by Hanna Komorowska. Her contribution attempts to answer some important questions relevant to young language learners such as "What is recommended in the European policy documents" and "What are the reasons for this-called early start "? She is also interested in looking at what is actually happening in the educational system as well as looking at how to best define "successful" early language learning and extract a model that is more likely to ensure success. Komorowska then looks at how these questions and controversies have been dealt with in the Polish context and offers an outline of the Polish model for course planning, syllabus and materials design for young learners.

Next, Mihaljevic Djigunovic describes the language teaching context of Croatia and how the long tradition of foreign language teaching has provided valuable input for the development of an early language learning approach —an approch that is now firmly entrenched in the Croatian educational system. The author exemplifies some of the different aspects of teaching and learning strategies through several case descriptions.

Finally, we end this book with an article by Eduarda Melo Cabrita in which she briefly describes the theoretical foundations of Howard Gardner's Multiple Intelligences theory, followed by a practical example of how this theory was used to engage learners in a multidisciplinary case study that combines literary, cultural and political perspectives. Not surprisingly, the orientation of these last articles traverse other teaching and learning approaches already described in this book, such as CLIL or TBL. After all, the theories advocated here promote a learner-centred, hands-on approach. This rounds up nicely the socio-constructivist, multi-faceted perspective which has been the back-bone of the book.

Works Cited

Bamford, Kathyrn W. and Donald T. Mizokawa. 1991. "Additive-Bilingual (Immersion) Education: Cognitive and Language Development." *Language Learning* 41 (3): 413–429.
Cooper, Thomas. C. 1987. "Foreign Language Study and SAT-Verbal Scores." *Modern Language Journal* 71 (4): 381–387.
Curtain, Helena. 1997. *Early Start Language Programs*. Unpublished paper. Madison, WI.
Curtain, Helena and Carol Ann Pesola. 1994. *Languages and Children: Making the Match. 2nd edition*. White Plains, NY: Longman.
Deardorff, Darla. 2004. *The Identification and Assessment of Intercultural Competence as a Student Outcome of Internationalization at Institutions of Higher Education in the United States*. Unpublished doctoral thesis. North Carolina State University.
Gardner Howard. 1993. *Multiple Intelligences: The Theory in Practice*. New York: Basic Books.
—. 1999. *Intelligence Reframed: Multiple Intelligences for the 21st Century*. New York: Basic Books.
Garfinkel, Alan and Kenneth Tabor. 1991. "Elementary school foreign languages and English reading achievement: A new view of the relationship," *Foreign Language Annals*, 24, 375-382.
Jensen, Eric. 1995. *Brain-Based Learning and Teaching*. Del Mar, USA: Turning Point Publishing.
Komorowska, Hanna. 2005. Linguistic policy effects of the European Union enlargement. In *Mehrsprachigkeit und Kommunikation in der Diplomatie,* ed. R. Festauer, 35-51. Vienna: Diplomatische Akademie, Favorita Papers 04/2005.
McGlothlin, Doug. 1997. "A Child's First Steps in Language Learning." *The Internet TESL Journal*, Vol. III, No. 10, October.
Milton, James and Vassiliu, P. 2000. Lexis and the content of EFL textbooks. *Proceedings of the 13th Symposium of Theoretical and Applied Linguistics,* Thessaloniki: Aristotle University.

Patkowski, Mark. S. 1990. "Age and Accent in a Second Language: A Reply to James Emil Flege." *Applied Linguistics* 11 (1): 73–90.

Thomas, Wayne P. and Virginia Collier. 1993. "Academic Achievement Through Japanese, Spanish, or French: The First Two Years of Partial Immersion." *Modern Language Journal* 77 (2): 170–180.

Vilke, Mirjana and Yvonne Vrhovac, eds. 1993. *Children and Foreign Languages I*, Zagreb: University of Zagreb.

—. 1995. *Children and Foreign Languages II*, Zagreb: University of Zagreb.

CONTROVERSIES IN TEACHING ENGLISH TO YOUNG LEARNERS: THE POLISH SOLUTION

HANNA KOMOROWSKA

Reasons for an early start

According to the Council of Europe, every citizen in the EU should acquire at least two foreign languages, apart from his or her mother tongue. One way of ensuring that these objectives are fulfilled is through an "early start" for the first and second foreign languages. The early start certainly conveys a strong message that languages are important and that the school system treats them as such, but its symbolic value is only one reason among many for lowering the starting age for foreign language learning. Another reason is connected with the longer period of time for language learning —in other words, "the longer the better" (Johnstone, 2002). Moreover, it is also believed that motivation is easier to raise at a younger age as most teaching methods are based on play. A third reason for an "early start" is that "education for tolerance" (an important part of intercultural communicative competence of foreign language learning) is also believed to be much easier to promote at an earlier age when curiosity and openness prevail and stereotypes have not yet been formed (Doyé, 1997). Finally, a language taught at an early age helps the children develop transversal competences —generic skills that support plurilingual competences and enable inter-comprehension of people speaking different languages (CEFR, 2001). This is especially valuable across languages which are typologically related, e.g. Spanish, Italian and Portuguese; or Polish, Slovak, and Russian. This fact takes on increased relevance when teaching young learners in multilingual and multicultural schools.

Confronting controversies

Despite these benefits, the idea of "early start" has raised some controversy, especially as far as a very early start goes, e.g. the kindergarten age. Indeed, problems arising in the process of teaching very young learners have been widely researched and discussed (Blondin et al. 1998; Edelenbos et al., 2006). One of the most important issues has to do with the consequences of insufficient input. Most kindergartens and primary schools cannot offer more than one or two contact hours per week and with this limited amount of exposure there is not much chance for foreign language acquisition similar to that typical of the mother tongue.

However, very young learners are not cognitively prepared for formal learning, and they also lack supportive strategies based on literacy. Introducing limited input at a young age usually results in vocabulary learning but does not lead to the formation of syntax. Likewise, with such limited input spontaneous speech does not usually develop and labels, e.g. for people and objects, are produced instead (Rokita, 2007). Inevitably, permanence of knowledge and skills becomes an issue —children learn quickly, but they also forget quickly. This is due to the dominance of mechanical over logical memory and thus the question arises whether investment in a very early start is worthwhile, at least from the point of view of the learning output.

In most cases, the answer is a resounding "yes", because difficulties are compensated by overall educational gains in the long-run, promising satisfactory achievement in later years. Yet a number of questions remain to be answered by psycholinguists and second language acquisition researchers. For instance:
- How much input is needed for acquisition to take place?
- Is there a road from vocabulary to syntax?
- What is the road from reproduction to spontaneous use of a FL?
- How does the age factor influence answers to the three questions above?

Inevitably, the main issue educational decision-makers will have to consider first is how much input can be realistically offered, taking into account the most feasible amount and frequency of language sessions. If the amount and frequency is not enough to provide sufficient input for language acquisition to take place, then formal language learning must be the alternative. This means that educational decision-makers will have to decide if the children are actually prepared for formal learning. If, however, it is decided that language acquisition through language exposure and authentic interaction is a realistic goal, then time for interaction must be factored into the eventual planning.

If the size of the group does not accommodate interaction and communication, then repetition, labelling and/or production without comprehension may prove to be the only realistic outcome. This begs the question of whether such an outcome is really worth the effort. Two final questions remain for educational decision-makers. Under the conditions in which early language learning is promoted, is strong motivation for language learning likely to be fostered? Do educational benefits compensate for efficiency problems in large groups and within limited learning time?

Depending on the answers to the questions above, decisions concerning the starting age and the type of programme can be made. In many cases, these decisions are related to financing. Thus, the decision may be made to either offer short language lessons in kindergarten or in primary or to introduce expensive but much more efficient immersion or bilingual kindergarten programmes. Evidently, in this situation controversies over course planning and syllabus design in primary education arise. Curriculum implementation and recommended methods are not uniformly approached either. Basic controversies often relate to three crucial issues.

The first controversial issue in course planning is the actual aim of primary language teaching. Teachers are interested in methods which would support children's overall development and enhance motivation through play. Decision-makers and policy-makers, aware of budgetary constraints, are often more interested in the tangible growth of knowledge and skills. This raises the issue of whether the introduction of a foreign language in primary education should be process-oriented or product-oriented.

The second controversial issue concerns the teaching focus of primary language learning. Teachers and researchers opt for the development of listening comprehension and "education of the ear". Parents, however, as well as decision-makers are often more interested in the product and prefer the focus on speaking. Should, therefore, the teaching of a foreign language in the primary be focused on reception or on production?

The third controversial issue is connected with the type of teaching content to be dealt with at primary level. Those who opt for product-oriented teaching more often tend to stress accuracy of speech production, while those who opt for process-oriented teaching tend to stress the value of vocabulary and the quality of content. The question is, then, whether young language learning should promote a vocabulary or a grammar based approach? The Polish model will be presented below as a set of possible answers to all the above questions.

The Polish approach to early modern language teaching: course planning, syllabus and materials design

With these questions in mind, this section presents a model of the approach to early foreign language learning that has been promoted in Poland over the last decade. It should be noted, however, that this model has been worked out for the context of class-lesson teaching (however informal and play-oriented) and in the situation of low input offered during two to three 45-minute lessons per week, as these are the most frequent conditions for "young language learning" in Poland.

This approach began in Poland in the 90s and, after more than a decade, it is now widely promoted throughout the country. Roots of the Polish approach to early modern language teaching can be found in the work of two expert teams led by the author of this article. The first project was to design and implement a new system for foreign language teacher training in Poland, rooted in 3-year colleges. It was run by a team of experts linked to the Ministry of Education. This project was initiated immediately after the fall of communism and has since become part of a major reform of higher education.

The second project, started and completed in mid-90s, aimed at the preparation and promotion of an innovative series of modern language curricula for the whole school system. This project was run by a team of applied linguists and language teachers for the main educational publisher in Poland (WSiP) and has since influenced the thinking of many teachers and designers of language teaching materials.

Later two major government programmes firmly embedded the idea of young learners into primary education. One was the introduction of a specialised degree in initial education and ELT at educational departments; the other was the commencement of a nation-wide in-service teacher training programme run by the National INSETT Centre, the British Council, Goethe-Institut and Alliance Française.

The Polish approach takes the child's age as the main factor in differentiating the way the teaching is implemented, though other factors are also carefully considered:
- Language education can take place in kindergartens covering age groups of 3/4 to 6, in "adaptation classes" for 6 year-olds and in actual primary schooling which starts at age 7.

- Literacy skills are presented to the children in the "adaptation class" but are not formally taught until age 7.
- Initial education is provided by one teacher for children aged 7 to 10; "subject-area" education is provided by specialist teachers after the age of 10, though a foreign language can be taught by a specialist teacher if the class teacher is not qualified to do so.
- Obligatory foreign language education starts at the age of 10, though today almost 70% of the Polish schools offer first foreign language from the start, i.e. from the age of 7.

What seems crucial, whatever the organizational context, is convincing parents of the value of language education and involving them in the language education of their children. Parents need to be made aware of the value of the early start and of the continuity of language learning. They should also be convinced that language education does not take place at the cost of other subject areas.

An excellent example of how to do this is provided in a primary course entitled *SPARKS* by M. Szpotowicz and M. Szulc-Kurpaska (2004). Guidelines for parents on how to help their children are provided and a special brochure offers a set of sample letters to parents, examples of which the teacher also gets on a CD accompanying the course book. Parents are systematically informed of their child's progress; to help teachers inform parents the authors offer easy to fill in forms for descriptive evaluation of the child's progress.

The national INSETT YOUNG LEARNERS programme offered ample information for teachers on how to plan meetings with parents to make them aware of the value of language education for the overall development of the child –especially for memory training, for the development of critical thinking and for children's self-expression. The programme helped teachers develop skills to give simple and clear presentation of the content and expected outcomes of the course. It also provided information on how individual differences are accounted for in language teaching and what it means for the development of learning strategies their children will be able to employ while learning other school subjects.

The Polish solution to the controversy over process-oriented vs. product-oriented language education

In the kindergarten group, (ages 4-6), process-oriented education has been adopted. Examples of this approach can be seen in a syllabus by K. Nicholls (2003), approved by the Ministry of Education. It demonstrated a positive approach that is holistic and incorporates "multi-sensory" learning through play, songs and rhymes which is encouraged in order to show language learning as a pleasurable experience. The main aim is to motivate young learners for both present and future language learning. This approach has also been adapted by Czos (2005) for language teaching through story-telling and drama in bilingual kindergartens and primary schools.

In the 7 to 10 age group, the approach shifts towards more product oriented learning, although there is an attempt to maintain a balance between product and process-orientation. An English course entitled *BINGO* developed by Anna Wieczorek (2005) can serve as a good example here. The student book offers child self-assessment sections in the form of three icons: a happy face (I can), an unhappy face (I cannot) and a straight face (I have to practice a bit more) after each sequence of five lessons. A parallel icon-based assessment by the teacher is presented to be filled out in the course book. A place for a parental signature acknowledging both types of assessment (student and teacher) is provided, which enables parents to reflect on similarities and differences between the two assessments. While the methods and techniques remain much the same as in the previous age group, there is more expectation of achievement. This is supported by Polish versions of the European Language Portfolio designed for very young (aged 3 to 5) and for the young learners (aged 5 to 10), published and widely promoted by the Polish INSETT.

In the teaching of children above the age of 10, a complete change of focus can be observed. At this point, product-oriented teaching prevails over process-oriented teaching. Motivating methods and classroom techniques are, of course, recommended, but achievement in terms of pronunciation, vocabulary, grammatical correctness and skills development is considered of significant importance. This is explicitly stated in the curricular guidelines (podstawa programowa) included in the Parliamentary Act on the Polish Educational System. This is also stressed in the Polish preparation for national language competence testing to be launched in 2009.

The controversy over reception-oriented vs. production-oriented teaching has led to solutions which again gradually change across age groups. In the 4 to 6 age group, reception-oriented teaching prevails and production is limited to repetition, or "joining in" of the examples provided in the target language. Although children are encouraged to repeat and say things, listening is the leading language skill aiming at "education of the ear". This can be seen in the management of class time, as has been recommended in teacher's guides for Wieczorek's *MINI BINGO* (2001).

In the 7 to 10 age group, reception-oriented and production-oriented modes of teaching are balanced out. "Education of the ear", although still present in the classroom method, gradually gives way to listening comprehension and to non-verbal and verbal ways of demonstrating understanding. At the same time more speaking than in the former stage is encouraged. A special programme integrating music into early language learning shows how to link reception of e.g. Debussy's *Dance of the Doll* or Prokofiev's *Peter and the Wolf* with work on rhythm and intonation (Pamuła, 2005).

For children older than 10, production-oriented teaching is predominant. More time is dedicated to the development of speaking skills than time spent with listening skills. Nonetheless, listening is not neglected; there is more varied input via audiocassettes, videos and DVD materials, which is explicitly recommended in the national core curriculum for the second stage of education (ages 10-13).

The controversy over lexical vs. grammatical syllabus: fewer obvious and clear-cut solutions

In the 4 to 6 age group, a lexical syllabus dominates in most of the materials available in the Polish market. Vocabulary is presented in situated contexts and in topic-based groups, e.g. colours, body parts, animals, etc Moreover, words are introduced in sentences and not as isolated items, phrases and chunks being carried by songs and nursery rhymes.

In the 7 to 10 age group, a combination of a situational and a task-based syllabus replaces the former purely lexical one. Children are encouraged to participate in activities which end in a tangible product, such as a paper doll, a toy, a mask, as well as problem-solving tasks such as completing a chart, often while listening to songs and singing for which ample materials are provided as e.g. *The Singing Class* by J.Zaranska (2003). Tasks are integrated with the work of the class teacher as demonstrated in the integrated courses, such as *SPARKS* or *BINGO*.

For children over the age of 10, a mixed syllabus is recommended which combines the teaching of lexical groups with the acquisition of certain grammatical structures, focused on a number of communicative functions within certain topics and themes (Otwinowska-Kasztelanic, 2007). These are chosen according to their level of interest for the children and support their learning strategies, as described by Szulc-Kurpaska

(2001) in her small scale research which also shows a dominant tendency to promote cross-curricular and content-based teaching.

Discussion

Although a lot of support is offered to teachers through special training packs, e.g. *Teaching English to Young Learners CODN Trainer's PACK* (2003), with a variety of materials and tasks to help observe, plan and conduct lessons according to the needs and capabilities of particular age groups (Szulc-Kurpaska 2003), not all the difficulties have been removed –ensuring continuity seems to be the most important of them.

The issue of continuity of language learning is principally linked to the role of transition between schools and/or educational stages. The change from lower to upper primary means moving from one class teaching into "subject-teaching" by several specialist teachers. The change from primary into lower secondary schools often includes a geographical change, along with the subsequent change in teaching staff. Ensuring the same choice of languages, providing qualified staff and enabling children to continue language learning rather than to make them start from scratch is a logistical problem (Komorowska, 1997). Paradoxically, the situation is often even more difficult for those children who initially benefited from the early start as their knowledge and skills are higher than those of other children in the same grade of a new school. A proper placement of children in groups and appropriate materials design with starter units recycling the language acquired earlier help a bit. Yet success depends on whether the teacher knows how to use appropriate methodologies and appropriate forms of work.

Continuity is more likely to happen when headmasters and teachers of other subjects are reassured that language education supports rather than undermines education in other subject areas. In Poland this issue is countered by collaborative projects which encourage autonomy, since children are allowed to choose topics that interest them and then search for, locate and organize information in order to present their work to others. Projects make language learning more attractive and they facilitate teaching, especially in schools trying to cope with broad-banding and mixed ability in oversized classrooms.

Teachers of other subjects are invited by language teachers to cooperate in projects promoted through the European Language Label (ELL) and ICT-based programmes such as e-Twinning. Both programmes are increasingly popular in early language education. Each year kindergartens and primary schools are among the winners of the European

Language Label, while the number of cross-curricular e-Twinning projects in kindergartens and primary schools in Poland in 2005/06 reached one hundred (Gajek 2006). A strong contribution of modern language learning to a more general "learning to learn" approach helps teachers of non-language subjects introduce alternative assessment and promote learners' self-assessment, at the same time proving that language education does not take place at the cost of the subject areas they teach.

Inevitably, the Polish campaign to promote early language learning brings up questions which must be carefully considered. Is it better to invest in the early teaching of one foreign language or to introduce a second FL as early as possible? Should we promote an early start irrespective of continuity assurance or to limit it accordingly? Continuity will remain a difficult issue, although it seems easier to achieve when methodologies for primary and secondary education are separate, yet a smooth transition between them is guaranteed. This happens when modern language teaching moves from the different stages explained above: a motivation-through-play approach and then on to the use of a foreign language to investigate interesting topics, to solve problems and to cooperate with peers in completing stimulating tasks.

Whatever the answers given in the context of a particular school or region, it is worth reminding decision-makers in our product-oriented era that educational investments are not meant to bring about immediate outcomes, nor are their outcomes easily measurable. Education in general and language education in particular are long-term projects which bring highly gratifying results, yet it takes years of effort and investment before their outcomes are clearly visible to the taxpayer. Tolerance, openness to experience, readiness to cooperate with others, creativity and the ability to use communication skills to solve problems are not easily demonstrated in educational "business plans". Promotion of early language education depends on how successfully this message is communicated.

Works Cited

Blondin, Christiane, Michael Candelier, Peter Edelenbos, Richard Johnstone, Angelika Kubanek-German and Traute Taeschner. 1998. *Foreign Languages in Primary and Pre-School Education: Context and Outcomes. A review of Recent Research within the European Union.* CILT: London.

Czos, Dorota. 2005 "Drama w nauczaniu dwujęzycznym w szkole podstawowej w klasach I-III. Ramowy program nauczania jezyka angielskiego w nauczaniu dwujęzycznym w szkole podstawowej w

klasach I - III" Unpublished materials for kindergarten and primary school teachers.
Doyé, Peter and Alison Hurrell, eds. 1997. *Foreign Language Learning in Primary Schools (age 5/6 to 10/11)*. Education Committee. Council for Cultural Co-operation. Council of Europe Publishing: Strasbourg.
Edelenbos, Peter, Richard Johnstone and Angelika Kubanek. 2006. *The main pedagogical principles underlying the teaching of languages to young learners. Final report of the EAC 89/04. Lot 1 Study*. European Commision.
http://ec.europa.eu/education/policies/lang/key/studies_en.html
Gajek E. 2006. "e-Twinning Partnerships in Polish Schools."
www.e-learning.org.pl
Johnstone, Richard. 2002. *Addressing the Age Factor: Some Implications for Languages Policy*. Strasbourg: Council of Europe.
Komorowska, Hanna. 1997. "Organisation, Integration and Continuity." In *Foreign language learning in primary schools (age 5/6 to 10/11)*, ed. Peter Doyé and Alison Hurrell, 51-62. Strasbourg: Council of Europe.
Nicholls, Katarzyna. 2003. *Program nauczania języka angielskiego w systemie zintegrowanym*. Warszawa: PWN.
Otwinowska-Kasztelanic, Agnieszka. 2007. "Programy i materiały nauczania w szkolnictwie podstawowym." In *Nauczanie języków obcych. Polska a Europa,* ed. Hanna Komorowska, 117-134. Warsaw: Academica.
Pamuła, Małgorzata. 2003. *Metodyka nauczania języków obcych w kształceniu zintegrowanym*. Warsaw: Fraszka Edukacyjna
Rokita, Joanna. 2007. *Lexical Development in early L2 Acquisition*. Krakow: Akademia Pedagogiczna.
Szpotowicz Magdalena and Małgorzata Szulc-Kurpaska. 2004. *Sparks*. Warsaw: Oxford University Press (Poland).
Szulc-Kurpaska, Malgorzata. 2001. *Foreign Language Acquisition in the Primary School. Teaching and Strategy Training*. Krakow: Oficyna Wydawnicza ATUT.
—. 2003. *Teaching English to Young Learners. Observation Tasks*. Warsaw: CODN.
Wieczorek, Anna. 2005 *BINGO*. Warsaw: Wydawnictwo Szkolne PWN.
—. 2001. *MINIBINGO*. Warsaw: Wydawnictwo Szkolne PWN.
Zaranska, Joanna. 2003. *The Singing Class*. Warsaw: CODN.

YOUNG CROATIAN LANGUAGE LEARNERS

JELENA MIHALJEVIC DJIGUNOVIC

The Croatian foreign language education context

It is not uncommon for countries whose national languages are not widely spoken abroad to strive to learn foreign languages, in particular those languages which are considered "world languages". This is true of Croatia, which helps explain why foreign language teaching has a century-long tradition. Up to World War Two, the most frequently taught foreign languages were German and French. Until then, English was taught only sporadically, and was introduced on a regular basis only after the war. At the same time, Russian became a compulsory foreign language in school, starting at age 11 (beginning of lower secondary education) and at age 15 (beginning of upper secondary) learners could then choose another language among English, French, German and Italian. At present, as in most countries in Europe, English is considered a lingua franca and more than 90 per cent of learners choose it as their first foreign language.

Importantly, what has characterised the Croatian foreign language teaching scene from the very beginning are Croatian-made teaching materials. These materials reflected the current trends in language teaching elsewhere. This is especially true of materials developed for teaching English since foreign experts were provided by such organizations as the British Council to help and Croatian experts were sent abroad on training courses. Moreover, language teaching methodology was also introduced at the university as a course for future teachers more than five decades ago.

As regards early learning of foreign languages, this practice has existed in Croatia for more than sixty years now. In the 1950s foreign language learning in public schools was initiated at age 10 (wherever there were qualified teachers) and it was compulsory for everyone to begin foreign language studies at age 11 at the latest. With the introduction of private language schools in the 1950s, a general trend towards starting foreign language learning earlier began. Parents considered knowledge of a foreign language a great asset in their children's lives and, if they could afford it, were willing to invest in early language learning in private schools, where the teaching conditions were much better than in the regular state-funded schools. These better conditions usually meant smaller groups, but also new, colourful and flashy foreign teaching materials.

In 2003, foreign language learning became a compulsory part of the primary curriculum from grade one (age: 6-7 years). Any foreign language (subject to availability of resources) can be taken but nearly all learners choose English.

Characteristics of the Croatian approach to teaching young learners

The approach to early foreign language learning and teaching in Croatia is based on research into two processes – learning and teaching. First, insights into how Croatian young learners acquire English were obtained in a series of studies (Vilke, 1976) carried out in order to find out what the optimal starting age for foreign language learning might be in this particular socio-educational context. The results showed that age 8 was optimal for the majority of children, while high-ability children can be successful in learning English if they start at age 7. The most interesting findings of these studies were the following: a) young learners are motivated to learn foreign languages from a very early age with the appropriate approach; b) the teacher has a very important role in raising and maintaining their motivation; c) although most children are great imitators of speech models, those that are instructed explicitly on pronunciation are more successful than those that learn only by imitation; d) words and phrases that refer to concepts that are part of children's mental repertoire are acquired earlier and better than those that do not correspond to their current cognitive and experiential levels.

A more recent longitudinal experimental research project (Vilke and Vrhovac 1993, 1995; Vrhovac et al. 1999; Vrhovac, 2001) that included parallel studies in four foreign languages (English, French, German and Italian) has resulted in an approach that has a number of characteristics now featured in the Croatian context of early language learning. The "Croatian" approach highlights learner-centredness, content-related activities, a functional approach to grammar, and a focus on teaching learners to understand their own learning process. These are discussed in more detail in the following sections.

Learner-centredness and the teacher's role

Teaching and teaching materials are designed with young learners' cognitive, affective and social characteristics in mind. Studies indicate that young learners tend to initially hold positive attitudes towards foreign language learning, and are uninhibited, curious and eager to enrich their awareness of the world. This motivation must be supported by ensuring the child's feeling of success in learning a foreign language in the beginning stages. Croatian teachers often stress that even an illusion of success is beneficial for early language learning. Moreover, young beginners become very attached to their teacher and the teacher is a key influence on their attitude towards the foreign language —they often develop a possessive attitude towards their teacher. All these observations highlight the importance of the right type of teacher able to deal with young learners' needs.

Children work best when their basic needs are fulfilled. The needs that are the most relevant for foreign language learning are those for emotional security, for physical activity and for self-realization within the peer-group. Emotions seem to be the starting point for learning for young learners: they learn best what they like best. They usually like best what gives them pleasure and what fosters their self-esteem. Since they find security in belonging to a group, their self-confidence, to some extent, depends on being recognized by their peers. The means of becoming recognized by peers may include imitating peers, finding fault with them, mocking the less successful, or trying to catch the teacher's attention by being disruptive. The problems that ensue due to this require a teacher that is well-trained in developmental psychology.

As for their needs for physical activity, activity-based methodology is a must with young learners. Thus, during early years, large parts of foreign language classes in Croatia involve total physical response (TPR) activities.

Making the lessons learner-centred means recognising that some children can be very shy at the beginning of foreign language learning. As a Grade One teacher puts it:

> At this age some children often experience fear, real or imaginary. The child then becomes shy, speaks in a very low voice, refuses to talk or take part in class activities. He needs to feel protected by somebody. The brave ones will ask the teacher for help – whisper into the teacher's ear that he got new shoes from his mother, or that he wants to go out of the class. But some will refuse to come to the blackboard or answer a question by just nodding their head or simply showing no sign of comprehension. If the

teacher, who usually stands in front of some thirty pupils, decides to approach the shy one, then all the other pupils' attention will, by following the teacher, be turned toward the frightened child who is, thus, exposed to an unpleasant situation rather than protected. The fear of public appearance in front of other children and the teacher often prevents involvement in class activities. (Jagatic, 1993:154)

Within the Croatian approach such children are given an opportunity to join in when they are ready and are not forced to do it when it pleases the teacher. The same teacher suggests ways of helping such children:

If the teacher applies a CLL[1] technique – the teacher "whispers" a translated sentence to the pupil who repeats it after her – the teacher is no more a critic, a viewer, an audience; she becomes an assistant and a help, like a prompter in a theatre. The child feels that what he utters must be good because it was told him by the teacher. If theatre props (i.e. magic wand, hat, bag, doll, etc.) are used, children seem to forget about their fear – they are completely engaged in the object which attracts them and protects them; the object they hold seems to diminish their fear (a hat hides them, a doll takes care of them). And the rest of the class is not paying attention to the child but rather to the props he is using. (Jagatic, 1993:154-155)

The concentration span of young learners is very short and they easily become tired and bored after five to ten minutes. This has an important relevance for planning activities in class: they need to be short, the stir factor needs to be well balanced and it seems best if the process of language learning is perceived by children as a kind of game to which they want to contribute physically, emotionally and intellectually. A teacher reports:

It means a lot to a 7-year-old to come to the front of the classroom just to remove something on the board or take something out of a box. Physical involvement makes children happy because they can move and change position. But also because they are for a moment the protagonists of a classroom activity. Tasks which require change of place range from P.E. lessons and play-acting to miming, action songs and simulation games,

---

[1] Counseling Language Learning (CLL) is a humanistic approach to language learning, designed to reduce learner's anxiety. For further details, see Stevick, Earl W. 1980. *Teaching Languages: a Way and Ways.* New York: Newbury House. Also see Richards, Jack C. and Theodore S. Rodgers. 2001. *Approaches and Methods in Language Teaching.* (2nd ed.) Cambridge: Cambridge University Press, (pp 90-99).

such as: cooking, shopping or having meals. For the same reason all kinds of dramatic activities provide one of the most successful devices in foreign-language teaching. (Rijavec, 1993:150)

Another aspect reflected in the Croatian approach is the fact that children's experience of the world is holistic, not analytic like that of adults. One English teacher describes how this was reflected in her class:

> While preparing puppets and scenery for a puppet-show project based on Snow-White and the Seven Dwarfs, I asked my second-grade pupils to classify the following words into two categories: castle, mirror, Snow-White, dwarfs, queen, wood, prince, apple, hunter and cottage. My intention was to engage one group in designing scenery and the other in designing characters. To my surprise the children put the queen, the mirror and the castle into one group, the dwarfs, the wood, the cottage and Snow-White into the other group, but had difficulties with the hunter, the prince and the apple as to where they belonged. In line with this we can understand why children can easily remember clusters of contextually related words, which should be kept in mind when designing the syllabus. (Rijavec, 1993: 151-152)

The children did not group the words according to one characteristic feature (place or character) one would come up with through analysis, like adults would have, but viewed the characters and place as a whole.

Croatian teachers stress that young children have a different sense of reality and that the world of make-believe can be more real to them than the actual everyday world. (On the other hand, children easily sense a contrived situation, a false attitude, a meaningless task and are very quick to refuse collaboration in such cases.) What is often most relevant to them is having fun and satisfying immediate curiosity. This is why it seems important to link instruction to entertainment, to design fun activities with non-linguistic objectives and to ensure immediate results in the form of obvious outcomes or rewards for a successfully accomplished task.

Functional approach to teaching grammar

Since Croatian young learners are mostly exposed to foreign languages in formal school settings and for limited periods of time (usually two to five weekly class periods), we can hardly speak of exposure to natural communication situations that would activate their language learning process and lead to morphosyntactic development. Between the ages of 7 and 11, young learners are in the stage of concrete operations (Piaget, 1975) and grammar is approached in accordance with their level of cognitive development. As an abstract representation of the language system, grammar is taught through functional categories (Vilke, 1995).

This means that metalanguage, if used at all in teaching the 7-11 age group, is used with great caution. Children have been found to ask about the different language forms and what has been shown to work well as explantions were extralinguistic stimuli for explaining language regularities. In teaching German, for instance, capitalization of nouns appears as a problem for first graders. Some teachers solve the problem by resorting to a system of "stories" that can answer the children's queries in simple and amusing ways. Here's the description of what one Croatian teacher of German does:

> First graders are not familiar with the notion of the noun yet. Therefore we had to create the notion in their minds and make them aware of it. How? By means of a story. "I wake up in the morning. I stretch my two nouns, I enter a large noun and wash my sleepy noun with a running noun. My black, hairy noun comes in waving his noun, etc." "What are the nouns?" The answer was quick and clear: "We, things and animals". "What would happen if all the nouns disappeared?" There would be nothing left. So, are nouns important words? Of course they are, and that is why the Germans write them in capital letters. They do it out of respect. So, the rule was learned. (Bosner, 1993:230)

Categories to be taught to young learners should be carefully selected. Croatian research (Vilke, 1988) has indicated that concepts expressed by some grammatical categories are avoided by children in their language performance. For instance, they may avoid using pronouns and resort to nouns instead, because it is less abstract. A Croatian researcher reports on a study she did with 180 young learners of English, French and German learning about pronouns in foreign language learning (Vilke, 1995). Her results show that young learners do go through an initial period of confusion about this concept in the foreign language but this confusion diminishes with the length of exposure to the foreign language. The implication of this finding is not that pronouns should be left out, as indeed they cannot be, but that insistence on their correct use should be postponed to a later stage of young learners' cognitive development. This also implies that grammatical mistakes should be tolerated till young learners are ready to focus on formal and abstract aspects of language. In the Croatian approach to teaching grammar to young learners all such abstract parts of the grammatical system of the foreign language are tackled as vocabulary items.

Another characteristic of the Croatian approach to teaching young learners is using contrasts —both at the linguistic and the sociocultural levels. Similarities between Croatian and the foreign language are capitalized on (e.g., starting a sentence with a capital letter and ending it with a full stop). Equally, differences can be highlighted —explanations of false pairs and differences in respective semantic fields are deemed highly relevant. Again, the functional approach is used in such explanations.

Teaching how to learn

A study on Croatian young learners' vocabulary learning strategies (Mihaljevic Djigunovic, 2001) has pointed out that children do use strategies. The type of strategies that children report using show that they pick up the strategies they are exposed to or are taught how to use. Here are a few examples of transcribed interviews with Croatian young learners of English in which the use of strategies was elicited by means of the projection technique: children were asked to describe in their L1 how they would teach their Dalmatian dog or their doll the English word for a particular object.

Stela – 7 years, female

> Interviewer: What would you tell your doll, what should she do to remember that "jabuka" is "apple"?
> Stela: To.. hm.. to draw an apple... I'd draw her an apple and she should write under the drawing... but not... not the way it is spelt but the way it is pronounced.

Petra – 9 years, female

> Interviewer: And what would help her (=the doll) to remember that word (=kite)?
> Petra: I'd tell her to read it many times till she remembers it...

Jelena – 8 years, female

> Interviewer: Well, and what would you tell the Dalmatian to do to remember that word (=present). It's a hard word for him to remember.
> Jelena: Present... well... hm... (smiles) I'd draw him a present as a gift, and then I'd write the word "present" under it and then I'd tell him. ... I'd... first I'd ask him how all these letters are said in English and then he would put the word together. Next time I'd give him a test, I wouldn't

write the word "present" but he'd have to put the word together from... jumbled letters, for example "r", "e", "s" and so on...

Children reported using a number of types of strategies: the TPR group involving the learner's physical interaction with what the word means; the formal learning strategies implying the typical classroom learning activities such as writing, reading and writing, drawing and writing, drawing and cutting out, etc., memory strategies implying repeating words, or reading or copying them many times; social strategies including learning or revising vocabulary with someone, often for testing purposes; and metacognitive strategies implying the subject's wish to organise learning. The students also differentiated between what we could call media context— referring to learning by watching cartoons and educational programmes focusing on the English language; and academic context which included the learners' suggestions that the doll/Dalmatian should learn the English alphabet first, should study books, go to school regularly and the like.

The use of TPR strategies seemed to decrease with age. Formal learning strategies showed a tendency to increase with age, except for the eight-year-old group, where it was lower and where memory strategies seemed to be very frequently reported. It is interesting that social strategies decreased with age as well. Since these strategies involved studying with members of the family, maybe this shows that the child's knowledge of English slowly surpassed that of the family members, or that such collaboration was not necessary any more because the young learner could manage on his/her own.

It is interesting to note that the less successful language learners reported using fewer TPR strategies and more formal strategies than the more successful language learners. The former reported using memory strategies more often than the latter and they also seemed to employ metacognitive strategies more often. The same is true of the media group of strategies.

This has been taken as proof that even very young learners can profit from strategies-based-instruction (SBI). Teaching learners how to learn, that is, how to use learning strategies efficiently and effectively is one of the components of the Croatian approach. It is implemented through modelling by the teacher, discussions in class about how learners go about learning and through raising self-awareness of the strategies employed by filling in the young learner language portfolio.

Teachers and teaching in the Croatian Context

One of the qualities of teachers of young learners that is stressed in the Croatian context is an excellent command of the foreign language, especially at the phonological and communicative levels. Also, love for children and enjoying teaching young learners seem to be as crucial for performing this job successfully. Within the Croatian approach to teaching young learners a new acronym has been coined – TER (total emotional response) denoting the desirable teacher behaviour (Vilke, 1995). The term reflects the need to be able and ready to play, dance, sing, draw, act —to do things that are not only intellectual but also emotionally highly demanding on the teacher.

The dilemma about the type of qualification young learner teachers should have is still not quite resolved in the Croatian context. At the moment, both class teachers and foreign language specialist teachers are formally qualified to teach young learners. However, observation of teaching in lower primary grades generally points to class teachers as a better solution. They are young learner specialists as their initial teacher training focuses on this age group, they know their young learners better than a specialist foreign language teacher can (spending only a few hours a week with young learners during foreign language classes) and they can integrate the foreign language into the curriculum more flexibly since they do all the other teaching in a particular class.

Although it is not implemented on a national level (yet), the Croatian approach to teaching foreign languages to young learners is based on suggestions from the Croatian longitudinal experimental project (Vilke and Vrhovac, 1993, 1995; Vrhovac et al. 1999; Vrhovac, 2001). These suggestions stress four requirements for ensuring successful early learning of a foreign language. The first is starting in grade one of primary school. The second is intensity of teaching: the Croatian experience, contrary to some other contexts, shows that it is vital to have more intensive teaching (ideally one class period per day five days a week) at the beginning than in later stages. Thirdly, foreign language teaching, especially in the first three to four years, should be carried out in groups that would not exceed 15 learners; this means splitting a class into two for foreign language classes. Fourthly, the teacher should possess the necessary qualities described above.

So far, only the first requirement has been fully met at the national level. The fourth one has been partially fulfilled as new initial teacher education programmes have been introduced for class teachers who wish to teach foreign languages to young learners. The second and the third requirements are still wishful thinking but, since foreign language learning is one of the country's priorities, it may not be too optimistic to hope the time will come soon when intensity and small groups will be a reality.

Works Cited

Bosner, Silvija. 1993. "How to understand German grammar before knowing the grammar of one's mother tongue." In *Children and Foreign Languages I* , ed. Mirjana Vilke and Yvonne Vrhovac, 229-235. Zagreb: University of Zagreb.

Jagatic, Mija. 1993. "Are available teaching time and the number of pupils important factors?" In *Children and Foreign Languages I* , ed. Mirjana Vilke and Yvonne Vrhovac, 153-161. Zagreb: University of Zagreb.

Mihaljevic Djigunovic, Jelena. 2001. "Do young learners know how to learn a foreign language?" In *Children and Foreign Languages III* , ed. Yvonee Vrhovac, 57-71. Zagreb: University of Zagreb.

Rijavec, Maja. 1993. "Fitting the syllabus and method to the young learner." In *Children and Foreign Languages I* , ed. Mirjana Vilke and Yvonne Vrhovac, 229-235. Zagreb: University of Zagreb.

Vilke, Mirjana. 1976. "The Age Factor in the Acquisition of Foreign Languages", *Rassegna Italiana di Linguistica Applicata*, 179-190.

—. 1988. "Some Psychological Aspects of Early Second Language Acquisition", *Journal of Multilingual and Multicultural Development*, 115-128.

—. 1995. "Children and foreign languages in Croatian primary schools – Four years of a project." In *Children and Foreign Languages II*, ed. Mirjana Vilke and Yvonne Vrhovac, 1-15. Zagreb: University of Zagreb.

Vilke, Mirjana and Yvonne Vrhovac, eds. 1993. *Children and Foreign Languages I*. Zagreb: University of Zagreb.

Vilke, Mirjana and Yvonne Vrhovac, eds. 1995. *Children and Foreign Languages II*. Zagreb: University of Zagreb.

Vrhovac, Yvonne, ed. 2001. *Children and Foreign Languages III*. Zagreb: University of Zagreb.

Vrhovac, Yvonne, Mira Kruhan, Marta Medved Krajnovic, Jelena Mihaljevic Djigunovic, Smiljana Nrancic Kovac, Inia Skender, Mirjana Vilke, eds. 1999. *Strani jezik u osnovnoj školi [= Foreign Language in Primary School]*. Zagreb: Naprijed.

Using the Multiple Intelligences Theory to Teach Intelligently: Literature, Poetry and Art in an EFL Classroom

Eduarda Melo Cabrita

> He who learns but does not think is lost. He who thinks but does not learn is in great danger.
> —Confucius

This paper aims to give a brief outline of the theoretical foundations of Howard Gardner's Multiple Intelligences theory and to supply a practical example of how to use the MI theory to engage independent to proficient learners in a multidisciplinary approach to literature, poetry and the arts in the EFL classroom at the University of Lisbon, Portugal. It also describes a unit built around a short story by contemporary US writer Richard Olen Butler so as to give learners valuable insight into the United States of America from the literary, cultural and political perspectives.

Introduction

In 1983, Howard Gardner published *Frames of Mind: The Theory of Multiple Intelligences*, the book where he introduced a view of intelligence that questioned the commonly accepted idea that intelligence could be measured and given a number. Indeed, ever since French psychologist Alfred Binet and Theodore Simon, his collaborator, published the first IQ tests, in 1905, to identify children who needed special help in coping with the school curriculum in France, IQ tests have been associated with classification and selection based on school performance. The IQ score quantified intelligence as the ratio of mental age to chronological age multiplied by 100, and was widely used for decades to determine who should benefit from advanced schooling (Arends 2007:48).

In *Frames of Mind* Gardner defined intelligence as "the ability to solve problems or to create products that are valued within one or more cultural settings" and challenged the common assumption that "most theories of intelligence (...) looked only at problem solving and ignored the creation of products, and (...) assume that intelligence would be evident and appreciated anywhere, regardless of what was (and was not) valued in particular cultures at particular times" (1999: 33-34).

Nearly two decades after his initial definition, Gardner redefined intelligence as "a biopsychological potential to process information that can be activated in a cultural setting to solve problems or create products that are of value in a culture" (1999:35). He argues that "human cognitive competence is better described in terms of abilities, talents, or mental skills" (1995:15), all of which he calls "intelligences", which "are not things that can be seen or counted" (1999:33) and that IQ testing is not a good indicator of an individual's intellectual abilities but merely the "tip of the cognitive iceberg" (1999: 3). Gardner also argues that IQ testing limits the definition of intelligence in that it measures only the fields in which literacy and mathematical ability are of great importance.

In Gardner's view, human beings possess not one but several types of intelligence "in a unique blend"; he claims that "although we receive our intelligences as a birthright (...) no two people have exactly the same intelligences in the same combinations" (1999:45). Inevitably, as happens in other fields of human knowledge, there is great disagreement about the degree of influence played by genetic and environmental factors in shaping human intelligence but one thing is certain: intelligences "are potentials (...) that will or will not be activated, depending upon the value of a particular culture, the opportunities available in that culture, and the personal decisions made by individuals and/or their families, school teachers, and others" (1999:34).

The eight intelligences

When Howard Gardner first proposed the seven, later eight, separate human intelligences he defined them in the following way (1999: 41-43; 48):

- The logical-mathematical intelligence involves the capacity to analyse problems logically, carry out mathematical operations, and investigate issues scientifically;
- The verbal-linguistic intelligence involves sensitivity to spoken and written language, and the ability to learn and use language to accomplish certain goals;

- The spatial intelligence features the potential to recognise and manipulate the patterns of wide space (...) as well as the patterns of more confined areas;
- The musical intelligence entails skills in the performance, composition and appreciation of musical patterns;
- The bodily-kinesthetic intelligence entails the potential of using one's body or parts of the body (...) to solve problems and fashion products;
- The interpersonal intelligence denotes a person's capacity to understand the intentions, motivations, and desires of other people and, consequently, to work effectively with others;
- The intrapersonal intelligence involves the capacity to understand oneself – including one's own desires, fears, and capacities – and to use such information effectively in regulating one's own life;
- The naturalist intelligence designates the human ability to discriminate among many living things (...) as well as sensitivity to other features of the natural world.

Learning styles

These intelligences translate into eight different types of learners which correspond broadly to the above-mentioned eight categories of intelligence. A brief description (Gardner 1993; Jensen 1995) of learners' particular likes and dislikes, the things they are good at and how they learn best is essential if one wishes to understand why the MI theory is of particular relevance in the classroom.
- Logical-mathematical learners like to do experiments, figure things out and work with numbers; they are good at mathematics, reasoning, logic and problem solving and learn best by categorising, classifying, analysing, and working with abstract patterns and relationships.
- Verbal linguistic learners like to read, write, argue debate and tell stories and jokes; they are good at memorising names, places, dates and trivia and learn best by saying, hearing and seeing words.
- Interpersonal learners like to have lots of friends, talk to people and work with others; they are good at understanding and leading people, organising, communicating, mediating conflicts, and learn best when they can share, compare information and cooperate with other learners.
- Spatial learners like to draw, design, build and create things; they like to look at pictures and slides and watch movies; they are good at imagining things, sensing changes and reading maps and

charts; they learn best by visualising, working with colour and pictures.
- Musical rhythmic learners like to sing, hum tunes and play a musical instrument; they respond to music, pick up sounds, remember melodies, notice pitches and rhythms and keep time; they learn best by associating rhythm, melody and music to the subjects they are studying.
- Intrapersonal learners like to work alone and pursue their own interests; they are good at understanding themselves, following their own instincts and being original; they learn best when working individually because they like to define their own pace and space.
- Bodily kinesthetic learners like to move around, use body language, touch and talk; they are good at physical activities and crafts and learn best by moving and/or interacting with space.
- Naturalist learners like to categorise species and find patterns in things; they are good at recognising and classifying the numerous species of their environment; they learn best by observing, studying, and charting out relations between flora and fauna.

Questionnaires like the ones devised by Smith (1997:60-61) and Wingate (2000: 34-35) are useful tools to find out each learner's preferred ways of learning. The *Common European Framework of Reference for Languages*, published by the Council of Europe in 2000, can also be used to try to help learners understand how they may know and improve their learning styles.

Once each learner's cognitive strengths and weaknesses have been identified and his/her individual intelligence profile has been built, teachers who decide to put the MI theory into practice can no longer go on ignoring the differences they see in the learners before them. They should try to provide *an individually configured education*, a phrase coined by Gardner to mean "an education that takes individual differences seriously and, insofar as possible, crafts practices that serve different kinds of minds equally well" (Gardner 1999: 151) and provide an alternative to standardized testing (1993:161-183).

Entry points

The traditional view of teaching —and assessing— aimed at the verbal-linguistic and logical-mathematical intelligences has to be radically changed so as to activate the other intelligences as well; learners need to understand beforehand what is expected of them, the objectives of the course, the issues under discussion, and how they are going to be assessed. The MI theory argues that teaching should be learner-centred and task-based. It identifies seven entry points which can be used to engage learners and which roughly correspond to the specific intelligences and types of learners briefly outlined before: the narrational (addressing learners who learn best by topics through stories with problems and conflicts to be solved and goals to be achieved) the quantitative/numerical (for learners who are engaged by numbers, the patterns they create and who are good at size, ration and change perspectives) , the logical (addressing the capacity to think deductively), the foundational/existential (appealing to learners who are intrigued by fundamental issues and who can argue about them), the aesthetic (addressing learners who are inspired by art and materials which display balance, harmony and composition) , the hands-on (motivating learners who approach a topic through an activity they can engage in) , and the social (for learners who learn more effectively in a group, where they can exchange ideas, see different perspectives and interact) (Gardner 1999:169-172).

These entry points coupled with the learning profiles should integrate the teaching and learning process because they establish a theoretical framework for enhanced co-operation between teachers and learners, on the one hand, and between theory and practice, on the other.

From theory into practice: A way into a short story

I will now attempt to show how the MI theory may be put into practice in the EFL classroom with independent to proficient learners (the B2 and C1 levels according to the *Common European Framework of Reference for Languages: learning, teaching, assessment*) in a unit about the United States of America built around the short story by Richard Olen Butler "JFK secretly attends Jackie auction" (Butler 1996:169-184). This experiment was carried out with two groups of students from the Faculty of Letters of the University of Lisbon, Portugal, in the first semester of the academic year 2006-2007.

As a way into the story, learners are first asked to read the poem "Early Sunday Morning" by John Stone, imagine it is not a poem but a painting and describe it. Individual learners may be asked to try to roughly sketch on the board what the class "saw" in the poem:

- physical elements (entrances to four stores; the awnings rolled in; ten windows; a barber's pole; a fire hydrant; the sun; the red of the building).

While engaged in the visualization of the painting, the following elements suggested by the poem can be discussed as they are elicited from or suggested by the learners themselves:

- **subjectivity** given by adjectives (the "*faceless* windows"; the "*imagined* East");
- **rhythm** and **movement** (the listing of elements with adverbs, conjunctions; pronouns; the repetition of parallel grammatical structures like "as if" and "on just such a day/morning"), the background sound ("practicing the flute");
- **colour** and how relevant it is (not just any red but "*Chinese* red");
- **reality** ("what is happening") and
- **appearance** ("what is not").

While the class members are sketching their painting based on Stone's poem, reference is usually made to Edward Hopper because his name is mentioned in the poem. Portuguese learners, and I would imagine other learners as well, do not as a rule know much about this famous 20th century American painter and this is when the actual painting (Hopper's 1930 "Early Sunday Morning") is finally shown. Learners are asked to compare and contrast their own drawing on the board with Hopper's painting, discussing any elements which may have been left out or added.

The next step is to show them another painting, this one by Taiwan-born painter T.F. Chen, called "Sunday Morning, Liberty!" (1986). This is a good example of a new art form: neo-iconography. Lawrence Jeppson first coined the phrase "neo-iconography" to describe Chen's art because the artist appropriates familiar "icons" from East and West, past and present, and creates a new painting by giving the final product, his work, a novel meaning.

In this particular example, T.F.Chen changes Hopper's painting by adding the shadow of the Statue of Liberty hovering above the building and an unidentified skyscraper barely discernible in the top right-hand corner.

Learners are asked to discuss the similarities and differences between the two paintings and the poem. They are then invited to prepare a dramatized reading of another poem, "The Lonely Street" by William Carlos Williams, splitting into groups or working individually, and to present it in class. Learners are encouraged to continue to use their creativity by adding

- sound (using background music),
- colour (using prompts evoking the duality white/black, white/pink, which may be associated with the feeling of innocence/awareness pervading the poem),
- movement (by choreographing their reading so as to emphasise the general mood of the poem).

As these activities are devised as a way into Olen Butler's story, which focuses on the history of 20th-century America, the next step is to awaken learners' interest in such issues by asking them to do some research on one of the elements added to Hopper's painting, the Statue of Liberty. They are invited to read and work on "The New Colossus" by Emma Lazarus, the poem inscribed on a bronze plaque which was added to the Statue in 1930.

The poem is handed out and seven groups are formed to spell the word LIBERTY[1]. Each group will deal with different aspects:

L: the title of the poem ("The New Colossus");
I: the poet (Emma Lazarus);
B: the Statue ("a mighty woman with a torch..."; Bartholdi)
E: cultural references ("the new colossus"; "the giant of Greek fame")
R: historical reality ("Mother of Exiles"; conflict in Europe; immigration into the U.S.A.)
T: social reality ("the tired, (...) the poor,(...) the homeless, tempest-tost");
Y: the poem as a whole: finding music to illustrate the poem.

The final goal for each group is to create a poster and present it to the whole class. Learners will engage in different activities to carry out their project with each group tackling the issues they have been allotted in their own preferred way. Some may wish to rely on the visual part of the poster with references to:

- the cinema (either to films showing the immigration issue as, for instance, Chaplin's *The Immigrant* dated from 1917, or to those where the statue is used as background as in Hitchcock's *Saboteur* dated 1942);
- the Statue as art work (e.g. by showing how it came to be made by Bartholdi);
- the political meaning (e.g. the gift of friendship from the French people: why? when?).

---

[1] Many of the resources used make reference to New York City, including the poem by Emma Lazarus, which is engraved in the pedestal of the Statue of Liberty. Thus, the word "liberty" was chosen as the acronym. Each team's name is a letter.

Time management and poster presentation are essential skills that learners are expected to develop while carrying out this project; a deadline is set for posters to be printed and ready for display in class.

With all the information gathered, presented orally in class and discussed, learners now have come to the end of the art-oriented introductory activities to the Olen Butler's short story "JFK secretly attends Jackie auction". Before reading the short story, learners are asked to play a game (Guess who/Find who) during which they learn about several important 20th century American politicians and events, all of which are mentioned in the short story. Learners are told that they will be focusing on:

- events, places (e.g. votes in the cemeteries in Chicago; assassination; Nobel Peace Prize; Dallas; Memphis; Chappaquiddick);
- names of American politicians; dates (e.g. Richard Joseph Daley, JFK, Martin Luther King, Ted Kennedy; 1960, 1963; 1964; 1994);
- photographs of American politicians (Richard Joseph Daley, Ted Kennedy, etc.), all of which have been taken from the short story.

By asking around and drawing on their general knowledge, learners have to match the information provided with the photographs and the names of the politicians by putting different items (names, events, dates, pictures) together. Incorrect matches are not set right; instead learners are asked to do research at home and then to report on their findings. Next step is to imagine what might have happened if John F. Kennedy had not died in Dallas. Learners have to come up with different suggestions and choose the most plausible one in view of the political and cultural contexts of 20th century America. Next they role-play an auction of Kennedy memorabilia. They have to find pictures of objects owned by John F. Kennedy and Jackie Kennedy and set up a mock auction.

This is another project for which time management and specific skills are essential. Selling and buying are part of everyone's daily life and an auction is just another important sales tool nowadays. With this activity, learners are encouraged to develop and enrich their auction-related vocabulary by taking part in a hands-on approach to auctioning practices and procedures and learning how to make a bid.

Discussing the short story

With all the cultural and political information gathered and discussed, it should now prove easy to read the story and fully grasp the plot and how it is developed. Discussion of the story will focus on presenting the facts as told by the original narrator but seen from different narrators' viewpoints:

- Jackie;
- the head of the intelligence services;
- Lyndon Johnson;
- Bob Kennedy;
- the man in the street.

Learners have to account for their choice of narrator, for the different views each narrator has and for the changes made to the original story. They may use the information supplied by the activities they have been engaged in (the guess who/find who game and the mock memorabilia auction). Other language-related activities (identifying phrasal verbs or examples of irony in the story and giving examples of how and when to use them in real life) may be carried out to round off the discussion of the story.

Follow-up

As a follow-up, learners bring to class any item they think might be used to further discuss important events of 20th-century America: for example, a newspaper clipping on any of the events dealt with in class; a site reference where events mentioned in the story can actually be seen (e.g. a virtual tour of the Statue of Liberty, the formal reading of Lazarus's poem); a scene from Chaplin's or Hitchcock's films where you can see the Statue of Liberty; a scene from Oliver Stone's *JFK* with the directors' perspective of what happened in Dallas;or an auction brochure.

As we see, using the MI theory in the classroom means more work for teachers and learners alike, but it also fosters more motivation and better performance. Learners are actively engaged in meaningful activities which they can use in their life outside the school; they know they are being assessed on a daily basis, as a whole, not only by the results, i.e. the work submitted in class, but also by the process leading to that presentation.

Having briefly outlined the activities designed for this unit, I will now show how I have tried to tap into the eight intelligences and the different types of learners.

Examples of intelligences and learning styles

I have outlined different entry points into the short story "JFK attends Jackie auction" by Richard Olen Butler. Consider the ways these entry points tap into the multiple intelligences in the preliminary activities:

- Reading and describing "Early Sunday Morning", a poem by John Stone utilises verbal linguistic, spatial, naturalistic, intra and interpersonal, bodily kinesthetic intelligences.
- Comparing and contrasting Stone's poem and working with the learners' drawing with Edward Hopper's painting "Early Sunday Morning" engages the learners' logical mathematical, bodily kinesthetic, inter and intrapersonal, verbal linguistic, spatial, naturalistic intelligences.
- Discussing Hopper's painting together with Chen's neo-iconography version of "Sunday Morning, Liberty" involves spatial, verbal linguistic, logical mathematical, naturalistic, inter and intrapersonal intelligences.
- The dramatised reading of "The Lonely Street" by William Carlos Williams taps into bodily kinesthetic, musical rhythmic, verbal linguistic, spatial, inter and intrapersonal, logical mathematical intelligences.
- The poster display and presentation on the Statue of Liberty (starting point "The New Colossus" by Emma Lazarus) works with the learners' verbal linguistic, bodily kinesthetic, logical mathematical, inter and intrapersonal, spatial, naturalistic, musical rhythmic intelligences.

Working with the short story itself also engages the students' multiple intelligences.

- "Guess who/ find who" game on 20th-century American politicians (matching pictures with people and events) works with the learners' verbal linguistic, logical mathematical, bodily kinesthetic, spatial, naturalistic, inter and intrapersonal intelligences.
- A mock auction of Kennedy memorabilia can be used to engage the learners' verbal linguistic, logical mathematical, spatial, bodily kinesthetic, inter and intrapersonal intelligences.
- Reading and discussing the short story in reference to the activities engaged in before the actual reading experience will employ logical mathematical, verbal linguistic, inter and intrapersonal, spatial, naturalistic, bodily kinesthetic intelligences.
- Other language-related exercises that students work on during the reading experience will potentialise verbal linguistic, logical mathematical, intra and interpersonal, bodily kinesthetic intelligences.

- Follow-up activities will ensure the use of verbal linguistic, bodily kinesthetic, logical mathematical, intra and interpersonal, and spatial intelligences.

Conclusion

The brief outline above tries to show that, although it may not always be easy or feasible to tackle all intelligences in one class or lesson, it is not only possible but also desirable to draw on at least three or four different intelligences at a time. Learners with different cognitive and learning styles will strongly benefit from diversified strategies to meet their varying needs so that they can link new information to already acquired knowledge in meaningful ways and be able to create their own meaningful representations of knowledge (Arends 2007:127).

I have, I hope, made the case for the MI theory in the EFL classroom.

Works cited

Arends, Richard. I. 2007. *Learning to Teach*. New York & Boston: McGraw Hill.
Butler, Robert Olen. 1996. "JFK Secretly Attends Jackie Auction" in *Tabloid Dreams: Stories*, 169-184. Henry Holt & Co.
Council of Europe. 2001. *Common European Framework of Reference for Languages: Learning, Teaching, Assessment*. Cambridge: Cambridge University Press.
Gardner, Howard. 1983. *Frames of Mind*. New York: Basic Books.
—. 1993. *Multiple Intelligences: The Theory in Practice*. New York: Basic Books.
—. 1999. *Intelligence Reframed: Multiple Intelligences for the 21st Century*. New York: Basic Books.
Jensen, Eric. 1995. *Brain-Based Learning and Teaching*. Del Mar, USA: Turning Point Publishing.
Lazarus, Emma. 1883. "The New Colossus". New York City: poem engraved in pedestal of the Statue of Liberty.
Smith, Alistair. 1997. *Accelerated Learning in the Classroom*. Trowbridge Wilts: Redwood Books.
Stone, John. 1985. "Early Sunday Morning" In *Renaming the Streets*. Baton Rouge: Louisiana State University Press.
Williams, William Carlos. 1921. "The Lonely Street" in *Sour Grapes: A Book of Poems,* Boston: Four Seas Co.

Wingate, Jim. 2000. *Knowing Me, Knowing You: Classroom Activities to Develop Learning Strategies and Stimulate Conversation*. Addlestone & London: Delta Publishing & English Teaching Professional.

RECOMMENDED READING: EXPLORING NEW HORIZONS

Baum, Susan, Julie Viens and Barbara Slatin. 2005. *Multiple Intelligences in the Elementary Classroom: A Teachers Toolkit.* New York, NY: Teachers College Press.
Curtain, Helena and Carol Ann Pesola. 2003. Languages and childen: Making the match. (3rd ed.). Boston: Allyn & Bacon.
Doyé, Peter and Alison Hurrell, eds. 1997. *Foreign language learning in primary schools (ages 5/6 to 10/11).* Strasbourg: Council of Europe.
Edelenbos, Peter, Richard Johnstone and Angelika Kubanek. 2006. *The main pedagogical principles underlying the teaching of languages to young learners. Final report of the EAC 89/04. Lot 1 Study.* European Commission. Available at http://ec.europa.eu/education/policies/lang/key/studies_en.html
Gardner, Howard. 2006. *Multiple Intelligences: New Horizons.* USA: Basic Books (Perseus Books Group).
Marinova-Todd, Stefka, Bradford D. Marshall and Catherine E. Snow. 2000. "Three Misconceptions about Age and Second-Language Learning." *TESOL Quarterly* 34 (1):9–34.
McKay, Penny. 2006. *Assessing Young Language Learners.* Cambridge: Cambridge University Press.
Nicholson-Nelson, Kristen. 1998. *Developing Students' Multiple Intelligences.* New York, NY: Scholastic Press.
Nikolov, Marianne and Helena Curtain. 2000. *An Early Start: Young Learning and Modern Languages in Europe and beyond.* Strasbourg: Council of Europe Publishing.
Vilke, Mirjana and Yvonne Vrhovac, eds. 1993. *Children and Foreign Languages I.* Zagreb: Faculty of Philosophy, University of Zagreb.
Vilke, Mirjana and Yvonne Vrhovac, eds. 1995. *Children and Foreign Languages II.* Zagreb: Faculty of Philosophy, University of Zagreb.
Vrhovac, Yvonne, ed. 2001. *Children and Foreign Languages III.* Zagreb: Faculty of Philosophy, University of Zagreb.

APPENDIX A

DEPICTION OF A POWERFUL LANGUAGE LEARNING ENVIRONMENT (VAN GORP)

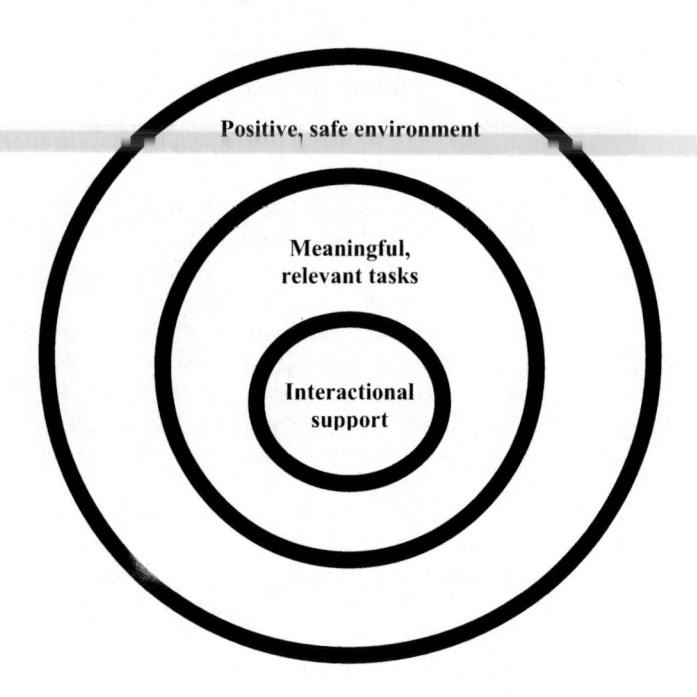

Positive, safe environment

Meaningful, relevant tasks

Interactional support

(Verhelst, 2006, based on Gysen, Rossenbacker & Verhelst, 1999)

APPENDIX B

THE THREE CIRCLES ACCORDING TO LEARNER AND TEACHER PERSPECTIVES (VAN GORP)

The 3 circles from the learner's perspective
(Based on Van Gorp, 2004; Verhelst, 2006)

Circle	Meaning
Within a positive and safe environment …	The learners feel safe, involved and competent. They are allowed to take the initiative, to make mistakes and to experiment with language. They feel motivated to engage in tasks and to explore particular aspects of the world. They are allowed control over their own learning process, and are stimulated to bring in their own knowledge of the world, values and opinions, and to utilize their full (multi)linguistic repertoire in the classroom.
… learners are presented with meaningful and challenging tasks, in which language use is a means to reach motivating, relevant and functional goals. These tasks contain a bridgeable gap between the demands of the task and the learners' current level of language proficiency.	The learners invest mental energy in performing the tasks: they confront and explore the world of the task, they engage in collaborative dialogue and try to comprehend and produce meaningful language while performing the task.
The learners are provided with interactional support from other learners and/or the teacher.	The learners try to tackle the problems that they meet along the way. They ask for help when this is not spontaneously provided, try to identify their problems and try to solve these with the help of others. The learners reflect upon the performance and outcomes of the task.
→ The learners use and learn language in social interaction.	

The 3 circles from the teacher's perspective
(Based on Verhelst, 2006)

Circle	Meaning
Within a positive and safe environment ...	Teachers take care that all learners feel safe and well. They support their learners' self-confidence and involvement by providing positive feedback, taking them seriously, listening to them ... Teachers allow the learners to take initiative, to make mistakes and to experiment with language. They motivate their learners to engage with tasks and to explore particular aspects of the world. They allow the learners to take control over their own learning process, stimulate them to bring in their own knowledge of the world, values and opinions, and to utilize their full (multi)linguistic repertoire in the classroom.
... teachers present the learners with meaningful and challenging tasks, in which language use is a means to reach a motivating, relevant and functional goal. These tasks contain a bridgeable gap between the demands of the task and the learners' current level of language proficiency.	Teachers select and/or develop meaningful and relevant tasks. They give clear instructions about the tasks. If necessary, they prepare learners for the task by building up their knowledge of the world, by motivating the learners or by brainstorming on the process of task performance. They respect the essentially functional and meaningful (language) goals of the task.
Teachers provide the learners with interactional support themselves, and give learners the opportunity to give each other interactional support.	Teachers provide interactional support to those learners who need it (the most). They adapt the quantity and quality of their interactional support to the particularities of the learners' task performance, and of the learners themselves. They negotiate about the meaning of incomprehensible input and push output, they provide feedback to the learners, and they mediate between the task demands and the learners' level of language proficiency. They do not take away all learner initiative while interactionally supporting task performance. They stimulate peer interaction and cooperation, and exploit the potential of working with heterogeneous groups. They stimulate learners' reflection on task performance and outcome.
→ The teacher provides and supports language learning opportunities in a collaborative social setting.	

APPENDIX C

RADIO TIKA TASK (VAN GORP)

Task: The pupils create a radio news bulletin for the fictitious radio station "Tika".
Goals: (1) The pupils create a radio news bulletin; (2) The pupils are able to obtain information from a radio news bulletin; (3) The pupils work together constructively in small groups.
Materials: Source card and work sheet for the pupils

Task description
1) The teacher tells the pupils that they are inhabitants of the fictitious country "Tikaland", where many languages are spoken. Radio and television is broadcast in several languages, so nobody is at a disadvantage. Pupils are asked to create a radio news bulletin for the fictitious radio station of Tikaland. The news bulletin should be in different languages. The teacher should try and stimulate the pupils' motivation to perform this task by asking the pupils if they know what kind of topics are covered in a news bulletin: domestic news, foreign news, sports, weather, etc. **Suggestion:** If pupils are not familiar with a news bulletin, they can listen to a real news bulletin on the radio.

2) Form groups of four pupils, making sure that there are different language speakers in each group. Give every group the source card with the different news items and the work sheet. Explain to the pupils that each group is going to create a news bulletin that should be no longer than three minutes. Each news item should be in a different language. Ask the pupils to use as many languages or dialects as possible, allowing the pupils to decide which language(s) or dialect(s). Move about the classroom and support the groups if necessary. Tell the pupils that they also have to come up with three quiz questions (in Dutch) for their audience. Collect the quiz questions and distribute them at random among the other groups. Each group gets three questions. **Suggestion:** Pay attention to the free rider effect (one pupil does all the work). Make sure that all the pupils contribute to the group work. Stimulate the pupils' exploratory thinking by asking specific questions: "Do you know another topic for the news bulletin?" "In what language are you going to tell this?"

3) Each group presents its news bulletin. The other pupils listen and try to find the answers to the questions.

4) Discuss the task. Did the pupils enjoy making a news bulletin in different languages? Could they understand everything? Would they like to have such multilingual news broadcasts in Belgium?

(Berben, Van den Branden, Van Gorp, 2007)

APPENDIX D

EXAMPLE OF CLIL TASK (BARRULL I GARCIA)

> More than 2000 years ago, Rome was the capital of the largest Empire of the Ancient World, the Roman Empire. Thanks to a powerful* army they conquered all the Mediterranean area, from the North of Africa to Europe and west Asia. Most of our culture comes from the Roman legacy and we have a lot of material and written sources to study them.
> "Since the Fall* of the Roman Empire the idea of unity has been present in European culture. The creation of the predecessors to the present European Union was however specific to the years immediately after the Second World War[1].

Look at the map: The extent of the Roman Republic and Roman Empire. [NB: the map has been removed because it was too large. The original map was colour-coded to show the Roman Republic and Roman Empire]

[Red area] 133 BC

[Orange area] 44 BC (late Republic, after conquests by republican generals)

[Yellow area] AD 14 (death of Augustus)

[Green area] 117 (maximum extension)

Compare this map with an actual map of Europe. Here you can have a look at a map in English:

Map of the World:

http://www.yourchildlearns.com/europe_map.htm

---

[1] Adapted from: http://en.wikipedia.org/wiki/Fall_of_the_Roman_Empire

"How we're going about it": Teachers' Voices on Innovative Approaches to Teaching and Learning Languages   289

- Write the names of 5 present European countries conquered by the Romans.

  I ………………… II …………………… III ………………………
  IV ……………………… V ………………………………..

Look at this map of the European Union Expansion[2]:
[NB: the map has been removed because it was too large. The original map was colour-coded to show the European countries.]

Compare it with the map of the Roman Republic and Roman Empire:

- Write the names of 5 present European countries conquered by the Romans and who are members of the European Union.

  I ………………… II …………………… III ………………………

  IV ……………………… V ………………………………..

- Write the names of 5 present European countries conquered by the Romans and who are not members of the European Union.

  I ………………… II …………………… III ………………………

  IV ……………………… V ………………………………..

Stop the recorder

Listen to your 3 recordings. Did you speak in English? Listen to the tape and complete the Speaking evaluation chart 1.

---

[2] Map from: http://www.ecb.int/ecb/history/ec/html/index.en.html

APPENDIX E

AWARENESS-RAISING TASK
(DELLEVOET & MUREŞAN)

On the scale below, only the descriptors for C2 and A2.1 are in their correct place. All the others need entering and re-ordering in relation to the corresponding reference levels. Once you have done this, compare the outcome of your selection and sequencing with that of your peer and discuss the specific elements that contributed to your decision-making. (The descriptors are on the next page.)

		FORMAL DISCUSSION AND MEETINGS
C2		Can hold his/her own in formal discussion of complex issues, putting an articulate and persuasive argument, at no disadvantage to native speakers.
C1		
B2	B2.2	
	B2.1	
B1	B1.2	
	B1.1	
A2	A2.2	
	A2.1	Can say what he/she thinks about things when addressed directly in a formal meeting provided he/she can ask for repetition of key points if necessary.
A1		No descriptors available at this level

Descriptors

(i)

Can follow much of what is said that is related to his/her field, provided interlocutors avoid very idiomatic usage and articulate clearly. Can put forward a point of view clearly, but has difficulty engaging in debate.

(ii)

Can participate actively in routine and non-routine formal discussion. Can follow the discussion on matters related to his/her field, understand in detail the points given prominence by the speaker. Can contribute, account for and sustain his/her opinion, evaluate alternative proposals and make and respond to hypotheses.

(iii)

Can generally follow changes of topic in formal discussion related to his/her field which is conducted slowly and clearly. Can exchange relevant information and give his/her opinion on practical problems when asked directly, provided he/she receives some help with formulation and can ask for repetition of key points if necessary.

(iv)

Can keep up with an animated discussion, identifying accurately arguments supporting and opposing points of view. Can express his/her ideas and opinions with precision, present and respond to complex lines of argument convincingly.

(Activity based on descriptors taken from the **CEFR**, pp 78.)

Try to identify now, which of these level descriptors would best describe your own performance in a formal discussion situation. Where would you set your further improvement targets?

[NB: Some of the descriptors have been removed for sake of space]

APPENDIX F

QUESTIONNAIRE (DELLEVOET & MURESAN)

Questionnaire re the implementation of the European Language Portfolio at the Academy of Economic Studies

Dear colleague,
As the EuroIntegrELP Project is approaching its end, could you please take a few minutes to reflect on your experience with the European Language Portfolio and your involvement in this LINGUA 1 project, and answer
at least some of the questions below. The outcome of this survey will be included in the final Project report and will be made available to all those interested.

1. Have you introduced the ELP in FL-teaching?   yes❏   no❏

If yes, which ELP version(s) have you introduced?

- EAQUALS/ALTE
- EUROPASS Language Portfolio
- other (please specify)

2. In what context:
  (a) Faculty/specialization

  (b) Level/year of study?

  (c) With how many groups?

  (d) When?
  - at the beginning of the course
  - later during the course
  - at the end of the course

3. What ELP component was most readily accepted by the students?

- the self-assessment component
- awareness-raising to the value of intercultural experiences

- the possibility of recording courses attended, certificates obtained
- the European dimension?

4. Have you recorded any interesting, suggestive, recurrent questions? Please give some examples.

5. As a teacher, which area / component do you see as having the highest effectiveness?

6. Support materials (textbooks, hand-outs, etc)

a) Have you used support materials for introducing the ELP?   yes❑   no❑

b) If yes, what materials have you used / adapted / developed?

7. Have you encountered any difficulties in implementing the ELP into the teaching / learning process? Please give two examples of challenges and solutions you have found.

8. Please comment on methodological aspects regarding its applicability in your class context, e.g.
- the ELP's role in the area of assessment, incl. the acceptance of the partial competences
- the impact of the students' familiarization with self-assessment on their progress
- the ELP's impact on syllabus design
- …………

9. Any further comments and suggestions that you would like to share.

CONTRIBUTORS

Editors

Melinda Dooly (Ph.D) is a lecturer at the Faculty of Education, Autonomous University of Barcelona (Spain). Melinda is the author of various journal articles and chapters and has co-authored several books on education. She has been a guest teacher at universities in Europe and the USA and has participated in many international educational projects.

Diana Eastment (MA) has lived and taught in many countries throughout the world. Her books and articles on ICT and education are world-renowned. Her most recent co-authored book *The Internet. Resource Books for Teachers*, was published by Oxford University Press. Diana has been a guest teacher around the world, most recently at Cambridge University (UK) and Padagogishe Akademie des Bundes in Wien (Austria).

Contributors

Francine Arroyo (MA) holds a Post-graduate degree in *Didactics of Foreign Languages*. She has been a lecturer at the Faculdade de Letras, University of Lisbon (Portugal) since 1983. She has written various articles and books about Didactics of French language and co-authored the French programs for Secondary Education in Portugal. Francine is currently the publication director of the Portuguese Association of French Teachers (APPF) and of UNIL (Grupo Universitário de Investigação em LínguasVivas),a research group belonging to the Faculdade de Letras, University of Lisbon.

Cristina Avelino (M.A) holds a Post-graduate degree in Didactics of Foreign Languages. She has been on the teaching staff of the Departamento de Linguística Geral e Românica, Faculdade de Letras, University of Lisbon since 1982. She is a teacher trainer and has written various articles and books about Didactics of French and co-authored the

French programs of the Secondary Education in Portugal. She is consultant for the Education Ministry and since 2006 she has been President of the Portuguese Association of French Teachers (APPF) and member of the board of the Language Centre of the faculty.

Mercè Barrull i Garcia has a teaching degree in Primary Education and a Bachelor of Arts degree in Geography and History. She also took a Postgraduate degree in "Didactics of foreign languages" (Didàctica de les llengües estrangeres) and has attended several courses on Teaching English as a Foreign Language. She had fourteen years experience working as a primary school teacher before moving into secondary education (as an English teacher) in 1995. During the academic year 2006/07 she has been doing research on teaching communicative strategies in the English classroom. Mercè is a member of the research team named ArtICLE (Universitat Autònoma de Barcelona) whose principle focus is on collaborative CLIL tasks.

Jennifer Bruen (Ph.D) is a Lecturer in German in the School of Applied Language and Intercultural Studies at Dublin City University (Ireland). Her research interests are primarily in the area of language teaching and learning and include, in particular, the following: language learning styles and strategies, German for academic purposes (business), the European Language Portfolio and language planning and policy.

Gabriele Budach (Ph.D) is a lecturer at the Department of Romance Languages and Literatures at Frankfurt University, Germany. In her teaching and research she specialises in sociolinguistics, studies on literacy, bilingual education, migration, multilingualism and transnationalism. She has several publications in these areas.

Do Coyle (MA) is Associate Professor in Education at the University of Nottingham, UK. She has been involved in developing CLIL research and pedagogies for many years, having led and participated in a wide range of European CLIL projects in teacher education and CLIL learning communities. She has many publications on CLIL theories and practice. She is an international advisor and consultant for national governments and agencies. Her special interest is in technology-enhanced learning and the use of video conferencing to build "borderless classrooms". She also researches the role of thinking skills and intercultural learning in CLIL.

Liliana Dellevoet is assistant lecturer of Business English and Portuguese at the Academy of Economic Studies and an active member of PROSPER-ASE Language Centre, Bucharest, Romania. For the last nine years she has been an oral examiner for Cambridge exams and her professional interests include evaluation and self-evaluation of language skills. She has also been involved in the coordination of EuroIntegrELP, a 3-year Socrates Lingua 1 project for the dissemination of good practice in the use of the *European Language Portfolio*.

Carmen Ellermann is currently researching computer-mediated communication and telecollaboration for her doctoral dissertation. She has been a member of several international projects in education, one of which won the German Cornelsen award for "best future project 2005". Carmen teaches English as a foreign language at Grund-und Hauptschule Neckargemünd (Heidelberg, Germany) where she organised an international "field day" between her German students and their international peers from France in 2007.

Betil Eröz (Ph.D) is Assistant Professor at the Foreign Languages Education Department at Middle East Technical University where she trains English language teachers at undergraduate and graduate levels. She received her MA in English Language and Linguistics and PhD in Second Language Acquisition and Teaching at the University of Arizona where she taught freshman composition to native and nonnative speakers of English. Her research interests include language teacher training, qualitative research methodologies in the classroom, computer-mediated communication, L2 use and pragmatics, and cross-cultural communciation.

Cristina Escobar Urmeneta (Ph.D) has worked as both a secondary teacher and as a teacher trainer. She recently participated in the piloting of the Catalan version of the European Language Portfolio, financed by the Spanish Ministry of Education. Cristina is currently employed at the Education Faculty, Autonomous University of Barcelona (Spain) where she is a member of the GREIP research team. Her research interests lie in assessment and self-assessment of oral interaction as well as the use of CLIL in multilingual contexts. She has published widely in these areas.

Claude Germain Ph.D. (Philosophy and Linguistics) is Honorary professor, Department of Linguistics and Second Language Teaching, University of Quebec at Montreal. He is an authority on teaching and learning of second languages and is well-known for his research and publications, such as *Évolution de l'enseignement des langues: 5000 ans d'histoire* (1993, Paris: CLE International) and *Le point sur l'approche communicative* (1993, Montréal: Centre Éducatif et Culturel). He is currently involved in a project with Dr. Netten on Intensive French in Canada.

Nicolas Gromik is a senior lecturer at the Center for the Advancement of Higher Education at Tohoku University. He teaches English with an emphasis on multimedia operation as a tool for communication, with a particular interest in content based learning, prior knowledge reinforcement and independent use of technology for the purpose of self-expression. He has provided teacher training workshops on movie making and editing in Poland, Bangladesh, India, the United States and Japan, as well as participating in online teacher training.

Melanie Kunkel (MA) is scientific collaborator at the Department of Romance Languages and Literatures at Frankfurt University, Germany. Her teaching and research is mainly in the areas of sociolinguistics, bilingual school projects and language history.

Hanna Komorowska (Ph.D) is professor of applied linguistics and language teaching at Warsaw University. After the fall of communism she headed the Expert Committee for foreign language teaching and teacher education reform in Poland. Former vice-President of Warsaw University and the Polish delegate for the Modern Languages Project Group of the Council of Europe, she is now a member of the EU High Level Group on Multilingualism, consultant to the European Centre for Modern Languages in Graz and co-author of the *European Portfolio for Student Teachers of Languages*. She publishes widely in the field of FLT methodology and teacher education.

Folkert Kuiken (Ph.D) is professor of Dutch as a second language at the University of Amsterdam (the Netherlands). He is (co-)author of several text books on Dutch as a second language and of various teacher training methods. His current research focuses on the relationship between cognitive task complexity and linguistic performance in second language acquisition. Other research interests include the effect of language policy, task-based language teaching, focus on form, interaction and collaborative learning.

David Marsh (Phil.L.) has worked on bilingual education since the mid 1980s. He was part of the team which conducted groundwork leading to the launch of the term Content and Language Integrated Learning (CLIL) in 1994. He has extensive experience of teacher development, capacity-building, research and consultancy in a range of different countries in Africa, Europe and Asia. Operating from the University of Jyväskylä (Finland) as an Academic Project Manager he undertakes advisory and consultancy tasks for international agencies and national governments worldwide. He has published widely on bilingual education methodologies and currently works on integration and curricular development, cognition, and the use of converging technologies in education.

Eduarda Melo Cabrita is lecturer in the Departamento de Estudos Anglísticos, Faculdade de Letras, Universidade de Lisboa. She is co-author of several articles on students' learning styles.

Jelena Mihaljevic Djigunovic (Ph.D) is SLA and TEFL Chair at Zagreb University, Croatia. She has been involved in a number of national and international projects focusing on early FLL, affective learner factors, initial language teacher education and FL education policy. She has published two research books and more than 70 papers.

Laura Mureşan (PhD) is professor of business English and German at the Academy of Economic Studies in Bucharest, Romania. She is Director of PROSPER-ASE Language Centre and Founder President of QUEST Romania. Former Secretary General of EAQUALS, she is now a member of the Inspections Sub-committee and an inspector trainer. Her professional activities include teacher training and research in areas such as CEFR and ELP implementation, quality assurance in education, transferability of best practice from language education to other academic fields. She has co-ordinated ECML projects (*Quality Management in Language Education* and *QualiTraining*) and has been involved in the Lingua 1 project *EuroIntegrELP*.

Joan Netten (C.M., Ph.D.) is Honorary Research Professor, Faculty of Education, Memorial University of Newfoundland and Visiting Professor, Graduate Education, Université Sainte-Anne, Nova Scotia. She has done extensive research on classroom processes in immersion education and is currently active in research to improve core French. She was co-editor, with Claude Germain, of a special issue of the *Canadian Modern Language Review* on Intensive French in Canada. She was awarded the

Order of Canada for her contribution to research and development of French education.

Randall Sadler (Ph.D) is an Assistant Professor in the Division of English as an International Language at the University of Illinois at Urbana-Champaign. His research interests include L2 writing, the use of technology in the classroom—including the place of computer-mediated communication in the L2 learning process, and combining qualitative and quantitative research methodologies in the classroom. He is the author of several publications in this area of teaching and learning.

Marta Seseña Gomez (Ph.D) was the 2003 winner of the prestigious ASELE award, which is given to researchers for outstanding dissertations by the Centro de Investigación y Documentación Educativa and the Spanish Ministry of Education and Culture. She has co-authored several articles on task-based language learning and has developed materials for the Instituto Cervantes (Spain). She has taught Spanish as a foreign language at Antwerp University (Belgium), Universitá degli studi di Milano (Italy) and is currently a lecturer at the University of Salamanca (Spain), in Cursos Internacionales.

Koen Van Gorp is a staff member of the Centre for Language and Education. He is currently conducting his Ph.d. research in the classroom variables that have an impact on second language learning and school success. He has published a wide range of articles and syllabuses with regard to task-based language education. He also supervises the development of a new task-based syllabus for the teaching of Dutch at primary school level. His main research interests are with the impact of classroom variables on content-based language learning and on peer interaction as concerns learning in general and language learning in particular.

Andrea Young (Ph.D) earned her doctoral degree from Aston University in 1994. She is currently a lecturer in teaching English to young learners at the Institut Universitaire de Formation des Maîtres (IUFM) in Alsace, France. Andrea is a member of the research group PLURIEL (plurilinguisme, dialogue interculturel et enseignement des langues) at the IUFM of Alsace, of the LILPA/ EA 1339 (Linguistique, langue, parole) research group at the Université Marc Bloch, Strasbourg and also of the Multilingual Europe research group established by the Department of Education at Goldsmiths College, University of London. Within the framework of a European project (www.tessla.org) she has recently co-edited and contributed to a publication dealing with teacher education for the support of second language acquisition.